COMPARATIVE TOURISM MARKETING
Case Studies

COMPARATIVE TOURISM MARKETING

Case Studies

Alexandru Nedelea
Babu P. George

ABHIJEET PUBLICATIONS
Delhi 110 094

ABHIJEET PUBLICATIONS
2/46 Tukhmeerpur Extension
Delhi-110 094
Phone: 011-22960492, 65698474
E-mail: abhijeetpublication@gmail.com

COMPARATIVE TOURISM MARKETING: CASE STUDIES

First Published 2010

ISBN 978-93-80031-62-0

PRINTED IN INDIA

Published by J.K. Singh for Abhijeet Publications, Delhi-110 094, Lasertypeset by Gaurav Graphics, New Delhi and Printed at Himanshu Printers, Delhi.

PREFACE

In its days of infancy, tourism marketing theory was nothing but simple applications of the generic theory of marketing. Over a period of time, it has grown as a disciplinary area worthy of studying itself. Yet, what came to mind when we thought about tourism marketing was a set of universally applicable theories and their unproblematic applications in the specific case of the tourism industry. However, many recent studies have highlighted the fallacy of this approach.

Social science theory in general is culturally sensitive. In relatively stable and slowly evolving cultures, theories may take more static forms. But, tourism theory mostly is about dynamic, floating, and every changing populations and these characteristics donot lend themselves to rigid frameworks or universality. The relevance of the present book, aptly titled "Comparative Tourism Marketing" should be viewed in this context.

We understand the fallacy of the hope of generalizability and have not attempted it as an overarching sheme. Instead, we asked the contributors of this volume to go into the depths of specific marketing situations to identify what is unique and what is more general. To the critic who might ask what the purpose of science is when the kernel is unique, our response is two-fold: one, the potetic pleasure of realizing uniqueness in phenomena; two, getting exposed to uniqueness in different contexts will help to sharpen our senses to anticipate, find out, and respond to uniqueness in phenomena that we will encounter in the future. Case studies presented here are generally meant to train the right brain, even though the exact mechanism by which that training is imparted is beyond the scope of this discussion.

The first paper, titled "Tourism in Crete: A SWOT Analysis" by Karagiannis Stefanos examines the evolution of tourism in Crete, Greece. The author has provided a detailed analusis of the intrinsic strengths and weaknesses of Cretan tourism. Tourism offers a great potential for Crete, but the changing geo-political and cultural dynamics might just put hindrences in its growth trajectory, it is observed.

"Tourism Marketing Cases from Albania and Macedonia"by Liljana Elmazi and and others is an excellent example of two researchers from two different coutries joining together to write a comparative narrative about tourism marketing practices in those countires. Despite the geographical nearness, the differences in marketing practices are amazing at times. The number and variety of cases presented make it a compulsory reading for anyone interested in tourism in these coutries. These case studies touch upon a range of theoretical issues in tourism marketing, too.

While most of the case studies in the present volume focus on Eastern Europe, "Strategic Tourism Marketing in Kenya: Reflections on the Nyanza/Western Region" by Roselyne Okech offers an entirely different perspective. Her paper is an eye opener for those who think that nothing in the African continent happens with a strategic vision. Despite formidable challenges, the Western Region of Kenya exemplifies a generally successful tradition in tourism marketing. Based on her analysis of the current practice and well informed by the theory of strategic marketing, she has proposed a number of strategic guidelines. These guidelines should be of great use for many stakeholder groups, the public policy makers in particular.

Slobodan Èeroviæ, in the paper titled "Marketing Management of Serbian Tourism" offers a glimpse into the macro level management of tourism marketing in Serbia. It also depicts the political transition of Serbia and and how that changed the nation's approach towards tourism marketing. It is indeed an interesting reading to see how socialistic ideas of tourism marketing differed markedly with more free market oriented ideas of marketing. Amusingly, Serbia is trying to preserve the positive elements of its historical practice of tourism while simultaneously embracing western marketing concepts. It is ironic how communist objects, which are remnants of an anti-market philosophy, became the objects of market driven touristic gaze.

"Application of Marketing Concept within the Airline Industry: The Case of Albania" by Areti Stringa critically looks at the marketing activities of the airlines operating on the Albanian market and establish their strengths and weaknesses. This case in particular highlights that marketing orientation is the result of a complex set of forces and does not come overnight. To break away from the clutches of a general apathy towards customer orientation, the best way is to break away from the traditional way of doing business: say, going online. Albenian airlines, for instance, has grown high-tech in its customer service as any other major airliner in the world.

The paper by Tatjana Mirchevska and Nada Sekulovska titled "Online Advertising and Distribution of Touristic Services" is a relatively context independent analysis of the impact of electronic promotion and distribution of the tourism product. World over, customers are increasingly turning towards e-travel agents for their various travel related needs and this analysis summarizes some of the recent trends in e-travel. While traditional distribution might not be wiped out, it definitely will be transformed in the onslaught of the technological revolution that we envisage now.

"Community Based Tourism: Bringing Marketing Closer to the Society" by Babu George attempts to weave together the theory and practice of community based tourism. Though the idea of community based development is age-old, its adoption into tourism is relatively recent. The paper examines how community based tourism can be a panacea for many of the evils of the mainstream industry driven mass-tourism.

"Comparative Tourism Marketing Case Studies" by Liljana

Elmazi and Alexandru Nedelea is an assemblage of various short case studies. These case-lets are prepared for short classroom discussions in mind. Cases on a range of organizations, located in various continents, are provided. Each of these cases can easily be related with one or the other of themes in tourism marketing.

"Kalypso Adventures: A Case Study of Innovation, Entrepreneurship, and Niche Marketing" narrates how a tourism start up has progressively tailor-made a unique marketing strategy. The authors, Manoj Edward and Babu George, argues that necessity often gives vital clues to innovations. Kalypso did not have the luxury nor the market demand to become everything for everyone and it slowly settled into a niching strategy. This made it not only successful in the short term but also helped to fortify its foundations.

With a wide variety of papers over an equally wide variety of marketing related themes, the present volume aims to satisfy the diverse needs of a diverse audience. We wind up this section with the earnest hope that we have been successful in this endeavor.

Alexandru Nedelea, PhD

Babu P George, PhD

CONTENT

1

Tourism in Crete: A SWOT Analysis

Crete Case Study

*Karagiannis Stefanos**

Introduction

The rapid evolution that has been redounded in the last 30 years in the tourist sector of Greece, our country, is an undoubted fact and is certified by the positive evolution of a great number of pointers that are directly related to the processes and changes of our national income. The rapid rise in the international demand for tourist travels, however, is only a capable convention for the change in the production terms of the tourist travels outside ones homeland, and not the necessary convention which is something more than the tourist demand rates.[1]

The domination of the spirit of "Hospital Zeus" in our country—with the high spirit of hospitality of our people, the natural advantages of the Greek landscape as opposed to other countries, the rich archaeological, historical and cultural heritage of the greek land and its people, the subtle climate conditions with the "long-lasting Greek summer" (for the pleasure of the sea, sand and sun), the interesting

* Ph.D., Technological Educational Institute of Crete, GREECE.

flora and fauna of the "Greek country" etc., have been the major factors for the development of the Greek tourism, for all the post-War seasons.

One should not be an economist to identify that the basic problem of the Hellenic Finance is exporting and that the most important exported product is tourism.[2]

It is characteristic that the basic components of the advantages of the country remain the same. The greater mass of the visitors sustaining tourism comes to Greece for the sun, the sea, the environment, the hospitality and the authenticity of people, moves on for holidays in seaside areas and islands and moves on in an organized manner. This demand dominates to other alternative forms of tourism. As a result, the greatest part of the Greek tourism offer is targeted on satisfying this demand, since the danger of being substituted by other countries is apparent. Therefore, we should concentrate on supporting the main form of tourism product, by engaging actions of differentiation and enrichment of the composition of the tourism product, in order to sustain and levitate the proportionate factors in the global tourism market. This should lead to the evolution of tourism from the dominant form (depicting low yield levels) to the demand of higher level tourism or even to demand for alternative forms of tourism. As a result, the threat of the domination on tourism terms of the neighboring competitive countries is more than apparent. Also, the problem of supporting family business in the mountain areas becomes harder due to fewer chances for people of agriculture for employment apart from their own work.[3] Last but not the least, the constant improvement of the quality, which can only be achieved on a limited degree and demands long-term actions and resources, is concentrated on a quicker "improvement of the tourist offer", so as to satisfy the increased demands of consumer of greater income scale and concurrent "differentiation" of this offer so as to cover the needs of the customers of alternative forms of tourism.[4]

1. Tourism Characteristics

Our country in just a few years moved from the edge of the

world tourist market to the most influential tourism economies and holds a great position in the global tourism demand ladder. Some areas of the country, as e.g. Rhodes, Corfu, and especially Crete, are considered as great tourist attraction poles, while some may even characterize them as satiate on tourist terms. Despite, however, the fact that they are considered to have "large apothems" of tourism development, something like this has not happened since they were occupied by massive tourism. Consequently, this led to unfortunate effects to the landscape and the people working on Crete's mass tourism industries; a fact that should not be disregarded. Another factor that affects tourism in Greece, is the change of the terms of tourist flow after globalization and its effects on the Greek tourism, after the inclusion of Greece in the EU. All these demand counteractions, as changes in the social and economical map of Crete and the search of developing strategic and financial policies in order to achieve viable development. Another approach is the common belief that tourism can become a primary and important lever of development of the Cretan economy, as long as it is orthologically organized on novel base, ignoring from the dominant aspect of "mass tourism" and "tourism industry".

In the formation of the tourism policy and planning, it is very important to understand the different forms of tourism development and the forms tourism that are connected with the special travel motives that are taken into consideration for the prefecture.[5]

We understood this problem and decided to dedicate some hours of fertile conversation and research, in order to conceive the extent of the problem, and through our scientific knowledge to assist in the following direction: to provide a scientifically validated aspect on the route the Cretan tourism should follow during the 21st century in order to be competitive enough and meet the expectations of the local authorities and people, in an era of intense international competition in the global tourist market. This was how "Tourist Crete and its perspective through SWOT analysis" arise, a deposit of knowledge and faith in Crete's power.

A great number of factors affected the vast development of tourism globally, and mostly the need for relaxation and escape from the daily routine for the people of financially and industrially developed countries. Curiosity, the joy of change, the attraction of the unknown always appealed to people.[6] Other reasons that assisted in tourism's development is trend, the dominating tendency of touring, and the will to escape the usual in combination to the will of change and acquaintance with the unfamiliar. An important portion of the tourist current, disregards the length of free time ands space, while also is interested in entertainment experiences and actions. The convergence in tourism experiences is intensified by the place ant way with which tourism invades everyday lives and free time. As it has been stated by[7] "*...Against the background of unparalleled growth in the latter half of the twentieth century, tourism now finds itself at a crossroads in its development. On the one hand, it is heralded as the word's biggest industry' by a number of global organizations including the World Travel and Tourism Council (WTTC) and the World Tourism Organisation (WTO), which highlights the fact that tourism overtook both crude petroleum and motor vehicles to become the world's number one export earner in 1994. Its economic significance it also illustrated by the fact that tourism receipts were greater than the world's exports of other selected product groups, including electronic equipment, clothing, textiles and raw materials.*" We indicatively mention that the development of world tourism, in terms of arrivals was the best of the last 30 years. All the primary tourism destinations featured a rise, that varies from 4% for Europe to 29% for Asia–Pacific.[8]

2. European and Mediterranean Tourism

Despite the fact that tourist activity internationally has successfully dealt with, to a certain extent, any problems were inherited by 2001, and managed to depict a raise of 3% in 2002, the incomings were lowered due to the great pressure imposed on the prices of the tourist services.[9] The most tourism development pointers of Europe, however, are positive and will lead in an impressive uprising in tourism, according to a relative study of the World Tourism Organization (WTO). The arrival of international tourists during 2000 were 224,640,000 tourists, while the same figures for other great regions on the same year were: America 20,080,000, Australia/Japan 7,490,000, Latin America/ Caribbean 2,650,000, Asia/Pacific 1,540,000, Africa 2,050,000, Middle East 1,410,000, South Asia 650,000, Eastern and Central Europe 41,920,000, other countries 14,910,000 tourists.

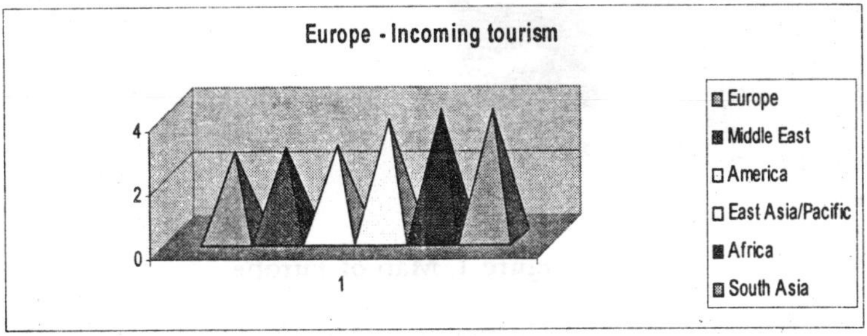

Diagram 1: Europe Incoming Tourism

The fact that according to WTO, Europe holds 43.6% of the world hotel potential (11,257,000 beds out of a total of 25,640,000 in the end of the 20th century) is indicative. To be more specific, the 15 country-members of the EU (12 of which are included in the 40 most popular destinations) depict 185.000 hotels and other lodging facilities featuring 9.000.000 beds, according to Eurostat. Other studies state that Eurostat provides "short-term statistics for organizations and businesses" targeting mostly on assisting business cycle analysis. These studies-reports use data from EBT (European Business Tendencies) Database. Europe, as it is obvious, still dominates as the most important tourist destination in the world, holding 58.8% of the global arrivals in 1997 (360.816.000 arrivals), despite that since 1980 it has lost 6.2% from its portion. Its participation on the global incomings from international tourism is 49.2% (218.046 billion dollars). The portion of tourism as opposed the exportation of goods, has increased in all European countries (from 7.51% in 1988 to 8.80%). Recreation and its variation based on traveling, that is tourism, undoubtedly hold a fundamental social role offering a contradiction to the daily activities. In addition to that, there are a number of factors that lead to the result that the current extension of the entertainment activities will continue.[10]

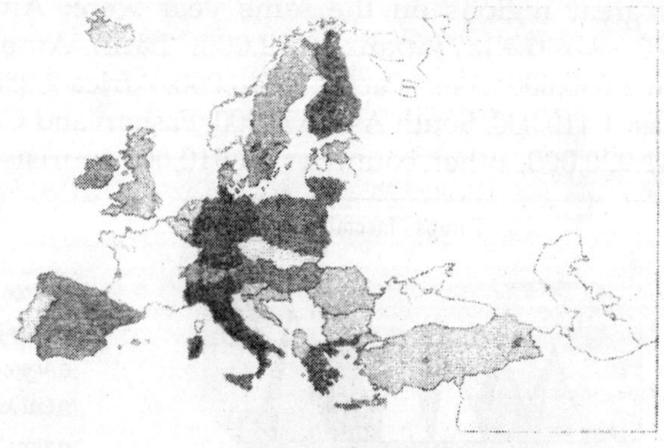

Figure 1. Map of Europe

3. Research and Development in Member-countries of the European Union

From the available information of our laboratories, we conclude that the Greek public expenses for the Development of Research come up to 0.38% of the GNP and are among the lowest among the 15 countries of the European Union (EU). The leader is Finland with 0.95% and is followed by the Netherlands (0.87%) and Sweden (0.86%). The last country is Ireland with (0.35%). The mean value of the Union is 0.66%. In USA this percentage is 0.56% and in Japan 0.70%. The Greek pointer is about 58% of the average value of the EU.

In Greece, the high risk investment capitals in the higher technology represent only 0.04% of the GNP. The first in this category is Great Britain with 0.26% and it is followed by Sweden 0.2% and Belgium 0.17%. Portugal is placed last with 0.01%. The EU's average is about 0.11%. Greece holds only 40% of this average.

This theory urges the research for the sustainable tourism development. It also stands for a great part of the UNESCO projects for the protection of the cultural heritage and tourist evolution (The first declaration was signed in May 2001 in UNESCO headquarters, the 2nd in November 2003 and the 3rd in 2005). It should be outlined that the same ideas are shared by the United Nations that consider the sustainable development as the foundation especially in developing and marine prefectures.[11] In Greece, the new derived capitals for enterprises represent 1.5% of the GNP. The Netherlands are first with 5.6% and is followed by Denmark with 4.5% and Spain with 4.4%. Italy is last with 0.1%, followed by Austria and Finland with 0.3%. The community average is 1.1%. Greece surpasses the average and is around 136% of it.

Only 12% of the Greek houses have Internet access. This is the smallest percentage in the EU. The Netherlands is first with 55% and is followed by Sweden with 54% and Denmark with 52%. In the USA this percentage is 47% and in Japan 28%. The community average is 28%. The Greek value is just the 43% of the average.

In Greece, the expenses for information and communication technologies represent 6% of the GNP. In the first position with 7.4% and is followed by the Netherlands and Portugal with 6.6%. Ireland is in the last position 4.8%. The community average is 6%.

From the aforementioned problems a number of weaknesses arise that should be dealt with especially on the tourism sector, since we are referring to high technology tourism. The EU is aid-giver in the technological convergence attempted by the country-members as it can be shown by the new European framework and its directives for years 2000-2006.

Under this framework the priorities for greek tourist prefectures are set:

1. Increase of arrival in 20m visitors
2. Increase of the overnight stays in 87m
3. Increase in the fullness of the hotels of the developed tourist areas by 10%.
4. Increase in the tourism income to 20b €
5. Increase in the average per head expenses to 1000 €
6. Increase in the number of the tourist workforce by at least 20%
7. The regional increase in the participation of tourism in the GNP by at least 2%
8. Promotion of the sustainable tourism[12]

4. The importance of tourism in Greece

From the available statistical information it is verified that the prime role in the Greek economy holds the tourism sector, since during the last 2 decades (1980–2000) the participation of the tourist industry in the financial development of the country was 12 times as much as the participation of industry.

In addition to that, during the last 25 years (1980-2005), the increase in employment in the tourist economy was 87.0% against only 9.2% of the total employment and against the decrease by 15.0% in the manufacturing industry. Furthermore, the pointers of the tourism sectors in our national economy, according to the findings of a recent (2003-2004) scientific research regarding the contribution of tourism in the GNP proved that tourism holds 53.0% of the GNP as opposed to 4.6% of the Industry and that the tourism currency was 2.5 times greater than the industrial exports and 1.8 times greater that the total export values.[13]

Direct	*Indirect*	
• Contribution in the GNP	4,5%	14,6%
• Contribution in Employment	5,0%	16,8%
• Contribution in Investments		22,5%

This related research (conducted by the Aegean University and University of Piraeus) predicts that by 2010 tourism will create 150.000 new work positions and that it could absorb 35.0% of today's unemployed people. Of course, the tourism sector of our country is far from being announced the "steamroller of the Greek economy", but it seems as though it could play a crucial role. A lot of elements help us conclude that this attempt will succeed and provide results. First of all, tourism employed 808.000 people, which is about 18% of the total workforce. This implies that 1/5 of the Greek workforce is either directly or indirectly related to tourism.

It should be made clear that tourism is not a business activity but a national cause. It is only then, that we can find the solutions to limit the losses and provide the opportunity for future steps; when we prove that we can come out of the crisis reinforced. This, of course, implies that we can deal with the crisis, take the necessary measures imposed by the circumstances, instead of remaining unresponsive to cancellations of reservations in Crete, for example. The Mediterranean basin is the place where the modern phenomenon of recreation travelling was initiated. Nowadays, 1/3 of the annual number of tourism globally is travelling in the Mediterranean. In this tourist area, Crete is justly considered the "air-force of the Mediterranean". Its distance from Asia is 175 km and from Africa 300km, and is naturally considered special as it is Europe's 5th island in size.[14]

Tourism development, as with any other financial activity, is not an end in itself. The target is the development to assist in the financial and social development of the reference area, improving both the income and the living conditions (short-term targets), and the general development perspectives of the area through a process of capital, knowledge, skill and future alternative solutions amassment (long-term targets).[15]

Nowadays, the perspectives for 2007 are auspicious, implying that the development rate will increase and confirm the initial predictions. WTO long-term predictions state that international tourism development will depict an annual development rate of 4.1% until year 2020. The number of tourists traveling around the world in the next 15 years will be 3 times as much as the concurrent. The Organization predicts that the boost in traveling will assist the economies of all the areas around the globe. It is also predicted that the number of people travelling abroad will be around 1b in 2010 and 1.56 b in 2020.

5. General Aspect of the Greek tourist phenomenon

However, modern war conflicts in the Gulf (Afghanistan, Iraq) and Kosovo, or the terrorist actions in Egypt, showed that tourist activity begins with skepticism. This is intensified by Crete's particularity that it is both very close (geographically) to the belligerent countries and the fact that it is an island providing only airplanes and ships as transport means. However, the rapid raise of tourism is not a Cretan phenomenon only. Nowadays, the circumstances are welcoming a global tourist development, as the evolution of the transport means, the validation of extended worker leave. According to the World Travel and Tourism Symposium, the traveling-tourist activity constitutes the greatest production sector on a global level, according to any financial pointer. It is estimated that it represents 12% of the private consumption, 7% of the total global employment and 6% of the global GNP. The same numbers for Greece, despite not being very specific, are probably higher than the global average.[16]

Figure 2. Map of Greece

The modern image of the financial aspect of greek tourism and its organic relation to the structure and operation of the greek economy, that is the production and promotion of an annually especially formulated private consumption for the living of about 13m incoming visitors has the following form and measures:

The modern capabilities of the country's hotels that surpass 8000 units, with more than 312,000 rooms and more than 600,000 beds constitute the most fundamental element of the tourist upper-structure on which the structural development of the global tourist production and promotion level is based upon and defined.[17]

The lodging, traveling and most of all the consumption of the annual 13m tourists end up in more than 100m overnight stays. In the aforementioned activity of the tourist production, one should include the seasonal goods and services from a number of non-tourist production enterprises as Banks, Road, Sea and Air Transportation enterprises, Mail and Health Services, Gas Stations, Food and Goods Shops, Airport, Port and Station Services, and all the manufacturing consumption goods production, as well as an important part of the capital good productions.

According to this information it may be understood the "error" in defining tourism as just "industry" or "service sector" and not on its real financial size as an annual specifically formulated private consumption. This implies that tourism should be financially and politically defined as the fundamental factor of the complete final demand of the domestic products and consequently the fundamental factor of the viability and competitiveness of the Greek economy.

This productive structure for the supply and administrative regulation of the annual consumption of the 13m tourist; that is for an important part of the domestic production, depicts certain characteristics, whose credible approach (see Table 2) and constant observation constitute the fundamental condition for every intervention in the tourist and generally financial policy, targeting on the increase of the competitiveness both of tourism and its participation in the financial competitiveness.

So there is, a financial phenomenon as the so-called tourism industry is operating, while at the same time a social phenomenon is under way as tourism implies the communication of people having different mental aspects and what this leads to. Through our country's global recognition for its tourist attractions, the island of Crete is an especially wanted tourist destination, as it attracts annually a large percentage of the visiting tourists.

Table 1: Tourism Affected Sectors

Tourism affected sectors	
Part of the income comes from tourism	*The whole income comes from tourism*
Nutrition	*Lodging*
Restaurants	Hotels
Coffee shops-Pubs	Pensions
Food industry/shops	Rooms to let
	Camping
Staff	
Public market goods	Travel Bureaus
Souvenirs	Domestic tourism
Clothes	Abroad tourism
Entertainment	*Transports*
Theatres/Cinemas	Air companies
Night Clubs	Recreation yachts
Local shows	Rent-a-car
Transport	*Tourist visit areas*
Public means of transport	Parks
Taxi	Museums
KTEL	Historical monuments
	Monasteries

6. The importance of Tourism for Greece, Tourism in Crete

The last two years tourist flow in Crete has developed, since it holds 20% of the total hotel units of the country and 25% of luxury and 'A' class hotels.[18] So the overly raised number of tourists formulates a new order. Crete's visitors in their majority come from high technical, scientific and mental development. These people provide the natives with specimens of culture, balanced and lawful behaviors. The same aspects are shared by the United Nations, because they adore the landscape, want to be hosted here, establish enterprises and offer employment to properly-trained natives.[19]

However, not such kinds of tourists visit Crete, and the consequences from tourism tides are not always positive. The negative consequences of the phenomenon are also important:

a) Tourists transfer, as already mentioned, new behaviors, ways of life and foreign habits, fact which causes tendencies for mimicking that leads to the engagement of those of less developed areas, without thought while at the same time relishing traditional values of our culture. E Papanoutsos in[20] wrote that "... I will not agree with those who care about the lack of moral purity of our farmers and especially islanders. Tourism does not bring degradation [...] but it might accelerate and worsen the fact that the living prototype causing mimicking, leads young people to conditions where they would be led on their own, but it now happens a lot quicker with less maturity, and therefore with a greater danger of getting humiliated...". To be more specific, a mimicking of loose morality that is presented by the tourists is observed, resulting in a blooming in short-term love affairs and problems inside the cretan families. A very big percentage of the loss of morality will consider everything traditional as anachronistic so a modernization is observed in dressing, nutrition, and entertainment. We should not omit the rise in drugs abuse, crime rates as well as diseases passed on through sex.

b) The contradiction between the natives and rich tourists, as it may be depicted by our common European Currency, creates the tendency for over-consumption and is responsible for the natives' greed for big and easy earnings, even through the violation of the rules of social behavior, or even worse speculation and illegitimacy. However, the natives seem to disregard the fact that during holidays, tourists are more susceptible to their consumption tendencies, as opposed to their countries where they follow a stricter financial programme.

c) Another unwelcome outcome of tourism is the fact that a lot of native people sell land to foreigners, to such an extent that in some years we may become foreigners in our country. This turn to tourist employment is part of a more general change of employment pattern for the young people of Crete, who unfortunately have been impressed by the immediate earnings of tourism and defy agricultural and other traditional jobs.

d) In addition to that, some profiteers, in order to attract and take advantage of the vast number of tourism, adapt the offered hospitality and entertainment, to the foreigners habits, use foreign means, imitate their language, organize shows and decorate the entertainment rooms and hotels with irrelevant elements, while also engage a number of bad-taste analogous actions. According to the results of a field research that was realized by gathering information from all the interventions of the island, it should be stressed out that they should not alter the characteristics of the island (cultural, environmental or historical) on their attempt to increase their earnings.[21]

Another problem was added to our tourist island regarding the pointers during period 1998-2002. First of all the number of overnight stays in 1998 was 11.830.707 with a change factor of +2.9% as opposed to the previous year. The same figures on 1999 were 13.116.526 overnight stays with a change factor of +10.9%. In the year of 2000 the figures were 12.457.367 overnight stays with a change factor of -5.0%, in year 2001 12.579.897 overnight stays with +1.0 change factor, while in the year of 2002 12.206.133 with a change factor of -3.0%. Despite the increase of overnight stays the occupancy of the hotels have declining rates the last years, despite of the fact that Crete depicts the highest fullness rates in relation to the rest of the Greece the average fullness rates does not surpass 63.46%.

The island character of the prefecture and its geopolitical region define to a great extent its development figures and are taken into account during the planning of the development policy with regards to the workforce. The prefecture presents low unemployment figures with the characteristic of limitation of employment on the primary employment sector and great increase on the tertiary employment sector. The positive populational evolution of the last two decades is strongly affected by the temporal increase of the population due to the tourist inflow.[22]

7. Basic peripheral pointers of Crete

7.1 *Geographical-morphological information*

The region of Crete is made up of Heraklion, Lassithi, Rethymnon and Chania prefectures and is located in Heraklion, which is the capital of the homonym prefecture. The Aegean Sea is on the north of Crete, while The Libyan Sea is on its South. The size of Crete is 8.335 km^2 and covers the 6.3% of the total size of the Country. Gavdos, Dia, Koufonisi, Gaidouronisi or Chrissi, Dionysades, Spinalonga, and Paksimadi, also belong to Crete region. The morphology of Crete is characterized by the existence of three basic zones: the 400m and above zone, the 200-400m zone and the sea level to 200m zone. The first two zones take up the 3/5 of the island and are made up of a constant mountain chain going from west to east, with small valley and canyons. This mountain chain has six tops above 2000m.

7.2 *Population*

The population of Crete is 601.159 people according to the information of the census of the National Statistical Service of Greece for 2001. 303.871 are male while 297.288 are female. In addition to that, 294.312 people live in Heraklion prefecture, 75.903 in Lassithi prefecture, 81.781 in Rethymnon prefecture and 149.163 in Chania prefecture.

During the last census realized on 1991, Crete's population was of 539.304, meaning that the islands' population was raised by 11.5% in this decade, which is more than satisfactory, if we consider the fact that the total population of Greece was raised by 6.7% (10.939.605 people as opposed to 10.252.580 people in 1991). From these 10.939.605 people, the 5.424.089 are male while 5.515.516 are female. The increase in the number of the male population was 2.4% while the female population was raised by 6%.

According to the same official information, among the 4 prefectures of Crete the greatest raise was in Rethymnon prefecture with 16.7%. The next one is the prefecture of Chania, with a raise of 11.5%, Heraklion with a raise of 11.3% and Lassithi with 7%.

The urban population is 42% of the total population of

Crete and has an increasing tendency. The rural population is 46% of the total population with declining tendencies while the semi-urban population is remaining stable with 12% of the total population.

7.3 *Regional Production*

The Region of Crete produces 5.7% of the total GNP of Greece. 31% of the regional GNP is produced on the primary sector, 13% on the secondary and 56% on the tertiary. The respective percentages for the country are 15%, 25% and 60%. The greatest part of the regional GNP is produced in Heraklion prefecture (51.1%), which is followed by Chania prefecture (23.4%), Lassithi prefecture (13.7%) and Rethymnon prefecture (11.8%).

7.4 *Productivity*

As for the productivity, the region of Crete stands on the same level with the total country, while presents smaller figures than the EU productivity rates. More specifically, in year 1996 Crete's productivity was 72% of the EU average (Greece average = 72% of the EU average), presenting however an increasing tendency during the last years.

7.5 *Employment*

The financially active population of the region of Crete is around 229,600 people, while the employed ones are 219,100 around. The evolution of the active population and the employment is rising the last years, which goes along with the raise in the total population of the Region. 37.8% of the employed population is working on the primary sector, 12.5% on the secondary, while 49.7% on the tertiary sector, while the national percentages are 19.8%, 22.5% and 57.7% respectively. As for the evolution of sectoral composition of the employment, during the last period, we observe a tendency of intensification of the tertiary and primary sectors, while the secondary sector presents a small decline.

7.6 *Unemployment*

The unemployment rate in the Region is better than the country's as it is about 4.6% as opposed to the national rate which is 10.3%. Unemployment in the Region of Crete depicts a slight rising tendency during the last years. The situation for the special categories of unemployed is better in the region as opposed to the country.

The unemployment rate for women is 7.3%, while the young unemployed are 20.7% of the total number of unemployed, while the respective national rates are 15.9% and 32.3%. The long-term unemployment in Crete is 49.7%, while the national rate is 57.1%. The intense circularity and temporality of the fundamental actions of the local economy demand increased multi-specialization, targeting on the movement of the workforce.

7.7 Primary Work Sector

The GNP of the primary sector takes up 12% of the national primary sector GNP and 31% of the total regional GNP, thus implying the importance of this sector for the regional and national economy. Despite its important participation in the macro-economic metrics, the primary work sector is characterized by the long-term structural incompetence resulting from the small and multi-fragmented agricultural land. In addition to that, Crete is lacking of watered areas. The structure of cultivation in the Region leads to the specialization on traditional farming as Olive oil and Grape cultivations. Vegetable cultivation is just 3% of the total cultivated area, but Crete depicts 50% of the total number of greenhouses in Greece. Crete has comparative advantages for the cultivation of vegetables and flowers. Cattle-raising in Crete has a more extensible character, with a small number of organized cattle units. The greatest part of the animal capital is made up of free pasture sheep and goats. The development conditions for the production of hard cheese are important, as the region participates in 25% of the national production. Despite the island character of the Region of Crete, fishing faces problems, stemming mostly from the lack of infrastructure, manipulation and selling of the fishing goods, and modernization and reformation of the fishing fleet and methods. Last but not least, Crete presents advantages in the apiculture due to the climate and apicultural flora.[23]

7.8 Secondary Sector

The selling businesses are of relatively small sizes except for the associations. Crete has only 1.8% of large-industry shops and only 25 units that present a work cycle greater than 350m €. The selling of the primary sector goods has organization, quality, planning and standardization problems, which are intensified by the lack in the modernization of the infrastructure. The problems are also connected to the lack of commercial networks for the promotion of the local production to the international markets. The selling and services connection, networking, and connection to research centers are on low levels. The land/urban-planning organization of selling is inadequate, resulting in environmental burdens and pressure from the settling extension and the development of other sectors of the local economy.[24]

8. Tourist Infrastructure on an Island Level

On an island level we have 1.244 units with 59.125 rooms and 9.157 apartments and 111.547 beds. The competitiveness of the tourist regions is based on their capability of attracting, creating and sustaining businesses with a constant rising portion of the tourist market and a constant improvement in the living conditions of their workers. The general tourism bureaus in Crete are 411. The local tourism bureaus are 37. The unguided rent-a-car bureaus are 531, while the rent-a-moto bureaus are 137. Nowadays, the movement of charter-based tourists to the airports of Chania and Heraklion was 3.088.013 people.

Crete's participation in the basic pointers of the research activity is higher than that of other regions of the country. Crete Region holds the second position in the regional ranking according to the percentage distribution of the research institutes in Greece with 14% by 1993.

The research institutes have developed cooperation with industries residing outside Crete but the orientation to the local economy remains on low levels. Moreover, a satisfactory level of synergy has been accomplished between the research and university institutes of the region.

Table 2: Hotel Figures per Prefecture

Hotel unit category	*Heraklion*		*Lassithi*		*Rethymnon*		*Chania*		*Regional Total*	
	Unit number	*Bed number*	*Unit number*	*Bed number*	*Unit number*	*Bed number*	*Unit number*	*Bed number*	*Unit number*	*Bed number*
Luxury	7	4,866 (14,1)	9	2,893 (22,3)	1	318 (0,2)	-	-	17	8,077 (11,7)
Á΄ Class	46	17,74 (50,5)	17	5,994 (46,2)	17	7,030 (48,1)	9	2,175 (30,6)	89	32,940 (47,6)
Â΄ Class	37	7,900 (22,9)	16	2,710 (20,9)	29	4,861 (33,3)	20	2,907 (40,9)	102	18,378 (26,6)
OTHER	29	3,956 (11,5)	10	1,387 (10,7)	18	2,401 (16,4)	45	2,026 (28,5)	102	9,770 (14,1)
TOTAL	119	34,463	52	12,984	65	14;610	74	7,108	310	69,165
% on the total of the tourist period	38,4%	49,8%	16,8%	18,8%	21,0%	21,1%	23,9%	10,3%	100,0%	100,0%

Tourism in Crete is the most dynamically developing branch. The GNP of the sector presents a constant raise for Crete, which is greater than the country's. The employment on tourism is also raised (the hotels and restaurants of Crete employ 8.5% of the active population) with a percentage which is almost double from the national.

The increased demand of the last years has led to important investments in all hotel units, resulting in the quantitative and qualitative upgrade of the hotel infrastructure. The current spatial distribution of the hotel units having more than 100 beds, per prefecture and category, is depicted in the Table 2.

The tourism sector however, despite its dynamics, faces a lot of problems. The seasonality leads to inactivity on capital and workforce terms from November to the beginning of April, despite the actions for extending the tourist period.

9. Infrastructure—Quality of Life

9.1 Transportation

The ports and airports of Crete are a crucial parameter both on tourism and good transportation and the population transportation needs. The major ports are Kissamos, Souda, Rethymnon, Heraklion, Ag. Nikolaos, Siteia, and Ierapetra, while airports exist in Heraklion, Chania and Siteia.

Through the North Highway Axis the whole northern seaside zone, where 79% of the tourism GNP is produced, is served. Also, this national road serves 74% of the total regional population. It is important to improve and finalize the Southern Highway Axis connecting the spot tourist development and the areas of intensive farming to the transverse vertical roads.[25]

9.2 Mountain/Internal Zones

Three extended mountain zones are identified: the first one that is made up of the Lefka Ori and Idi, the second zone which is made up of Asterousia on the south of Heraklion prefecture and the third one extended eastern including Lassithiotika Ori. 49.4% of the region is mountainous. From the total of the former municipalities and villages (567) that are in Crete Region, 35.6% belongs to mountainous areas, while 17.1% of the total population lives on mountainous areas. The most important problems are spotted on the improvement of living conditions and the protection and show-off of the natural environment.

9.3 Small Islands

In Crete Region also belongs a number of islands as Gavdos, Dia, Koufonisi, Gaidouronisi or Chrissi, Dionysades, Spinalonga, and Paksimadi, most of which are not inhabited, the most important of which is Gavdos. In these islands a number of actions have been taken in the framework of earlier programme periods. The small size of these islands, the low productivity and their financial dependence, in relation to the lack of adequate transportation connection and low quality and quantity of infrastructure, results in the creation of acute problems, results in a gradual ageing, population shrinking and depopulation.

9.4. Urban Centers

Table 3: Urban Centres and Possibilities

Urban Centers	*Development Role*	*Business and Development Infrastructure*	*Promotional Activities*
Heraklion	National and International Development Pole, Governmental and Commercial Center, Sea transport center for the area of the SE Mediterranean	Port Airport University TEI Industrial Zone Northern Highway Axis	Higher Education Technological Research and Development Health Services Tertiary Industry (international commerce-transports) Tourism
Chania	Center of Prefectural Development	Port Airport University TEI Industrial Zone Northern Highway Axis	Higher Education Technological Research and Development Tertiary Industry (commerce-transports) Tourism)

Rethymnon	Center of prefectural Development	Port University TEI Northern Highway Axis	Tourism Higher Education
Other Cities			
Agios Nikolaos	Center of Prefectural Development	Port TEI Northern Highway Axis	Tourism Higher and Technological Education
Ierapetra	Center of Local Development	Port TEI	Tourism Higher and Technological Education
Siteia	Center of Local Development	Port Airport TEI Northern Highway Axis	Tourism Higher and Technological Education Energy Production

10. Marketing Science in Tourism

As stated by Kotler in[26] ,... *Marketing has been defined in many ways. Consider the following definitions:*

"Marketing is the performance of business activities that direct flow of goods and service from the producer to the consumer or user" (American Marketing Association).

"Marketing is the management process responsible for identifying, anticipating and satisfying customer requirements profitably" (British Institute of Marketing).

"Marketing is human activity directed at satisfying needs and wants through exchange processes."[26]

However, the most difficult part is to define marketing in the area of service offer, where its activities are multidimensional. Generally, however, tourist marketing deals with the business tourist activity, whose target is the viability of the hospitality business and its unique capabilities in the specific tourist market, where it is the most suitable for the better exploitation of its resources. In this definition we will attempt a small analysis:

a) There are specific capabilities of a tourist business that can provide special emphasis in claiming the tourist market with regards to time and financial capability of the tourists-consumers.
b) The definition of the targets should be specific; that is what the target group in the market is, because not all people are attracted by a tourist packet.
c) The relation between the two aforementioned parameters should be adequate.

The Tourist Marketing that is applied by the Greek Tourist Organization, to achieve the objective targets that have already been set by the National Tourism Planning must constitute a basic operation and tool of applied tourist policy.[27]

The term market placc is also open for definition. Most scientists agree that the market place is equal to the consumers: the buying or buying-capable population. This market place is also apparent in tourism, with the tour operators as the intermediaries that find the end-users (consumers). However, the most important success condition for a tourist business is a constant support on marketing that is required to sustain a viable hosting business. This is why marketing, along with Financial Management-Revision, have the profound effect on the performance of any tourist business.[28]

This is the situation regardless if a clearly identified marketing department exists in a tourist business or not. A hosting business in Crete, in order not to alter itself, or stop functioning, should first of all check if it would use marketing a sales approach or as something more than that. Generally speaking, this can be utilized in three ways:

a) For the description of an approach of a problem
b) For the creation of a unique department that has a number of responsibilities and actions
c) As just one part of the total works of a tourist business.

Marketing is of vital importance for the definition of the long-term future of a tourist business or area, especially in the distribution of the resources in certain operations. Marketing scientists and businessmen are interested in the study of the consequences of consumer dissatisfaction since the kind and intensity of these consequences have been studied with market feedback mechanisms in the foreign (Anglo-Saxon mostly) bibliography.[29]

Marketing acknowledges these needs so as to propose a series of actions that satisfy the choice of the most appropriate actions according to certain marketing factors.[30]

According to the general aspect, marketing in the area of service offering is not a neglected financial technique. The intangible values that often regulate the selection of the tourist product was directly equalized to the intangibility of a service.[31]

However, as it is widely known, a service offering provides memories, while a product durability. However marketing is not considered a peripheral skill and posture but a modern financial technique. For example, "the stabilization of packet booking-sales to the extent we want to be full" of the unit for the viability of a tourist business, contributes in the decline of the temporal gain, targeting on the long-term profits that remain a basic notion.

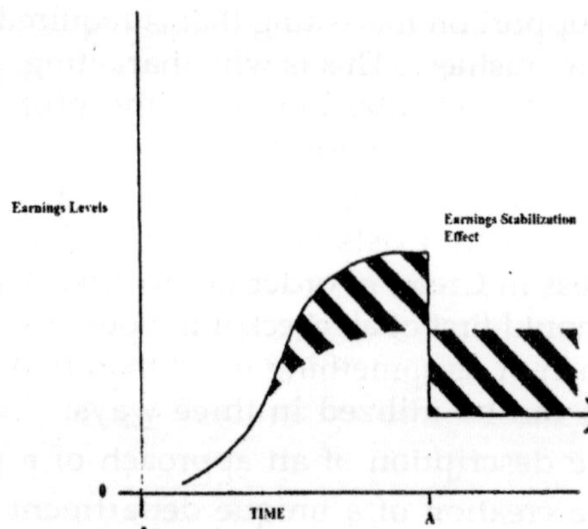

Figure 3: Stabilization of Fullness in Relation to the Increase of Booking[32]

The operation of the tourist marketing is applied either on areas or on distributed exploitation departments of a tourist business. According to the current data, the development of the tourist areas or businesses requires long-term marketing. For a sector that employs 290,000 people on prime season, there are no acceptable ignorance, omission, and delay thresholds ...we advertise tourism off-season using the same clichés.[33]

Despite the fact that the infiltration operation of the tourist packets in the tourist market existed in the early years as well, a supplementary sector of this operation was initiated called marketing. For example, we can infiltrate it to the tourist market through the appropriate channels, after we first advertise it in an appropriate manner. Competition results in such situations that even if we create a very good tourist product, we will not be able to sell it without the appropriate advertisement[34]. However, the global promotion of Myconos, Rhodes, Mallorca, Saint Trope, and especially Crete and the mass flow of tourists from other parts of the world in these areas, was not accomplished through complex and expensive tourist programmes, but was the outcome of tourist satisfaction from the offered service, resulting in a mouth-to-mouth advertisement.

The Gothic cathedral of Milan is undoubtedly the most wanted tourist spot in the city, but the second element is Virgin in Italy through a balloon. This was how the company salesmen believed they would infiltrate in the market.[35]

11. *Primary Viewpoint Registration Search*

The people working in tourism in Crete are again agonizing for the tourist season of 2007. The perspectives seem optimistic, yet a lot of people are troubled by the lack of infrastructure, the environment degradation and other familiar problems. Two years ago, everybody was referring to the flow deficit resulting from the decline in the arrivals in Crete, along with the 2.1b € for the installation costs and losses of around 450m € from the decline of tourism in Crete. The decline in the arrivals and overnight stays was less than 10% (4% and 8% respectively), but the earnings decline was around 20%-30% in a year that started with a number of problems. This deficit that became apparent in the local market, is the outcome of the decline in arrivals, in overnight stays an in imported tourist currency.

Our laboratory team considers Crete to be the most important tourist destination in Greece. It is the biggest island in size and population, depicting the longest coastline in Greece. One of the biggest congregations of archaeological, historical and religious monuments is located in Crete, with Knossos Minoan palace being the second in visitation in Greece, after Acropolis. The Heraklion Museum is the first Greek museum in visitors. The cultural and historical tradition of the island is special, while its contribution to the global history and culture with a rich folk tradition is great. In addition to that, Crete presents excellent tourist development perspectives, since it depicts numerous natural beauties, taking into consideration, however, that there should be a special planning and sensitization especially for the offer of high quality services and environmental respect. Last but not least, Crete has some of the most important natural monuments as the Samaria Canyon, with a great flora variety and some unique fauna specimen.

Crete also has an excellent, mild and tourism-favorable climate with the greatest climatic differentiations in Greece. It has two of the biggest international airports and ports of the country and a dense road network. The satisfaction and safety feelings of the tourists is observed at about 95%, while the most important satisfaction elements are the landscape, the natural environment, the sightseeing areas, the clear water and sea, hospitality and people, the quality of the provided services and the hotels. This is why the tourists that visit the island more than once are a lot (41% of the tourists have visited the island around 3.3 times). 23% of the visitors consider Crete the best holiday place. 72% is favorable to Crete, when comparing it to their favorite holiday area.

Crete is not considered by tourists as a touristically satiated place, when compared to other Greek tourist destination as Rhodes or Corfu.

The tourist sector, as already mentioned above, is one of the basic areas of Crete's economy and concentrates 25% of the private tourist infrastructure of the country. Generally, it presents a satisfactory yield the last years, despite the fact that the provided services do not always have the same quality. Crete's tourist product still operates on high competition markets, with the difference that from 1/1/2006 the decision taken by the German market about certified products, turned the Cretan producers to sales promotion techniques of certified products and the initiation of e-marketing. Crete remains a traditional recreation destination offering, sun, sea, beaches and cultural monuments. The tourist packet demand, which is based on the aforementioned, continues to increase on low rates, while at the same time the consumers' demands are rapidly evolving, for destinations that offer high-quality services regarding lodging, nutrition, natural environment, and alternative entertainment solutions. Little benefits have been gained by tourism on the local communities; very few of the desired results have been produced, while a number of harmful consequences have been observed.[36] Crete is undoubtedly a tourist island. The fear that all Cretans would become servants of the foreign tourists, in reality, is nothing more than an indirect recognition that tourism is the most positive profit source of the country.[37] Let us state clearly then that tourism is one of the most important branches for the development of the local Economy.[38]

12. The Tourist Product Sales Prediction

The most complex methods of predicting the sales of the tourist products take into consideration the different variables to formulate financial models. This, however, surpasses the capabilities of most tourist enterprises that tend to limit themselves to a hypothetical prediction of their sales; in other words, in a prediction that is based on hypotheses of what the world thinks would happen.

The prediction is based on marketing research, yet this is future-oriented and implies expectations, decisions and prediction for the same tendencies implied by the diagnosis. The diagnosis undoubtedly represents a factual platform that defines the base of tourism planning on a strategic or tactical level. The prediction methods are easy to be included in the marketing programmes of small tourist enterprises, while the prediction of the tourist product demand can be formed only on the basis of its demand on a predefined time on a tourist market place and specifically either on a part of the tourist market place or on a certain geographical area.

Despite the fact that the prediction of tourist product sales should be made an o tri-level approach (tourist environment, tourist industry and tourist enterprise), yet almost all of the short and middle term predictions are based on the use of statistical techniques to conclude in the sales tendencies of the past. Thus, the analysis of time sequences that levels the effects of circular or cyclic changes in sales is used to project the tourist product sales. These sales can be conceived as a linear or exponential tendency, where one expects to multiply them by a constant in order to acquire a stably increasing curve.[39]

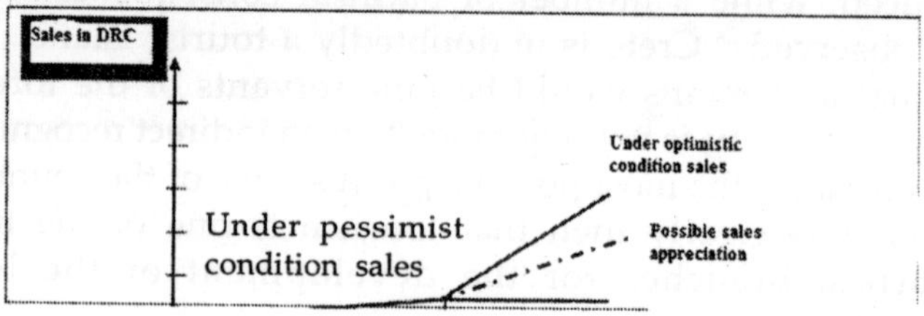

Figure 4. The prediction of a tourist product's sales[40]

13. The life-cycle model

One of the most controversial examples in the philosophy of developing a tourist destination as that of Crete, besides swot analysis, is the life-cycle model. The analyses of the life-cycle route are described when the evaluation of the current tourist situation has been included. The models tries to verify using large-scale time series, and the general conclusion is that the limitation imposed by the congregation process, limit the example of Crete life-cycle of Crete on a statistical framework, in the existence of not less than one statistical condition of the real tourist world.

Since 1980 when Butler wrote his first article for the development of tourism, the life-cycle model has been widely discussed, applied and has been accepted as a notional framework for the analysis of the historical evolution of the resorts and even tourist destinations through a wide variety of perspectives. The five stages are depicted on the following table. Few tourists, limited capabilities, unspoilt natural environment without masses of people on the local communities that are included in the stage of Research. On the next stage we have Participation, the local communities are bonded to tourism, the capabilities and infrastructure is built, the tourist conveyors are created, the tourist market place is defined, which later on increases the speed of tourism development. On Development stage, Crete as a tourist destination is defined correctly: the tourist attraction spots have been projected, the promotion campaigns have increased and the publicity of the area has been gradually raised, which is certified by the constant increase in the number of tourists' arrivals. In the stage of Stabilization, the number of tourists continues to rise, but to a smaller percentage than the past. Crete as a tourist destination is not easily sold and tourism is very important for the local economy, in an area identified as tourist. The last stage, Stability, Crete does not have the greatest number of tourists. It is outdated and it has obvious environmental protection problems, or even culture promotion and possible capabilities in the development of local industry structure. In this phase, the destination has two options: fall, or rebirth.

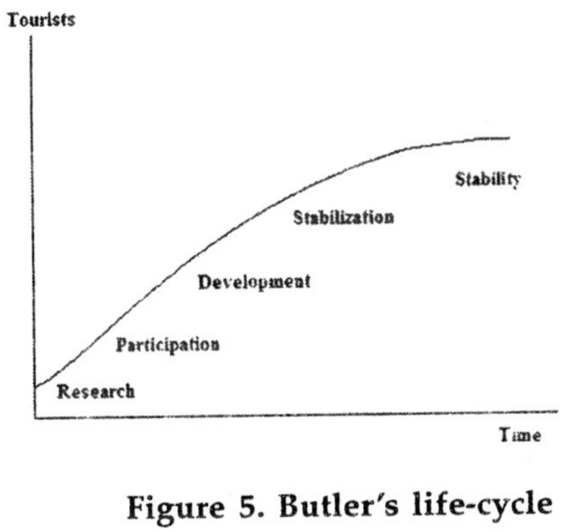

Figure 5. Butler's life-cycle

Through this philosophy, the test of the model has followed the path of element correlation from the case-work examples in the stages of the life-cycle curve. The general conclusion seems to be that the model is useful as a representation of Crete's development, but is rather descriptive than finite. However, a number of attempts have been made to check the model and describe the development in a different way than the theory. However, the model itself is still used as a descriptive framework, and under this background it is possible for one to explain the local characteristics that cause the deviation from theory.

In our study for the island of Crete, it is shown that international tour operators play an important role in the island's development. Generally speaking, it seems that the competition from other tourist destinations is a "shift factor" in the curve. As a result, different decisions between the tourist conveyors are important for the speed and form of the life-cycle process, but affect more as "subject variations" rather than general challenges. But it is a controversial point as to whether a model including the market place variations, the financial conditions, and the unspecified tourist product changes, can formulate the time route shown in the table, offering a "rich" theory for the development of the destination.

In our study for Crete, we present an example of an island that was not a mature destination in the 70s and has struggled for its rebirth since then. Generally, the descriptive sight of Crete's life-cycle is oriented on differentiation, with a concentration on the tourist product. The advantage of observing in the tourist offer is an implied challenge for the improvement of the product, especially if you are on the verge of the Stability stage. However, the number of tourists is the norm of the chronic route of Crete as destination, while also assisting the examination of the theoretical stages of the cycles from the tourist perspectives.

14. S.W.O.T. Analysis

Having assured the necessary data through the process of diagnosing secondary sources of information and future tendencies through the process of prediction, as shown from the next figure, the next step is to assess the importance of tendencies in strategic and tactical planning of the marketing project. An efficient way to assess objectively, is to use S.W.O.T. analysis, following the four steps: Strengths, Weaknesses, Opportunities, Threats.

S.W.O.T. analysis targets its interest on the elaborate work required to answer the question "Where are we now?". It is an efficient and sometimes laborious composition of the capabilities and weaknesses of the tourist destination in relation to the competition, as well as the opportunities and threats. With SWOT analysis one checks:

- The Strengths, in relation to the competition that were deduced by the internal analysis and can be classified or assessed in order to declare and present their importance.[41]
- The weaknesses, in relation to the competition that were deduced by the internal analysis and can be classified or assessed in order to declare and present their importance.
- The Opportunities, that were deduced by the outer analysis of the situation and can be classified by a time-schedule aspect (direct, middle-term, long-term), by the aspect of the profit importance on the tourist destination and by the aspect of success possibility.
- The Threats, that were deduced by the outer analysis of the situation and can be classified by a time-schedule aspect (direct, middle-term, long-term), by the aspect of severity in the framework of importance of the negative effects on the tourist destination and by the aspect of occurrence possibility.

The same applies for the strategic marketing plan where the same question should be answered, and in the tactical marketing plan the points of vital importance are presented on a concise way (see next diagram)

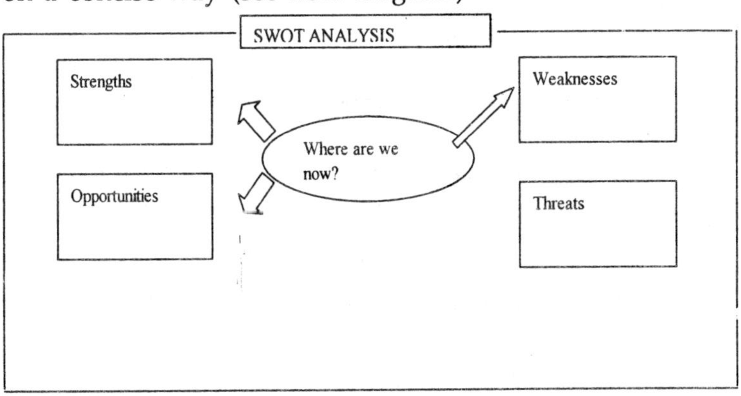

Diagram 1: SWOT Analysis

The marketing plans are expressed in a certain form as the situation in which the destination would like to be after a specific time period, e.g. three or five or even ten years. Marketing aims usually target their interest on markets and products, which are produced after the SWOT analysis.

The annual aims of marketing result from the long-term strategic targets and must be compatible and express quantitative and qualitative goals, be countable and as specified as possible, so as to be time defined (weekly, monthly etc.) and with an expiry date, so as to have a control mechanism, while also be realizable and efficient goals.

Marketing long-term strategic goals are related to:

a) the numbers of arrivals in the destination, expressed in real or absolute or percentage values and rises in the current values;
b) the costs of the tourist visits on the destination, expressed in real or absolute or percentage values and rises in the current values;
c) the length of stay of the tourists-visitors on the destination, the costs of the tourist visits on the destination, expressed in real or absolute or percentage values and rises in the current values;
d) the possible extension of the tourist season for the tourist-visitors on the destination, expressed in real values and percentage increase of the current business in the months with lowered flow;
e) the intensification of the level of services and results of the tourist destination;
f) the increase of the number of suppliers in the tourist destination.

The tactical (annual) goals of marketing are related to:

a) the number of tourist visits that are defined as the annual specified target with a "from-to" increase (e.g. from 5.000 people to 7.000 people), separated in local and international visitors per important tourist department, according to the visitor's nationality, in new or old tourist businesses;
b) the numbers of costs defined as the annual specified target with a "from-to" increase (e.g. from 100,000

to 300,000) separated in cost per person, per visit, per exploitation department, and according to tourist destination ingredients (stay, sightseeing etc).

c) the time of stay that is divided in the basic part an according to stay and overnight stay data (hotels, pensions etc) and distributed by month or season

d) the extension of season and tourist destination at the off-season months expressed by a "from-to" increase (e.g from 2m people to 5m people or from 2m overnight stays to 5m overnight stays)

e) the annual improvement presented in the measurements on the important exploitation departments (research results)

f) the annual improvement presented by the destination from the measurement of satisfaction levels, according to the ingredients of the destination and according to important results (research results).

Weakneses

The following have been observed as less strong elements of the Cretan Tourism:

- A great congregation of the tourist activity on the northern part of the island around the national road with an analogous congregation of transport means and hotel infrastructure.
- An especially large congregation of the tourist activity on the road connecting Heraklion to Agios Nikolaos, in the city of Rethymnon with an eastern direction and western from Chania.
- Disproportionate burden imposed on the Heraklion airport with the ¾ of the total tourist arrivals.
- Little satisfaction from the road signs and information system for tourists
- Environmental care, with special complaints for the presence of rubbish in streets, public places and beaches
- Limited preservation, in comparison to the rest of Greece and southern Europe, of the traditional

architectonical character and urban/rural style or the development of a "post-traditional" style.

- Tourism cataclysm, as extracted from statistical data (in year 2000, there were 12.457.367 overnight stays, while the hotel fullness was over 82% with increasing tendencies.[18]
- Increased seasonality of the offered tourist product, resulting in a great part of the workforce to stop working and going back to the farming employment.
- The development of tourism is unbalanced between the northern and southern coast with a high development rate on the north.
- The national infrastructure is not responding to the needs of the constantly raising visitor flow.
- In order to achieve high bed coverage and raise in tourist flow, the offered prices are falling resulting in lower profit margins for the enterprises and therefore lack of investments and limitation of the ability of attracting high tourism.
- The tourist product is based on foreign tourist businessmen and therefore the demand of novelty in the sector is declining.
- Insufficient educational system and constant learning of the employees on tourism.
- The certification and quality control systems are inadequate.
- No control in the rational housing development, resulting in an anarchic building and the alteration of the traditional image of the island.
- Lack of tourist marketing and market search as well as the application of e-commerce in the businesses.
- Non-existence in the peripheral structure of substantiation, research and planning of a complete strategy.
- A large addiction to foreign businessmen.
- Low average level of exploitation of the new technologies and inclusion of novelties that are connected the upgrade of the supplied services.

- Despite the great importance of tourism there is a lack of credible information or data for the tourist market, which results in the lack of strategic planning
- The anarchic building has imposed great burdens on the housing net and the nature, but also intense unbalance in peripheral structure economy, resulting in serious distortions that operate as anti-motive.

These contradictions are statistically presented, since during the last years Crete has fallen from the third to the fifth position of the per-head GNP. So, another important issue directly related to the future and Crete's orientation, but also the plans that will present the pragmatic capabilities and will bring Crete in the first gear of the European regions and convert it to a strong developing pole in the S.E. Mediterranean.

Important Opportunities

Crete has important opportunities of further tourist development in a series of axes. The first axis deals with the efficient exploitation of the important increase ratio. This is why the possibility of a third international airport should be considered, that would help relieve the congestion from Heraklion airport and serve the southern tourist destinations. In addition to that there should be an important improvement in the southern national road and the roads connecting northern national road with the southern national road. The second axis deals with the more efficient exploitation of the current infrastructure, with the extension of tourist season and the improvement of the level of tourists. Seasonality, which characterizes Cretan tourism, can be faced with the development of conference, school, naturalist, internal, "motivated", special-need and eco tourism. The development of eco-tourism will be based on the rich flora and fauna that is offered by the island. In addition to that, another opportunity for Crete comes from the development of new packets of tourist products for the winter period as the medical, conference and sightseeing tourism. Opportunities, also, arise by the development and promotion of agricultural tourism, which nowadays constitutes 2% of the tourism today. The next opportunity arises from the demand of the consumers for destinations and areas offering high quality tourist product, with regards to the stay of the natural environment and the offering of differentiated tourist services. The last opportunity arises from important financing and capabilities offered by the third Community Support Framework 2000-2006, with the aim of upgrading the tourist enterprises.

Strengths

At the same time, the directions for the promotion of greek tourism, stressing out that "the critical current coincidence is a chance for us to become stronger". There is the need for Crete to react directly to any negative fact that occurs and deals with tourism: "It is obvious that the success of factor safety is an important advantage for the island and we should not let anyone who is irrelevant to create impressions by stating anything he/she likes. We should not let anything drop and respond quickly and effectively for everything negative that is heard for our country."

The strengths of Crete are first of all a mild climate for any kind of activities, the existence of historical and cultural monuments, a great number of hotels offering high quality services and the existence of well-organized tourist businesses, while also a satisfactory level of offered services as well as the hospitality feeling and service willingness which is an inherent part of the cultural character of Crete. In addition to that, there is an intense tendency of market attraction in the traditional tourist product of Crete, while it also serves as a traditional, tested destination for tourism. These are intensified by the good air and sea transportation.

Crete undoubtedly has a strategic geographical position for the international and local (Mediterranean) passenger and commercial transportation. It is close to the great marine transport axis connecting the Indian Ocean with the Atlantic, while it also constitutes a crossroad leading to the Black Sea, fact which gives it the capability of being called as one of the greatest transportation junctions of the area. It is also the South-Eastern gate of the European Union and the point where the seas of three continents (Africa, Asia, Europe). It is also known, that from this marine space (from and to the Black Sea) are transported about 200m tons of goods.

Threats

The threats of the tourism sector are the following:

- The demand of Crete's tourist product is based on a limited market (small number of different origin countries of tourists)
- High competition from other Mediterranean destinations
- Cooperation between foreign businessmen are initiated and achieve better promotion prices for the tourist products than the local businessmen
- There is no governmental strategic planning for the development of tourism in Crete
- Degradation of the environment and no development of the transportation and hotel infrastructure of the island with ratios that keep up with the natural improvement ratios of tourism, are presented as the greatest threats imposed on the development perspectives of the future cretan tourism.

The experience gained by Crete the last 30 years of intense development is important. It is obvious that this kind of development solves short-term problems, but mortgages a difficult future. The degradation of the environment, the anarchic building and the disdain of the spatial aesthetics undermine the qualitative initiatives that are struggled by non-viable choices. A viable and operating spatial plan is absolutely required. The short-scale industry, mostly in the area of nutrition, is required to complete the quality of the tourist product. Agricultural production should focus on alternative choices and cultivation variety in order to retrieve its lost competitiveness and surpass the stalemates connected with the subsidy policy. Cattle-breeding will become a viable choice, if it focuses on high quality in conjunction with environmental protection.

Earlier in the 60s, the theory of stage development for tourism was supported. The stages referred to were three. The first stage includes the discovery of the area by some local or foreign tourists or businessmen. The second stage includes the positive reaction of the population to the tourist development and the creation of the infrastructure for the reception of a great number of tourists, while on the third stage, there is the building of large tourist clusters offering standardized and high specification hospitality in organized-traveling tourists and the transform of the tourist-native relation to the customer-salesman relation.[42]

In Crete, the transition from the first to the second stage was rapid, while from the second to the third we had mass tourism. This fact led us to create tables of some fundamental parameters of the island of Crete.

16. Work Plan

The team of our laboratory working on the applied research on the area of services proved that Crete's tourism is a positive factor not only for the financial development of the island but for its mental and social evolution, using the results of swot analysis. The belief shared by our laboratory team for Crete is that the island can take advantage of the situation if it first:

- Assures a number of employment positions for specialized and unspecialized workers or employees, with the aim to be the young people of the rural areas.
- Opens new employment chances for newly-employed people around the region.
- Finds a secure work alternative in the region, on areas of high restructural unemployment that comes from the shrinking of the primary sector and de-industrialization.
- Develops small and medium sized tourist enterprises of part-time or seasonal employment, of individual or family character, which would not undertake a high risk.
- Promotes directly and quickly the positive profits of the investments on an employment and income level.
- Assists the entrance of women from the agricultural or rural areas into a variety of tourist employment positions, even high responsibility ones, since it is known that despite the fact that certain progress has been made, yet women nowadays are employed on

15. *Table of advantages and disadvantages of Crete*

Financial characteristics		*Social Characteristics*	*Spatial Characteristics*
Strengths	• The dynamics of the local economy is balanced between two sectors (tourism and agriculture)· • In the sector of tourism we have created congregation economies and high quality hotel infrastructure· • Good quality and wide variety of local products· • Existence of an intense educational and research network and possibilities of development and novelty infiltration· • The position of the region in the SE Mediterranean· • The dynamic urban centers of Heraklion and Chania· • Its important place in the market· • The intense exporting orientation and dynamics on the primary sector and tourism	• The pointer of natural population increase has better values than the national average • Low unemployment rates (half the national average) • Population homogeneity • Discrete and alaready advertised living manner	• Important congregation of areas with remarkable natural environment elements. • Intense presence and spatial distribution with important historical and cultural elements • Capability of a total planning of an autonomous operating spatial unit due to the island character and great size

(contd...)

(Contd...)

Financial characteristics		Social Characteristics	Spatial Characteristics
Weaknesses	• Intense addiction to mass tourism· • Low level of agricultural standardization and weak mechanisms of commerce and promotion· • Low productivity and small specialization level of the workforce· • Low level of cross-sector synergy At the same time we present the current limitations that seek for a solution which are: ❖ The burden of the transportation cost due to the insular character of the region. ❖ Anarchic tourist congregation and strong connection with mass tourism ❖ Low level of secondary sector development ❖ Intense pressure on the environment by the overpopulation and the activities on the northern part of Crete ❖ Intense pressure and problems on the great urban areas (mostly in Heraklion)	• Increased pointers of ageing and addiction when compared to the national average • The educational level of the employees is worse than the national average • Limited social infrastructure network • Limited participation of women on the workforce and intense tendency of congregation of the female employment on the primary sector	• Difficulty in developing cooperation relations due to the insular character of the region • Intense pressure on the enviornment by the overpoulation and the activities on the northern part of Crete • Intense demands in infrastructure due to the diversity of the population on small scale settlements • Increased demands for the protection of the natural and cultural environment

Opportunities	• Stable quality, standardization and totalistic promotion policy of selected local products • Enrichment and differentiation of the tourist product • Intensification of enterprising and organizing of the units on a modern basis • The development of strong interconnections between research-technology and validated sectors of the local economy • The existence of a strong educational network and activity • The positive demographic evolution and small unemployment rate • The climate and natural environment	• Intensification of the multi-specialization of the workforce • Finalization of the social infrastructure nexus especially on the civil security sector • Social exclusion opposition • Intensification of the cultural structures	• Improvement of the spatial specialization • Intensification of the interconnection of the developed financial centers and entrance gates. • Promotion of the local urban centers and ensuring of their business relation with the rural zones • Totalistic administration intervention for the natural and cultural inheritance

low or medium work positions, while a very small percentage of them works in high responsibility places.

- Promotes the positive role of the Greek rural woman in small and medium sized of family businesses.
- Creates the suitable financial and social conditions of demographic improvement of the country, so as to stop the population decline of the rural areas, and have a real increase on these populations.
- Promotes all kinds of mild tourism (e.g. eco tourism, mountain-tourism, walkthroughs, traditional villages tourism, museum tourism, religious tourism, etc) so as to show both the natural and human-oriented environment.
- Provides the appropriate education to most of those who are employed in tourism.
- Corrects the lack of proper tourist program-planning that has led a great number of Cretan people among other natives to make wrong decisions that on a long-term manner will not help both the development of tourism and the local society.
- Increases both quantitatively and thematically the unemployment/employment specialization programmes on specific tourist sectors.
- Restructures the national tourist education, by modernizing and further specializing the programs of studies, as well as predicting new tourist jobs, and educating the workforce on a large scale.[43] Especially for Crete, its unrivalled in beauty and variety natural elements in conjunction with its unique in historical monuments culture, which are both globally known, can neutralize to a great extent the dissuasive for the tourist demand effect oh the human-oriented part of the total quality of the tourist product and classify it in the most wanted tourist destinations on a global scale.[44]
- Enables Crete to regain the lost time by converging gradually with its communal partners on the area of market research on tourism and information, despite the delays that still exist in tourism.

- Attempts, among others, a comparative evaluation of the tourist performance of the Crete areas, in which the achievements and tendencies will be shown, the strengths and weaknesses will be underlined and the tourist convergence route in the area of tourist market research by observation will be checked.
- Analyzes elements and pointers of tourist costs, arrivals, fullness, and per category of tourist enterprises in the areas of: Human workforce, creation of tourist knowledge, transmission and application of new tourist knowledge, tourist agents, and tourist markets.
- Makes attempts to reverse the tendency of delays or lacks in tourism, underlining that the tourist policy in Crete has been characterized by the Greek authorities as of crucial importance, while for the first time the authorities talk about the "Chart" of re-orientation of the Greek tourism with a perspective of 2020.
- Predicts for the following 5 years the alteration of Cretan tourism to a qualitative financial phenomenon so as to surpass the competition of the neighboring countries, and raise its demand in order to improve the levels of financial performance.

Conclusions

While the rules of the game that formulate the drastic changes in the outer environment are especially competitive, the basic composition of the tourist products in Crete is altered on very slow ratios. Tourism, as a modern socioeconomic activity, constitutes a post-industrial recreational society and it is foreseen that it can become the steamroller of the development and thus be used as an organic element for the planning of the peripheral tourist development. For that, it is required that the touristically developed regions that receive tourist flow to have the following conditions: natural, climatic, geographical, access, financial, living and cultural. But also in order to assure the stability of the peripheral development it is vital for the following elements to co-exist: numerous small enterprises with a local control, no superspecialization, environmental protection, assurance of constant demand, and appropriate tourist policy.[45]

These rates can not assure the maintenance of the peripheral income from tourism and Crete's share on the tourist market, if no upgrade services and enriching of the tourist product actions are taken. To that direction, the strategy for the improvement of the competitiveness of Crete's tourism should be structured. Under this prism the proposals aim to: upgrade the quality of the provided services in all sectors that constitute the tourist product and the maintenance of this quality through a totalistic modernization of the installations and hotel business of Crete. The enrichment of the composition of the Cretan tourist product with the development of special infrastructure that can differentiate the development of new tourist products of higher added value that are based on the exploitation of novelties and technologies that have already been developed in the Region of Crete, with the aid of research institutes of Crete (medicinal tourism, aquatic parks, museum tourism etc), and with the creation of special lodging infrastructure (agricultural tourism lodging etc.)

REFERENCES

1. Zacharatos G.(2002), *Tourist Financials,* Aegean University postgraduate programme, pp. 42.
2. Business and Tourism (2004), *Tourist Magazine,*Vol. 50, p.
3. Patronis B.-Papadopoulos A.(2001), 1st International Scientific Conference, (Proceedings), Preveza, p. 572.
4. Ministry of Development, Strategic Plan of Hellenic Tourism Development 2004–2010, September 2003.
5. Lagos D. (200), Financial Tourism Planning, Aegean University postgraduate programme, pp. 18.
6. Kotadakis A. (1974), *Tourism and Christian Belief,* I.M. Chalkida Publishing, p. 23.
7. Ray Youell (1998), *Tourism an Introduction,* United Kingdom, p. 2.
8. Greek Economy and Tourism Bank of Greece (2005) *World Tourism,* Vol. 19, pp. 59.

9. Money and Tourism (2003) from *Who Tourism Highlights* Edition 2003, Vol. 11, p. 203.
10. John M. Edington & M. Ann Edington (1986), *Ecology Recreation and Tourism*, Center for Environmental Studies, University of Wales, Cardiff, U.K pg. 1.
11. United Nations (2005), International Meeting to Review the Implementation of the Programmer of Action for the Sustainable Development of Small Island Developing States, Panel three: role of culture in the sustainable development of Small Island Developing States, Port Louis, Mauritius (1-14 January).
12. Strategic Plan of Development for the Greek Tourism 2004-2006, Ministry of Development–The predictions of International organizations for the development of the Greek tourism.
13. Strategic Plan of Development for the Greek Tourism 2004-2006, Ministry of Development.
14. Zopounidis K. et al (2004), Evaluation of the Financial Performance of the Tourist and Hotel Enterprises of Crete, Financial Administration Laboratory Cretan Polytechnic University, σελ. 4.
15. Spilanis G. (1995). The Tourist Developmnet of Lesvos with the Exploitation of Cultural and Natural Resources, Conference: Tourism and Environment on Insular Regions, Heraklion Crete, 17-19 March, p. 2.
16. Pavlopoulos P. (1999) Financial and Tourism Policy Issues, The Quality of the Greek Tourist Product, Pub. Institute of Tourist Research and Forecast, Athens, pp. 29.
17. Business & Tourism (2004), Strategic Planning for Long-term Benefits, pp. 27.
18. Skoulas N. (2000)., Financial Thinking, "The perspectives of Tourism of Crete in the new Environment", (Directive) Agios Nikolaos Crete.
19. Pavlopoulos P. (1999) Financial and Tourism Policy Issues, The Quality of the Greek Tourist Product, Pub. Institute of Tourist Research and Forecast, Athens, pp. 53.
20. Papanoutsos I. (1973)., Vima newspaper Article Tourism: The provocation of morals.
21. Tsukatos E., Exarhos G. (2004), Scientific Magazine, Research, Vol. 113, pp. 22.
22. Plan of Regional Decvelopment 2000–2006 of the Southern Aegean RegionPresent Situation.

23. Karagiannis St.-Apostolou A. (2004), The role of novelty in sustainable development of Crete Region, 2nd International Scientific Conference, (Proceedings), Preveza, p. 411.
24. Karagiannis St.-Apostolou A.(2004), The role of novelty in sustainable development of Crete Region, 2nd International Scientific Conference, (Proceedings), Preveza, p. 414.
25. Financial Data: Inoregio – Supporting sustainable development for the Region of Crete – A plan of regional action application and novelty –Crete Polytechnic – Laboratory of Information Analysis and Forecast (2002), pp. 46, 47, 48.
26. Kotler Philip 1986, p. 4 &Manuscript (1992) Hotelfachlehrgang fuer Maturanten, Hotel Modul. Wien, seite, 3.
27. Zacharatos G. (2003), *Tourist Policy,* Aegean University postgraduate programme, pp. 24.
28. Petrakis M. (2006), *Marketing Research-Research Methodology,* 2nd Publishment, Pub. Stamoulis, Athens, p. 119.
29. Sarmaniotis Chr. (2004), Consumer complaint behavior and methodological issues, *Review of Economics Sciences,* Vol. 5, p. 150.
30. Tsaras V. (1990), Export Promotion Organization, Educational Sector, Product Policy & Marketing Strategic Planning. Athens pp.
31. Dimitropoulos T. (1990), Export Promotion Organization, Educational Sector, Longterm Marketing Seminar. Athens p. 15.
32. Marketing K.W.N.IRONS the COLOGNE Re. Koelnishe Ruekversicherung-Gessellschaft 1963.
33. Tsanaka E. (1996)., Interview with the President of Association of Greek Tourist Enterprises on Conference: Greek Tourism & Marketing, ad BUSINESS, Vol. 75, Athens, pp. 24.
34. Karagianis S. (1993)., Tourist Advertisement, ELLIN pub., Athens, pp. 45.
35. Bromson R. (1991), *Marketing Report,* Vol. 112, sel. 6.
36. Exarhos G., Papailias T.(2004), *Tourist Scientific Review-*Semestrial Journal, Vol. 2, p. 59.
37. Alexandrou G. (1990)., *Marketing,* Athens, p. 45.
38. Skoulas N. (1987)., "How much do we know what are tourism is?", *Mag. Oikonomikos,* Athens, p. 26.
39. Igoumenakis N. (1999)., *Marketing in Tourism,* Interbooks Publishing, Athens, p. 125.

40. Holloway, I. & Plant, R.V., (1998)., *Marketing for Tourism,* Pitman Publishing, London, p. 40.
41. Xenia (2004). *Monthly Informational Review –Hellenic Hotel Chamber,* Vol. 222, p. 58.
42. Tsartas, P. (1988)., Planning of the tourism development stages in Cyclades Prefecture, *The Greek Review of Social Research,* Vol. 70, p.
43. Tourism Training Comittee (1999), Plan Proposal for Regional Development 2000-20006, Tourism Sector. Ministry of Development – Greek Tourism Organization, Athens, p. 24.
44. Komilis P-Vagionis N. (1999), Tourism Planning "Environmental Effects from Tourism", Pub. Propompos, Athens, p. 134.
45. Lagos D. (1998) Tourism and Regional Development, TOPOS Review of Urban and Regional Studies, Vol. 14, p. 57.

Literature

Karagiannis Stefanos, Papailias Theodoros, Panagou Vasilios, Zafiropoulou Anastasia, Development of Activities Friendly to the Eco-Tourism, *Journal of Finance and Informatics,* Vol 1 2005.

Stephanos Karagiannis, Development of Activities Friendly to the Eco-Tourism. The Region of Samaria Gorge. Journal of Environmental Protection and Ecology. *Official Journal of the Balkan Environmental Association,* Vol. 4, No. 4, 2004.

Nikos Pelekis-Haralampos Karanikas, 3D Class-Preserving Projection Technique for the Representation of N-Dimensional Classified Date and Association Rules. I. Journal j.ucs & Proceedings of I-KNOW' 05 International Conference on Knowledge Management–Graz Austria, June 29-Juli 1, 2005

Stephanos Karagiannis, Productivity and Managerial Efficiency in Hotel Industry. Crete as A case study. *Tourist Scientific Review-*Semestrial Journal. Vol. 2, Athens. 2004.

Stephanos Karagiannis - Apostolos Apostolou, Accomplishments in Tourism Management in Creta Island. Buletinul Stiintific al Universitatii "Politehnica" din Timisoara Romania. Tom 49 (63) 2004 Fasciola 1,2. Management. Engineering Economic. Transportation Enginnering.

Karagiannis Stephanos-Tsoukatos Evangelos, Spinaloga Heritage as an Alternative Tourist Product: The Case of the Spinaloga Islet in Crete. *Anatolia,* an International Journal of Tourism and Hospitality Research, Vol. 14, No. 2, Winter 2003.

Karagiannis Stephanos-Tsoukatos Evangelos, Marketing-Management in tourism enterprises, «EPEYNA», Vol. 47, November 2003.

Karagiannis Stephanos-Papailias Theodoros, The Influence of Tourist development on the social ethics of local communities of Hersonisos Municipality, on the island of Crete, Greece, Archives of Economic Historie, Volume XIX, No. 2, July–December 2002.

Karagiannis Stephanos, Natur und Kultur Griechenlands als unerscoepfliche Grundlagen des Zukunftsfähigen Tourismus, TOURISM, Review of AIST- International Association of Scientific Experts in tourism, Vol. 58, No 1., 2003.

G. Argiropoulou-Karagiannis Stephanos, Seasonality in Crete, Review of Decentralization Local Government and Regional Development, Revue de Decentralization d' administration Locale et de Development Regional, Vol. 24, 2001.

Karagiannis Stephanos: EUROPA IM AUFWIND-EG 1992/ TOURISMUS OHNE GRENZEN, Ïst -West Forum, Wien, 1992.

Karagiannis Stephanos: QUALITÄT, RPOFESSIONALITAET & PUBLIC RELATIONS, (Hotel Management & Marketing in Griechenland, Ïst -West Forum. Wien, Jul 1990-2 Jahrgang No. 3.

Karagiannis Stephanos: ÖKOLOGIE UND TOURISMUS AM BEISPIEL KRETA, ATHENER ZEITUNG, Die einzige deutschsprachige Zeitung Griechenlands und Zyperns, 1999.

2

Tourism Marketing Cases from Albania and Macedonia

Liljana Elmazi, Jovan Stojanoski***

2.1. USAGE OF PROPAGANDA TOOLS IN TOURISM—CASE OF ALBANIA AND MACEDONIA

Liljana Elmazi & Jovan Stojanoski

Overview

Usage of propaganda tools in tourism is widely found, beginning with tourists' domicile place. means of transportation, travel itself and the target place, i.e. tourist destination. Their importance in tourism is huge, because their role is to initiate, familiarize, interest and destine potential tourists with a given offer. We meet these tools every day in different places and in different mediums (posters, billboards, advertisements, windows of tourist agencies, TV and radio commercials, on fairs, CDs, in our mail- and email boxes, etc.). These tools are numerous, diversified, continual.

However, a question arises—how do passengers and tourists orientate themselves in this crowd of propaganda

* Ph.D. Head of Marketing—Tourism Department, and Director of Online Education School, Faculty of Economics, University of Tirana, Albania.

** PhD. Ohrid, Macedonia.

tools, i.e. which are the most successful tools among tourist that help them inform themselves and finalize their decision. For that purpose, we conducted a poll among interviewees who often travel, have a lot of experience in selecting tourist destinations and collecting information through various propaganda tools before, during and after a journey.

In that way, we tried to find at least a preliminary image about superior propaganda tools among our tourist population. This image could be very useful to all tourist employers as indicators how to best engage their human and financial resources in order to achieve larger financial effects.

Introduction

Which tools of tourist propaganda are most often used when a tourist destination is chosen and what a tourist clientele finds most motivating are only some of the questions whose answers we wanted to find out through the conducted poll. The goal of the whole research was to, on the basis of the data collected, determine attitudes and opinions of tourists about used tools of tourist propaganda and to get a clear idea about effects of propaganda through different medias. All tourist workers could use these information as a signpost indicating in which direction they should engage their human and material resources in order to realize greater economic effects.

A poll as a type of methodic procedure was used in data collecting. The poll was conducted in spring 2004. on a sample of 220 examinees; 100 of male sex and 20 of female. Results were obtained on the basis of a random chosen specimen and the type of polling was a written questionnaire that was filled in by poll-takers after an oral answer was given by a examinee (method of direct polling) (Curcic, 2000). Poll-takers were students of the final year of Tourism and Hotel Management, and they conducted the poll as part of their obligatory practical' researches in the subject Marketing in Tourism.

The analysis of questionnaires was processed according to a sex of examinees with an aim to determine whether there is a significant difference in usage of different tools of tourist propaganda between men and women, considering the fact that nowadays women are those who direct means of a family budget when traveling are in question. This knowledge could help the creators of tourist propaganda to direct themselves towards the right marketing segment that plays a crucial role when a tourist destination is chosen.

Structure of a Random Chosen Specimen

In the total number of people questioned there were 45.45% of men and 54.54% of women. The lower age limit was 15 years since it is considered that young people of that age already have certain tourist experience and can seriously, and with understanding answer the questions. There is no upper age limit. Representatives from the youngest and two oldest age groups were most difficult to find, which means that their participation is rather modest and it represents 9.09%.

Table 1: Age Groups

	Age groups							
	15-20	*21-30*	*31-40*	*41-50*	*51-60*	*61-70*	*70-up*	*Sum*
Men	4	49	18	15	11	2	1	100
Women	10	66	19	15	7	2	1	120
Total	14	115	37	30	18	4	2	220

The greatest part of the specimen is represented by examinees between 21 and 30 years of age, since that is an age closest to students who conducted the poll and population that they reached most easily. At the same time, this is a group that we can consider the most mobile, group with less obligations and more free to travel, which means that its considerable participation does not disturb the relation in the specimen and that it does not reduce the value of the results obtained. The participation of this age group is 52.27%.

The participation of other age groups is as follows: from 31-40 years of age 16.82%, from 41-50 years of age 13,64% and from 5 1-60 years of age 8,18%.

What are the Reasons for Traveling among the Interviewees?

The most often motif for traveling according to specimen questioned is rest and entertainment and that is 58.50%, followed by visiting relatives and friends (20.75%) and business trips (15.99%). Women travel more often for the reasons of rest and entertainment and visiting relatives and friends compared to the male part of the specimen. Apart from answers offered, interviewees were free to add their own motifs for traveling. Among men the following motifs are present: visiting historical places, education, playing sport games, and among women the other motifs for travelling are: advanced training in foreign languages and advanced study.

Table 2: What are the Most Usual Motifs for Traveling?

	What are the most usual motives for traveling?					
	Business	*Rest/ entertainment*	*Medical treatment*	*Visiting relatives*	*Other*	*Sum*
Men	30	72	4	26	4	136
Women	17	100	4	35	2	158
Total	47	172	8	61	6	294

Which propaganda tools do interviewees use?

Ways of informing, i.e. sources of information about different destinations differ among interviewees, where as answers were offered only those means that are widely accessible.

Apart from offered medias, it turned out, among specimen examined, that the greatest part is played by friends (30.46%) and travel agencies (29.02%) and that they are equally important to both men and women. Half as small importance in offering information about tourist destinations belongs to television and the internet, while the radio as a type of media almost entirely lost its importance and its participation in this poll reduced to minor 0.86%. It is interesting that in our country a lively human word still has a great importance, whether we talk here about conversations people have with their friends or about contacts they make directly in tourist agencies: fact which points out to a great importance of personal sale and so-called promotion "from mouth to mouth". On the other hand, a small presence of medias in this type of informing can also be the result of a rare information offering or of an unobjective, incomplete or superficial information offering. It is possible that there is certain distrust in that information i.e. there is a need to check them through direct contacts.

Group of answers named "other" also mainly includes information obtained from people that examinees were in contact with. Male examinees said that those are relatives and business partners they most trust and women said, apart from relatives and business partners, that those are parents, faculty, and colleagues (Table 3).

Table 3: How do you Inform Yourself about the Chosen Destination?

	How do you inform yourself about the chosen destination							
	TV	*Radio*	*News-paper*	*Internet*	*Travel agency*	*Friends*	*Other*	*Sum*
Men	29	1	12	23	40	47	3	155
Women	24	2	11	27	61	59	9	193
Total	53	3	23	50	101	106	12	348

In the group of printed propaganda tools, combined means have the greatest importance catalogues, informative prospect etc.) since 29.01% of given answers belongs to them. Very close are prospects with 24.69%. It is interesting that articles in newspapers, tourist stories and records are also judged as important sources of information (18.83%). In this poll, tourist maps were evaluated as a very bad source of information (3.70%). That can be a result of either a lack of wide spread of tourist maps or of their poor quality and inadequately presented facts. Thus, this practical and relatively cheap tool of propaganda lost its importance.

As part of this question, interviewees were asked to answer the question why the tools they chose offer all the necessary information. Most of examinees did not explain their answers.

However, certain answers were given. Combined means are thought to offer more facts if combined with photographs; because of a good layout and amount of information; they give a complete image idea about one tourist [place; because they have a complete offer etc. Prospect is thought to have short and complete information; that it is easily reached. Articles in newspapers, tourist stories and records offer a better insight into a destination and accommodation conditions since they are rather new; contain all the necessary details; are most often read; are most accessible. There is a small number of those who consider tourist maps to offer complex information. Newspaper advertisements are interesting because they have a complete offer and it is easy to choose a destination according to them. Postcards as sources of information are interesting because they are most accessible, and one female examinee is of opinion that that is how she gets the bet impression, while written brochures are interesting because they offer complex information (Table 4).

Table 4: What Type of Printed Material do you use to Inform Yourself?

	What type of printed material do you use to inform yourself									
	Post-card	*Broch-ure*	*Pos-ter*	*Arti-cle*	*Tra-vel guide*	*Com-bin. means*	*Tour-ist map*	*News advertis*	*Bill-board*	*Sum*
Men	15	34	3	30	7	40	6	6	3	144
Women	19	46	4	31	9	54	6	8	3	180
Total	34	80	7	61	16	94	12	14	6	324

Place where examinees usually come to get printed propaganda tools is a tourist agency (48.39%). That is understandable since tourist agencies are specialized for this kind of activity. Women in a somewhat larger number visit tourist agencies and take printed material (57.78%) than men. The second way of obtaining printed propaganda tools is from friends (33.69%). Specialized fairs and tourist stock markets do not play a significant role, and neither do travel companies that have even a smaller percentage in this poll.

In the group of answers named "other" male examinees mentioned: billboards, newspapers and magazines for newspaper advertisements, mail, the Internet and business partners. Women, as other sources of printed propaganda tool, mentioned: newspapers and magazines, relatives who send them, faculty or material they already have at home (Table 5.).

Table 5: How do you reach these propaganda tools

	How do you reach these propaganda tools?					
	Tourist agency	*Fair*	*Travel company*	*Friends*	*Other*	*Sum*
Men	57	13	2	47	9	128
Women	78	19	0	47	7	151
Total	135	32	2	94	16	279

Examinees usually keep printed propaganda tools (41.82%) as a memory to their trips, as one kind of a souvenir and this phenomena is more present with women which tells us about their stronger emotional characteristics (65.22%). A large number of examinees keep this material only sometimes (39.55%), i.e. they keep only some that they are especially fond of, that are important, nice, quality and long-lasting. In the examined specimen there is a small number of those (18.64%) who do not keep anything of printed material and this group is dominated by men (65.85%). On the basis of the answers given it can be seen how important propaganda tools are, and how quality and how carefully designed they should be, since they can last and carry a message for a long time (Table 6.).

Tablc 6: Do you later keep this advertising material?

	Do you later keep this advertising material?			
	YES	*NO*	*Sometimes*	*Sum*
Men	32	27	41	100
Women	60	14	46	120
Total	92	41	87	220

When printed material is concerned, apart from color and photography, one of the very important terms is the quality and type of paper that make tourists decide to take that material, look at it arid later keep it. As answers offered, there were four most usually types of paper used for making prospects, posters, catalogues, brochures, maps and other tools. Nowadays, the largest number of printed material is made of a niçe smooth paper with a greater or smaller shine. That gives the material made of this paper a touch of exclusiveness and a bit greater value, which makes the orientation towards this kind of material completely understandable (44.83%). Plasticized paper follows with 35.78%. It can be easily squeezed, it lasts longer and shines more that the previous one. Most answers in these two groups were answers obtained from women. which indicates that women are less choosy when these tools are in question.

16.81% answered they prefer matt paper with no shine on its surface, and only 2,59°o of examinees answered they prefer rough paper, that is firm and with no shine and that resembles thinner cardboard or recycled paper. Unfortunately, propaganda tools made of matt or rough paper are rarely found in our country, although they are, in combination with quality colors, much more esthetically sophisticated than those printed on smooth or plasticized paper (Table 7).

Table 7: What paper do you like this material to be printed on?

	What paper do you like this material to be printed on?				
	Smooth	*Plasticized*	*Matt*	*Rough*	*Sum*
Men	44	37	21	4	106
Women	60	46	18	2	126
Total	104	83	39	6	232

When the color of printed propaganda tools is concerned, absolutely the largest number of examinees answered they like them to be done in full color (91.03%), since such multicolored they are more attractive. Only a few examinees think that material done in a combination of up to three colors are attractive, and even smaller number thinks that black-and-white technique satisfies the needs for attractiveness of one prospect, catalogue, written guide or similar. Present tourist propaganda material on the tourist market is also mostly printed in full color, while other two categories are present in only a small percentage. So, the following question stays unanswered: Do materials that we place in front of the public form their opinions of those things are the result of the public's taste? (Table 8.)

Table 8: Do you Like the Material to be Printed in

	Do you like the material to be printed in:			
	Black and white	*Up to 3 colours*	*Full colour*	*Sum*
Men	4	7	90	101
Women	2	7	113	122
Total	6	14	203	223

First elements that tourist audience notices on printed propaganda materials are photographs, and as it can be seen from the previous answer, photographs in full color. They clearly and unambiguously send a picture of one place, beach, natural scenery, accommodation object etc. This answer proved the old marketing saying "one picture (view) is worth more than thousand words". One good photograph can send more different messages than the whole page of text. Through clearly directed massages on photograph we can inform our tourist clientele a lot and at the same time, we save space for a text and lessen the scope of propaganda material, which at the same time lessens the total expenses of propaganda. That is why we have to take care about the crucial role of photography when choosing a place, hotel, transportation mean, i.e. the whole selection of tourist arrangements, because a wrongly chosen image on the photograph can have a strong negative effect when choosing a tourist destination. 72.73% of examinees chose photography as the first element they notice, with somewhat larger number of answers obtained from female population of the specimen (55.73%). Is this kind of attitude the consequence of the fact that a large number of humankind belongs to the group that visually perceives information from the surrounding or is it the result of all-present overwhelmingness and everyday usage of visual medias, such as magazines and newspapers, TV and the Internet, or is it only the need to. in accordance with a fast way of living, get to know as much as possible with as little effort and time spent?

16.67% of examinees mentioned text as the first element they notice on printed propaganda materials and 9,4700 of them mentioned maps. According to answers obtained, it is concluded that almost no one first notices tables and graphs, especially in the female part of the specimen who find them completely irrelevant (Table 9.).

Table 9: Which Elements do you First Notice

	Which elements do you first notice?					
	Text	*Photo*	*Maps*	*Tables*	*Graphs*	*Sum*
Men	22	85	11	2	1	121
Women	22	107	14	0	0	143
Total	44	192	25	2	1	264

This was the key question connected with the importance of cartographic supplements to means of printed tourist propaganda where, through graphic measures, we saw nuances in using these supplements. The greatest number of examinees often uses geographical maps and sketches and they are of great importance when finding certain places or localities (45.00%). A great share belongs to those people who consider these supplements not very useful when orientating themselves in certain area (28.18%). Geographical maps and sketches are very useful to 17.27% of examinees, and completely unuseful to 9.55% of them, especially to men since there are double of them than women.

If we only look at the first two questions, it can be concluded that 62% of the specimen uses maps from propaganda tools; fact that can be a significant index about the importance of geographical maps and sketches in these tools. That is why marketing workers should carefully plan and design them in order to increase the total value of propaganda tools, and in order to make the printed space clearer and easier for orientation (Table 10.).

Table 10: Are geographical maps and sketches of use to you?

	Are geographical maps and sketches of use to you?				
	Very much	*Often*	*Rarely*	*Never*	*Sum*
Men	15	43	28	14	100
Women	23	56	34	7	120
Total	38	99	62	21	220

This question was asked with an aim to find out which audio-visual means mostly contribute to providing potential tourists with information. The results given indicate that the most important are electronic medias. The most important media is certainly television, and examinees answered that they obtain information about tourist destinations from specialized TV shows (31.94%) and that is equally important with male and female examinees. On the high second place is the Internet (20.90%) which was completely unexpected considering the fact that there is a small percentage of computer users in our country. It is interesting that women use this media almost twice as much as men. TV and the Internet are followed by TV advertisements I If. and then come tourist films (9.25%). Advertisements are equally important to men and women. While women use tourist films almost three times more than men.

Public announcements, slides and video cassettes are the least used for these purposes. Each of this material has a share of minimal 0.90%.

Two men and two women said that they do not inform themselves with neither of the mentioned means, while there were those men who answered that for obtaining information they use recommendations, tourist agencies, tourist magazines, while women said they use friends(3) and tourist agencies. This kind of answer is not relevant since we talk here about different types of audio-visual means and not about general information (Table 11.).

Table 11: Do you inform yourself by

Do you inform yourself by:

	Radio ad	*TV ad*	*Public annou-ncements*	*Tourist films*	*slides*	*TV shows*	*Sum*
Men	5	28	1	8	3	50	95
Women	10	27	2	23	0	57	119
Total	15	55	3	31	3	107	214

	TV commercial	*Lectures*	*Internet*	*CDs*	*Video cassettes*	*Sum2*	*Sum1*
Men	11	6	25	4	2	48	143
Women	16	9	45	2	1	73	192
Total	27	15	70	6	3	121	335

What Interviewees Like To Bring Home From Their Trips?

This question led to awareness which plastic means of propaganda tourists like buying and collecting. With the assumption that souvenirs would be the most often given answer through the next two questions, our aim was to analyze what kind of souvenirs and made of what our examinees prefer.

Our assumption pro to be correct and most answers showed that that is a souvenir (80.95%). We also found out that women buy them more often than men. Souvenirs are followed by badges, key rings, lighters, and similar small objects who participate with 14.29% of given answers, and are equally bought by men and women. At the end, there are mascots with only 4.76% of given answers, that men bring from their journeys four times more than women.

It is interesting to say that there were those who said

that they do not buy anything that was offered as an answer (two male and one women examinee) (Table 12.).

Table 12: On your trips do you buy

	On your trips do you buy:			
	Souvenirs	*Mascots*	*Badges and simp.*	*Sum*
Men	78	9	16	103
Women	109	2	17	128
Total	187	11	33	231

Most examinees, when travelling, like to buy souvenirs that are made of local, autochthonous material (32.20%), or souvenirs made of wood (28.79%). They are followed by souvenirs made of cloth, glass and clay or terracotta (9.47 to 8.33%). Souvenirs made of crystal and metal got the least votes, which is probably the result of their high price (crystal) and the fact that they are more rarely found. It is interesting that women are much more interested in souvenirs made of cloth, crystal and glass, while both men and women consider souvenirs made of local, autochthonous material and of wood as their favorite.

Moreover, there were certain answers where examinees claimed that they do not have favorite material they like souvenirs to be made of or that they simply do not care (7 male and 3 female examinees). 2 male examinees said they most like souvenirs made of plastic, and there were some answers where interviewers said they like souvenirs made of leather or of combined material, or that material is not important if it represents the place of stay. Women also had the following answers: different kinds of materials, what I like most, ceramics (Table 13.).

Table 13: What material do you like souvenirs to be made of?

	What material do you like souvenirs to be made of?							
	Wood	*Glass*	*Crystal*	*Clay*	*Cloth*	*Metal*	*Autoch-thnous*	*Sum*
Men	34	9	3	10	6	9	37	107
Women	42	15	12	12	19	8	48	157
Total	76	24	15	22	25	17	85	264

Most often, from their journeys tourists bring decorative (36.90%) and in somewhat smaller percentage, usable things (29.15%), since they are obviously longer lasting and authentic representatives of space and ambience they originate from. Other two groups, dressing (19.19%) and consumable (14.76□o) things are much less considered to be authentic souvenirs. This can be explained by general unification of the market of consumer goods with little accent on the autochthnousness of these products, their easier circulation, greater import on domestic market which means there is no need to go abroad to get them, as well as their shorter expiry date.

When sex structure of the examinees is concerned, women's answers tell us that they more often buy usable and decorative things. Men and women equally buy dressing goods, while men much more rarely buy consumable goods as souvenirs.

Some of the answers were: handicrafts, carvings, few of all. thing specific for region and cultural environment. However, these answers could either be included in the answers offered (handicrafts and carvings into decorative souvenirs) or are imprecise (few of all) since the goal of this question was to precisely learn what tourists gladly buy, i.e. towards what. direction we should develop souvenir manufacture in Serbia and Montenegro (Table 14.).

Table 14: What kind of things do you most usually buy as souvenirs?

	What kind of things do you most usually buy as souvenirs?				
	Dressinig	*Usable*	*Decorative*	*Consumable*	*Sum*
Men	26	28	43	24	
Women	26	51	57	16	
Total	52	79	100	40	

Conclusion

Usage of propaganda tools in tourism is widely found, beginning with tourists' domicile place, means of transportation, travel itself and the target place, i.e. tourist destination. Their importance in tourism is huge, because their role is to initiate, familiarize, interest and destine potential tourists with a given offer. We meet these tools every day in different places and in different mediums and that fact initiated the need to determine what are the most successful tools among tourist that help them inform themselves and finalize their decision.

Oral promotion "from mouth to mouth' is still most trusted and most reached when valid information about travelling to a certain destination need to be gained.

In the group of printed material, examinees find combined means and prospects most important because of their accessibility, richness in information and complexity. In the graphic means of propaganda tools, most intriguing are photographs in full color, whose adequately chosen motives give a complete, clear and true image and thus there is no need for so much text and their scope is economized.

Apart from printed material, medias that distinguish themselves when obtaining information and animating tourists are revered television, where almost equally important are all forms of propaganda (travel reports, tourist films, and commercials) and the Internet that represents a kind of a surprise since it is believed to be still rarely used in our country.

On the basis of sex analysis of the data from the poll, there is an impression that women are very active when choosing tourist destinations, movable, of a clear differentiated taste when using tourist propaganda tools, information channels, buying souvenirs etc. That is why, creators of tourist promotion and propaganda should develop a differentiated approach towards this segment of tourist demand, because women are, according to the poll conducted, active participants in tourist journeys and who also make final decisions not only when buying household goods and cosmetics, but also when choosing tourist destinations and deciding on travel expenses.

2.2. TOURISM SMALL BUSINESS STRATEGIES TO SURVIVE IN A COMPETITIVE ENVIRONMENT. CASE OF ALBANIA AND MACEDONIA

Liliana Elmazi &
Jovan Stojanoski

Introduction

During the last 15 year of capitalism system the Albanian and Macedonian tourism business among the success have also faced failure which are the result of some factors. One of the most important one is the lack of main concept about the capitalism rules. The opportunities that raised entering in the capitalism system made that lot of the tourism business in the lack of information they concentrated in same main activities. Some of them looked profitable but they were not. There are a lot of tourism enterprises in Albania and Macedonia. In this process some of them could not resist against the competition and so some of them failed, some of them change their activity or another one are going to be created. This inevitable process of the competition made the tourism businesses to know better the distinctive character of their business with their single purpose to achieve higher result and to survive in the tourism market. Their survive in the market was particularly depended from the differentiation in their features and the competitive advantages that their will create in their business. The purpose of this study has a double result:

> First is focus in the concept of distinguishing features and the ways by which the small tourism business in Albania and Macedonia may profit from adapting those theories and to give recommendation in different kind of strategies that in order to create competitive advantages. The concept of the distinguishing feature has been discussed as a strategy that takes in consideration the businesses that compete in high competitive market. The distinguishing feature is the way how we can develop a specific ability in a connection with a product or a service that is easily distinguishing from the customers. The application of this theory we will see in a service industry and will take in consideration restaurant service as one that has had a important growth during those years. The advantage of the economy of scale that have the major restaurant and their professional image has settled the small one in difficult position. The strong competition is meaningful especially in the service industry where the product served the channel distribution are the same although if they are big or small. When the customers are not sure for a service package, those businesses tends to be neglected.

Survey

It have been a lot of interviews with 60 managers of the restaurants in Albania and Macedonia with the aim to build a questionnaire which focus is in the distinguishing feature. The question were made in those main direction: the future of the small business, the competition perception, the publicity, media, activities projected to have more market share, the standard used for the effectiveness and the strategic management. For studies purpose those questionnaires where spreaded and filled in 120 different small restaurants and hotels in Albania and Macedonia. 50% of the employers where part of those businesses from 8 to 10 years. This indicator show that the service industry in stable, able to compete in the market. 63% of them offers specialized restaurants and hotel service and 18% where offering secondary service.

The Result of the Survey

The first question where concentrated in the management perception about the competitive environment within they operate. The way than a individ has perception about the environment, has influentation in the way he act. A manager that has the perception that the market is competitive for example may behave differently from another manager that see the market in a different way. When they were ask, 'which is the future of small restaurants?' 42% of the managers see the future of their business not good. However 36% of the managers see the market as a competitive one. It was no different competitive perception between the managers that see the future as not good and them that the future was seen in a positive view.

The other part of the 4 question focused in what a manager can do to be as much competitive as possible. The first two question where made about the publicity and media tools. For them the publicity purpose was to get known the name of their business, enlarge their image, and to get known from the general public. Media resources were newspaper, television and radio. 3/4 of the managers does not use media tools. The purpose of the other question was related to the fact: What management do to raise market share, and which where their activities they used. The managers mentioned activities like mouth to mouth marketing, special promotion for loyal customers. Only 15 businesses sad that they were segmented in a target with high income.

The other question where focused to: How they differently change from the competitor. 32% of the managers sad that they do a professional work and 16% pretended to have special service. To make a professional work cannot be considerated as a distinguishing feature because all the firm pretend to be professional .Among this is difficult to make known this concept to the customers.

The third group of question was focus in the management of the business to estimated and maintain the result. The main criteria used to distinctive the result, lead the main business activities in market. From the managers are distinctive three main concepts: sales, growth, and their image (the customers opinion sad in the public).

The managers where were asked also for the number and the frequency of the standard used to estimated the result. 61% of the business used only one criteria standards, the most used standard was the value of sales. 40% of the business estimate the results in monthly basis, and yearly basis.

At the end, the managers were asked about the strategic management. 74% of the business planned yearly objective. Although only 20% of them had written objective, 38% of the firm pretend that they have long term objective(not written)

The discussion of the Results

Small restaurants and hotels haven't been positioned in a market which change very rapidly. Even however the management see the restaurant and hotel service industry like very competitive doesn't see the market in this way does not exist any data to show that the management is changing behavior. The management of those businesses are acting like the environment has not change.

However, the marketers know the importance role of publicity, only few of them use it. Only few of tourism small businesses are involve in activities that make them different from the others businesses. The marketers does not know the meaning of distinctive features, Make ``a professional work`` is a distinguishing feature, evaluated by a great numbers of businesses. Being different from others must bee the goal of each business and for this reason we didn't consider like a distinguishing feature. Only a little % of this organization accomplish a special service to attract customers.

The capability to compete successful in a market is base on business results. As the firm use a limited numbers of criterions to distinguishing her results, this can not give a main frame, realistic of the activity of the business in front of the competition.

Generally a great numbers of firms involved to compose the future's plans. The goals of this strategic management focus on the final product and does not aim the creations of any distinguishing features.

Creation of a Distinguishing Feature

The small tourism organizations that operate in a competitive market which change very rapidly, does not repose on practices that times before has been successful. Those firms need to develop a quality to differentiate them from the others. But to differentiate a service organization is a complicate duty or obligation. The decision to change has consequences in hole fields of organization activity. There are two important points:

a. accentuation the quality of the service may result with the disparagement of the others services, which causes low results.

b. assessment of the process may come very close if we answer only the information about distinguishing features. In the case that the only criterion of the results is the value of sales during one month, then the way haw are achieve those sales is less important. But whole this can result in a small number of recurrent customers.

A small organization can follow four steps to determine or assign and develop a distinguishing feature.

First step involve the commitment of three sort of analyses:

- The first analyze focus the appearance, financial conditions, technology expertise and human resources.
- The second analyze must study the firm's conditions in the desire market from her. The demand of market for services determine from three elements: the number of potential customers, trendy which reflect from a growth market, stable market or from unsteady market and local markets.

- The third analyze include a very careful study of the competition, notably of the pioneer . The study must regard three elements: the reaction of firms against the demand; the way they create demands for their services and how the customers perceive the market leaders.

Those analyses provide the right information to pass in:

The second step: identify a distinguishing feature that organization is able to develop. The distinguishing feature must be: the new presentation of a new service which is request from a specific group of customers; readjustment of an existent service which is going toward the decline or elimination of the services that does not accomplish our needs.

The third step involve the projection and implementation of a plan for the positioning of the features of the firm. Except the questions : who will realize, what, when and how ought to considerate 3 elements:

a. communication's strategies of distinguishing features.
b. which is the message that organization desire to transmit.
c. selection the right media to communicate.

The fourth step include the composition of the delivery strategies, which are efficient for different target of customers.

The Creation of Competitive Advantages

The small business to be successful must create something new for their`s customers, different from theirs counterparts or to address others segments, names niche. Fulfillment of specifics needs of those segments is a focusing strategy which has been successful for small businesses.

Strategy of "cost leadership" is a general strategy use to produce of low costs. Businesses that apply this strategy are more protected by market fluctuations and more prepare against fluctuations of the market prices.

"Differentiation strategy" use by businesses that see themselves like unique in some specifics segments of the market. A business like this can use a monopoly price for it's products or services.

The last one is the "focus strategy". The businesses that apply this strategy, try to optimize services in a segment in which the large businesses can not serve. In this way the firm has the possibility also to know more deeply the specifics needs of the target segment.

Conclusions and Recommendations

Small businesses (example restaurants and hotels) have not positioning themselves in market which vary rapidly, even, however the management see restaurant and hotels service industry like very competitive, does not exist any data to show that management is change his behavior. The management is acting like the environment is not changing. However the marketers know the importance role of publicity, only few of them use it.

Only few of businesses are involve in activities that make them different from the others businesses. The marketers does not know the meaning of distinctive features. Make ``a professional work`` is a distinguishing feature, evaluated by a great numbers of businesses. Being different from others must bee the goal of each business and for this reason we didn't consider like a distinguishing feature. Only a little % of this organization accomplish a special service to attract customers.

The capability to compete successful in a market is base on business results. As the firm use a limited numbers of criterions to distinguishing her results, this can not give a main frame, realistic of the activity of the business in front of the competition.

The small services organizations that operate in a competitive market which change very rapidly, does not repose on practice that times before has been successful. Those firms need to develop a quality to differentiate them from the others. But to differentiate a service organization is a complicate duty or obligation. The decision to change has consequences in hole fields of organization activity. There are two important points:

a. accentuation the quality of the service may result with the disparagement of the others services, which causes low results.

b. assessment of the process may come very close if we answer only the information about distinguishing features. In the case that the only criterion of the results is the value of sales during one month, then the way haw are achieve those sales is less important. But whole this can result in a small number of recurrent customers.

A small organization must develop a distinguishing feature. The distinguishing feature must be:

- the new presentation of a new service which is request from a specific group of customers;
- readjustment of an existent service which is going toward the decline or elimination of the services that does not accomplish our needs.

The small tourism business to be successful must create something new for their's customers, different from theirs counterparts or to address others segments, names niche. Fulfillment of specifics needs of those segments is a focusing strategy which has been successful for small businesses.

Strategy of "cost leadership" is a general strategy use to produce of low costs. Tourism Businesses that apply this strategy are more protected by market fluctuations and more prepare against fluctuations of the market prices.

"Differentiation strategy" use by businesses that see themselves like unique in some specifics segments of the market. A business like this can use a monopoly price for it's products or services.

The last one is a "focus strategy". The businesses that apply this strategy, try to optimize her services in a segment in which the large businesses can not serve.

2.3. TOURIST PRODUCT AND THE CHOICE OF BASIC CRITERIA. THE CASE OF DESTINATION OF VLORA-SARANDA

Liljana Elmazi

Introduction

In order to determine and define the Strategy of Vlora-Saranda tourist product as a tourist destination in the conditions of globalization it is necessary to accomplish a number of pre-activities that are actually preconditions for making the mentioned strategy, its functioning in the tourist industry.

These preconditions can briefly be defined as follows:

- Marketing strategy of Vlora-Saranda region as a tourist destination and its tourist product consisting of several tourist subproducts, i.e. narrow products—segments that form the total product;
- Defining the tourist product of Vlora-Saranda region as an important destination;
- The choice of basic criteria in the Strategy of Vlora-Saranda tourist product
- The choice of strategic alternative to the tourist product of Vlora-Saranda as a destination
- The life cycle of Vlora-Saranda destination product as a tourist region;
- Supervision and control of functioning of the strategy of the touriat product of Vlora-Saranda as a tourist destination in practice, i.e. on the market.

Marketing Strategy of Vlora-Saranda as a Tourist Destination in the Conditions of Globalization

The marketing strategy of Vlora-Saranda as a region and an tourist destination in the 21 century consist of the following four important elements:

- ❖ Marketing positioning of Vlora-Saranda as a tourist destination in Balkan Region
- ❖ Tourist product of Vlora—Saranda as a destination and its subproducts

- Aimed markets and market segments as consumers of Vlora-Saranda as a product
- Strategy of promotion of Vlora—Saranda's tourist product as an important destination in our country, Albania.

Marketing positioning of Vlora –Saranda region as a tourist destination in Balkan Region, not only in Albania, has as a starting point the following marketing aims, missions and general visions:

- To perform a turnaround towards a higher quality of tourist service, since the existing level of quality of the tourist product does not fully satisfy the needs;
- To perform redirection of tourist demand to certain segments, instead of the mass tourist market as has been the case so far;
- To introduce new attributes for positioning on which the whole marketing activity of all the subjects-companies and non-profitable factors participating in shaping the tourist product of Vlora-Saranda region as a destination can rely.

The attributes for positioning Vlora–Saranda as a tourist destination can be graphically shown as well.

Vlora-Saranda region has accommodation, catering, sport and recreational facilities though it still lacks the facilities and supply of the high level of quality, with emphasis on selective forms of tourism, ecology, culture and entertainment for the guests of middle and high level of demand.

REST AND RECREATION – SELECTIVE FORMS OF TOURISM

QUALITY OF TOURIST PRODUCTS

SPORT AND RECREATION – CULTURE AND ECOLOGY

Figure 1: Desired Attributes for Positioning of Vlora—Saranda as a Tourist Destination

The basic attributes for positioning Vlora–Saranda as a tourist destination could be the following:

1. Vlora–Saranda is a wonderful place for rest, recreation and improvement of health.
2. Vlora–Saranda is a close and easily accessible tourist destination in the very favorable position of Balkan Region.
3. Vlora–Saranda as a region is an exclusive ecological destination with well-preserved nature, national and local parks, a very long coast, woods and hills.
4. Vlora–Saranda is a destination for sport tourism, recreation, hunting, angling, etc.
5. In the 21st century, Vlora–Saranda is becoming a destination of selective forms of tourism.
6. In the 21st century , Vlora –Saranda is becoming a destination "that offers the more on the Adriatic and Jonian sea"

The tourist product of Vlora-Saranda as a tourist destination implies a whole range of products as services a tourist can use or experience during his stay in Vlora – Saranda as a touriat destination

Tourist Product in the Conditions of Globalization

The definition of tourist product implies the observation and analysis of a tourist product from two possible points: one is from the viewpoint of the producer of products and their supplier on the market'. And the second is from the viewpoint of the consumer, i.e. the tourist.

In the authors' opinions, the second viewpoint is much more important since the consumers could have a different or opposite opinion from the supplier of the product or service. The tourist product of destination is indeed as whole (total, composite) product, consisting of a large number of elements, though they can be put into three groups forming their constituent parts.

Graphically, it can be presented as in figure 2.

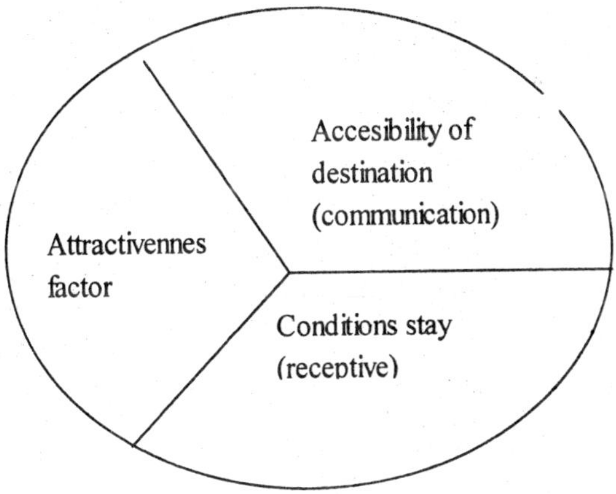

Figure 2: The Tourist Product of Destination with three Basic Groups of Elements

Conditions for the stay of tourist, i.e. Receptive factors, imply all those elements that represent the tourist supply of an area or destination. It is a whole set of services in the domain of accommodation, catering, culture, entertainment, sport and recreation, improvement of guest' health. It is necessary for the tourist destination to understand that it should offer the largest possible range of products, in order to offer the tourists a possibility of choice, through what we in marketing call a line of products in a tourist destination with an appropriate width and depth of assortment, can hypothetically be presented as in figure 3.

There is a number of different criteria that need to be taken into account while making the Strategy of destination as a tourist product as following:

1. There should be a considerable tourist demand for a chosen segment of the tourist product that is being developed.
2. The destination's tourist product should be in accordance with the image the destination has on the market.
3. Every new product should be well –planned, especially from the point of view of financial sources, human resources, natural resources, etc.,

WIDTH OF PRODUCT

A. *Cultural and historical heritage-monuments*	B. *General relaxation and recreation*	C *Interesting events*	D Conditions of stay
❖ Museums and galleries ❖ Forts and churches ❖ Theatres and operas ❖ Concerts of classical music ❖ Jazz, blues, rock.	❖ National &natural parks ❖ Beaches & indentation ❖ Woods and hills ❖ Hunting grounds ❖ Sea features	❖ Festivalsv Fairs ❖ Various events ❖ Folk festivities ❖ parades	❖ Hotels ❖ Camp sites ❖ Private accomm. ❖ Special offer

Figure 3

4. Every new product that is being developed should contribute to increase of profit or influence a faster development of tourism in the destination or the whole area.

From the standpoint of Vlora–Saranda as a destination, it is important for the successful strategy of the tourist product to answer the following questions:

❖ How to identify, run and direct the components of the products mix.

❖ How the destination itself can contribute to a more harmonious development of the strategy of partial tourist products

❖ How the destination should efficiently contribute to the development of new partial tourist products and its own product as well

❖ How to change the strategy of the destination product depending on the life cycle of the tourist product itself.

When we making decisions about a new destination's tourist product, it is extremely important to determine the following assumptions and answer the questions:

- ❖ What are the natural, social, economic, cultural and historical characteristics of the area or destination for which the tourist product is planned?
- ❖ Which are the features of tourist demand and needs in the segment for which it is planned to become a market target, i.e. the aimed segment of development?
- ❖ Which are the specific infrastructural demands necessary for the destination in order to fully satisfy the needs of tourist (marketing) segments?

Surveys and questionnaires to help learn about the state of resources in the destination, the drawbacks and tourist's wishes, especially those belonging to the more important segments, could be of great help.

A good analysis of resources in the destination, as well as the analysis of the existing, desired, and potential tourists for Vlora-Saranda as a tourist destination could be of crucial and long- standing importance. Having such information is already being "half-way" to the development of an adequate long-term strategy of Vlora-Saranda tourist product.

The Choice of Strategic Alternative to the Tourist Product of Vlora-Saranda as a Destination

The choice of an appropriate strategic alternative to the tourist product of a destination should rest on adequate and important criteria, such as:

- ❖ Are the intentions and procedures, plans and activities towards the development profitable?
- ❖ Which benefits are expected, both the total benefits and benefits for each participant separately?
- ❖ Will the new product be compatible in the social and economic senses?
- ❖ Will the new tourist product bring about new employment:

- How will the new product influence the natural heritage or the cultural and historical heritage of an area, destination or a place?
- Is the tourist product attractive in the natural and social respects?
- Is the tourist product in harmony with the infrastructure (local, regional, national)?
- Is the tourist product economically justified and profitable?
- Which market trends does the tourist product fit in?
- Which market segments (groups of consumers) does the product rely on?
- Which are the new needs, demands and wishes of the tourist product consumers, and which are their priorities?

The process of the strategy of a tourist product can be carried out practically on basis of good-quality information and on sound knowledge of fulfilling certain criteria. Theoretically speaking, the process have few stages:

The first stage: identifying the possibilities (defining the market, the development of ideas),

The second stage: defining the product (measuring the possibilities of the market for the tourist product, the development of the concept, the development of strategy),

The third stage: testing the product(promotion, predicting market trends, testing the market), introducing the product (planning and realization of the product).

The concept of a product's life –cycle can be very useful to the managers, planners, designers and marketing professionals in the process of choosing a strategic alternative to Vlora-Saranda tourist product. It would be very useful in practice of developing Vlora–Saranda tourist product as an important tourist destination in the 21 st century, to introduce and to carry out all the separate stages following each other:

1. The stage of introduction
2. The stage of exploitation
3. The stage of growth

4. The stage of consolidation
5. The stage of stagnation
6. The stage of revival or decline of the product.

However, in every case, the application of the above stated concept in the process of determining the strategic alternative should take into account a significant number of elements, relevant for the establishment of the strategic alternative and the strategy itself:

1. The level of analysis (an analysis for the destination as a whole, an analysis for some of its parts or for a single product of one tourist supply offerer),
2. The tourist market (foreign, domestic, segments)
3. The existing possibilities for the development of Vlora-Saranda tourist product,
4. The period in which the Vlora—Saranda's tourist product should be developed
5. Establishing the stage in the tourist product life-cycle in order to undertake measures for its development.

The Cycle of Vlora-Saranda's Destination as a Product and the Strategy of its Development

The destination of Vlora-Saranda as a tourist destination with ambitious plans, should be planned as a whole as well as in its parts. By doing so, it is extremely important that the destination as a whole, its individual parts and all the tourist supply bearers have a realistic picture of the importance of knowledge about the tourist product of Vlora-Saranda region that can be created by its life-cycle. Besides, it is also important to have such knowledge for each segment to which Vlora-Saranda's tourist product is directed or distributed. Since Vlora-Saranda's tourist product in this century can be in different stages of its life-cycle, it is necessary to plain it according to each individual segment (group or category of tourist). When doing so it is important to form a total tourist market, consisting of all segments that consume either the present or the future tourist product of Vlora-Saranda as a destination.

It is of extreme importance to correctly establish the stage in the tourist product's life-cycle, independently of the product being a partial or an integral product. It is necessary to have adequate measures and instruments in order to make realistic evaluations. The number of tourists, the tourist's spending, the seasonal quality of the tourist product consumption, the intensity of spending in time and space and similar parameters are great importance for the planning and development of the destination of Vlora-Saranda as a product.

Target Markets and Market Segments of Vlora-Saranda as a Destination in the Processing of Globalization

Tourist products differ among themselves regarding two important factors:

1. The existing attractions, natural resources and receptive capacity and
2. Preferences or consumer's wishes.

To make attraction marketing plans for Vlora-Saranda, the marketing strategy has to approach target markets; above all, it should address geographical markets to which a commercial message could be conveyed through the media and, secondly, to consumers segments.

Vlora–Saranda region in this century should look towards the following target geographical markets:

- Closer or exclusive markets of Macedonia, Kosovo.
- New markets of Balkan Region
- New markets of European countries (especially markets of Diaspora).

These markets have not been present in Vlora-Saranda and it is thus necessary to invest a lot of marketing and promotional effort to attract them.

Conclusion

There are different strategies concerning the manipulation of the tourist product. Here are some that Vlora-Saranda could and should apply in the development of its tourist product in this century.

To promote a frequent use of the product among the existing tourists. In addition, it should try to improve, by a better product assortment, the arrival and stay of high- quality tourists, to prolong the average tourist's stay, to encourage the frequent arrival of tourists in Vlora-Saranda and its micro regions, to improve the experience the tourists have as a benefit from the destination.

To develop different forms of using the product among the existing tourists. This will depend on the attractiveness, accessibility of Vlora –Saranda as a destination, but also on the conditions for stay the destination has. It is a combination of all the factors, some kind of a development tourist mix of service providers and product. It also involves tourists' different experience in the physical, social and economic, cultural and psychological viewpoints.

- To create a completely new possibility for use of tourist product of Vlora-Saranda.
- To find completely new segments on the emotive tourist market, the ones that would be the consumers of a new, high–quality and selective tourist product of Vlora—Saranda.
- To control and supervise the implementation of the tourist product strategy.

2.4. MARKETING CONCEPT APPLICATION WITHIN TOURISM INDUSTRY OF COUNTRIES IN TRANSITION: THE CASE OF ALBANIA

Liljana Elmazi

Abstract

This paper investigates marketing concept application in the most profitable of tourism businesses in Albania. The total population is defined according to the profitability criteria, whereby the stratified sample of 100 tourism businesses was applied. The research is aimed at gathering primary data by the questionnaire sent via mail.

The goal of each economic activity is creating value for the end users. In this context, profit is a measure of value which firm has created for the customer and indicator of how well the enterprise has understood customer needs and translated the understanding into products and services that deliver superior value. From the above stated, the conclusion can be made that the most profitable tourism businesses adopt marketing concept to the largest extent. For this reason the above mentioned tourism businesses are considered relevant for the assessment of internal and external factors in adopting marketing concept.

This research, which includes the explanation of methodology and the conclusion, comprises two significant sections. In the first section, significance of marketing concept application in Albanian economy is reviewed briefly from the theoretical point of view. The second section tends to be wider and more significant. It examines the peculation of adoption and application of marketing concept in Albanian economy in transition on the basis of analysis of empirical research.

The total population is defined according to the profitability criteria, whereby the stratified Sample of 100 tourism businesses was applied.

These tourism businesses have achieved the highest level of profit (earnings after tax) in Albania in 2005. The importance of stratified sample rests on the assertion that those companies make up only 6% of total entrepreneurs in Albania, and realize as much as 30.5% of Income after tax, 42% Earnings before Tax and 24% of total revenue of the Albanian economy. The same tourism businesses employ 22% of workers in Albania.

Research Methodology

The research is aimed at gathering primary data by the questionnaire sent via mail. The questionnaire includes questions about two essential areas of research:

- The degree of acceptance of the marketing concept, determined on the basis of 25 structured questions;

- Factors of adoption of marketing concept in transitional economies researched through: 20 structured questions about impact of internal and external factors. Furthermore, 1 non-structured question was asked with reference to the peculiarities of market-oriented business and adoption of marketing concept of designated tourism businesses operating within the transitional economy.

Findings of the Research

The findings of our research are: integrated customer-oriented approach, market focus and profitability.

The results of empirical research essentially confirm the hypothesis of work, which states more profitable tourism businesses tend to be more market oriented than the average of the Albanian economy as a whole. The sources of profit generation are in 52% of cases achieved customer satisfaction and quality of offer, which points out to the acceptance of basic hypotheses of marketing concept. Formal adoption of marketing concept in form of the existence of marketing department is present by 42% of tourism businesses. The previous findings are confirmed by the assessment of the surveyed population that in 34% of tourism businesses marketing concept is adopted in full or to the greater extent, which we consider to be objective.

Some of the thinking and empirical research about the application of marketing concept in Albanian economy lead to a conclusion that, Marketing, that is marketing logic and marketing way of thinking tend to be extremely limited, regardless of how business and non-business spheres of life and organized. Marketing is not adequately established. The reason for this can be prescribed to the surrounding conditions, as well as to subjective weaknesses. This indicates that the acceptance of marketing still remains in its infancy.

Introduction

The process of change toward market economy and democracy, generally known under the term transition, includes radical changes in the context of ownership pluralism, market pluralism and pluralism of political system. Although these processes are highly interdependent and as such need to be observed as a whole, we contend that the focus of this paper should be the market transition. In fact, market transition serves as a basis for the full application of marketing (as an instrument for reconciling production and consumption), i.e. a basis for satisfaction of social and individual needs of business entities and end users of goods and services.

With the development of theory and practice of marketing it becomes apparent that meeting the long-term goals of the above mentioned parties can be achieved with the application of the marketing concept. This concept became popular during the fifties of this century, when it started to be used by the business entities of the most economically development countries of the world.

Increasing earnings and generally increasing the value of equity by means of offering value and meeting expectations of users of goods and services tends to be an objective of any society. For this reason, the application of marketing concept is justified in transitional economies as well.

Intrigued by almost defeating results of the mentioned researchers, this works investigates the significant aspects of marketing concept application in Albania. Special emphasis put on factors of its adoption, have been little researched, in general, particularly under the transitional conditions.

This research, which includes the explanation of methodology and the conclusion, comprises two significant sections. In the first section, significance of marketing concept application in Albanian economy is reviewed briefly from the theoretical point of view. The second section tends to be wider and more significant. It examines the peculation of adoption and application of marketing concept in Albanian economy in transition on the basis of analysis of empirical research.

Research Methodology

This paper investigates marketing concept application in the most profitable of Albanian tourism businesses. The goal of each economic activity is creating value for the end users. In this context, profit is a measure of value which firm has created for the customer and indicator of how well the enterprise has understood customer needs and translated the understanding into products and services that deliver superior value. From the above stated, the conclusion can be made that the most profitable tourism businesses adopt marketing concept to the largest extent. For this reason the above mentioned tourism businesses are considered relevant for the assessment of internal and external factors in adopting marketing concept.

The total population is defined according to the profitability criteria, whereby the stratified Sample of 100 tourism businesses was applied. These tourism businesses have achieved the highest level of profit (earnings after tax) in Albania in 2005. The importance of stratified sample rests on the assertion that those companies make up only 6% of total entrepreneurs in Albania, and realize as much as 30.5% of Income after tax, 42% Earnings before Tax and 24% of total revenue of the Albanian economy. The same tourism businesses employ 22% of workers in Albania.

The research is aimed at gathering primary data by the questionnaire sent via mail. The questionnaire includes questions about two essential areas of research:

- The degree of acceptance of the marketing concept, determined on the basis of 25 structured questions;
- Factors of adoption of marketing concept in transitional economies researched through: 20 structured questions about impact of internal and external factors. Furthermore, 1 non-structured question was asked with reference to the peculiarities of market-oriented business and adoption of marketing concept of designated tourism businesses operating within the transitional economy.

Analysis of the research result was performed on the basis of 60 returned questionnaires (the rate of response is 60%). Received data is considered representative given that the returned questionnaires encompass equally well all business activities with the exception of one enterprise of other communal, social, personal and service business activities.

Marketing Concept and Albanian Economy in Transition

Due to its previous continual reforms, Albania has entered the period of transition to a market democracy notably better prepared than majority of transitional countries. However, the process of transition of the Albanian economy has proven significantly more difficult and slower than expected.

At the enterprise level the task is to design and offer those products and services that fully meet the needs of population. A precondition to all of the above is qualitative management and promotion of marketing function, which in its intermediary role enables tourism businesses to rely the needs of their customers and the delivery of what constitutes a value to the customer.

The feature of Albanian enterprise is that there is historically one 'completed' period in adoption, interpretation, and also in application of marketing. During the transitional period those activities have received and added impulse. In other words, the essential factor of enterprise transformation - a man, possesses certain knowledge, experience and abilities for successful operation, which is of course, necessary to utilize and continually promote. It is believe, however, that the acquired knowledge and the potential of educated marketing experts are not appropriately valued and utilized for economic development of Albania.

Thus, management, especially in big and medium size tourism businesses, following ownership transition and privatization, like in big state tourism businesses, has to create conceptual, intellectual basis of the business development on market postulates, following world trends and processes of globalization. With the adoption of marketing concept as a philosophy and business and the way the work is done dual interdependent goals are achieved: quantitative (increase in the market share, profit, the number of employees and other) and qualitative, such are structural changes of business process performance, new technology, product innovation, improved organization and management improvement.

For all that, successful application of marketing concept means the respect of the basic criteria of its applicability. This criterion is consisted of creating marketing value higher than the invested effort, and of adjusting marketing activities to the environmental conditions, like those apparent in Albania-doing business in time of recession.

In order for marketing efforts to contribute towards the process of transition the appropriate role of state is necessary. The state regulates relations at the level of the national economy, and it is also desirable that it positively acts at the level of international relations.

Findings of the Research

The findings of our research are: integrated customer-oriented approach, market focus, and profitability.

Integrated Customer-Oriented Approach

The application of marketing concept rests on several basic tenets.

One of essential requirements for the successful application of marketing concept includes integrated marketing activities, which means the respect for priorities, completeness and synergy. Such an approach assumes knowing and understanding the marketing system of the enterprise and especially potential customers. Moreover, long-term sustainability of the enterprise is contingent upon a successful delivery of value to its customers, which is at the hub of the marketing system and it accordingly represents a crucial subject in the assessment of the offered value.

Given that consumers define the value of competitive supply, the information about customers, inclusive of the of the assessment of all contributing factors of marketing environment, today becomes one of the key strategic resources of the enterprise.

According to the research results, 54% of respondents believe that market information constitutes one the most important strategic resources of their enterprise. In market oriented tourism businesses any important decision is made on the basis of the current, complete and correct information about the marketing environment. So, 61% of respondents think that previously mentioned assertion corresponds to the real situation, 33% stated that important business decision are made on the basis of incomplete information, while 6% of the respondents deny the presence of the above stated in their enterprise. Such a decision-making is possible, firstly, when there is the adequate marketing information system in tourism businesses.

Gathering information about marketing environment in researched tourism businesses is realized by daily monitoring of internal reports and the reports about developments in marketing environment. Almost all departments participate in preparing those reports. The most active is the marketing department (when there is one, in 60% of tourism businesses researched), with relatively high involvement of top management (32%). The information is also gathered via focused studies of specific marketing problems, which are conducted in 56% of the tourism businesses.

The Marketing department carries such research, either individually or with the participation of outside consultants. Customers' complaints may also serve as means for gathering customer information. They are used as e relevant source of information in 62% of surveyed tourism businesses. Related to this, particularly positive experiences have been observed in cases of introduction of toll free telephone lines. The result of active relations with reference to the marketing environment is knowledge of market position in relation to the competition (92% of tourism businesses). In order to derive use of the gathered information it needs to be systematized.

Nowadays, this greatly facilitated by the availability of contemporary computer technology. According to the research results only 15% of surveyed tourism businesses have structured and analytically processed system of information about the marketing environment. Furthermore, 45% of tourism businesses have no such a system in place and in the remaining 40% of tourism businesses this system is in the process of being established.

Based on stated results in surveyed tourism businesses it is believed that their marketing function (regardless of the form of organization) meets one of its essential purposes, that is, to be an expert about customer in 30% of cases. The same was negatively appraised in 25% of cases where the prevailing view was that understanding of the market in the surveyed tourism businesses is incomplete (45% responses).

Despite the previously stated results, in 46% of tourism businesses it is believed that marketing function successfully fulfils its second important role, which consists of supplying the decision maker with all necessary market information. In 44% of the tourism businesses it is believed that received data are not completely appropriate and in 10% of them marketing function does not supply decision makers with needed information at all.

Market Focus

Since no single enterprise has the ability to serve the entire market alone, one of the priority steps and critical strategic choice is orientation to those market segments whose requirements are compatible with enterprise resources. In this context, 95% of surveyed tourism businesses access the market like a heterogeneous group of consumers and 91% of the tourism businesses distinguish between major market segments.

This is done according to either the empirical or methodological procedure of market segmentation, which is certainly present by 12% of tourism businesses that use services outside consultants for that purpose. Furthermore, 62% of tourism businesses assess and carefully select the targeted markets. Based on the established target market, essential component of strategic determination of enterprise, consistent with the market orientation, is the development and design of offer consistent with customer demands and the enterprise's abilities.

Under present conditions of strong technological advancement and sophisticated customer demands, continuous innovations are necessary, which are considered, besides marketing to be the basic function of an enterprise. So, 61% of the surveyed population replies how the enterprise offer gets continually adjusted to the market requirements, 28% think that this is implemented in full, while 11% of respondents claim that this is not done.

Achievement of marketing goals means completeness and consistency of the total effort, which by its nature of interdependent marketing activities enables the achievement of synergetic effects.

With respect to this an opinion reveals (62% of surveyed population) that marketing functions tend to be only partially coordinated, while 28% of surveyed population thinks that they are consistent. Furthermore, 10% of the respondents claim that there is inconsistency with respect to the marketing functions. Generally, the difficulties arise from the business environment. Due to its turbulent nature, individual organizations have difficulties with organizational and personnel adjustments to it.

In particular, the surveyed population assess that in such conditions of business activity strategic market orientation tends to be more difficult, while the lack of financial resources and sometimes insufficient staff expertise makes gathering and processing of market information, development of appropriate offer and it's promotion more difficult.

Profitability

According to the marketing concept as a business philosophy, profit is generated upon customer satisfaction. In 66% of surveyed tourism businesses, income generating sources (the possibility of multiple answer) are met customers satisfied qualitative offer. However, offer is considered innovative only in 24% of tourism businesses. In 58% of tourism businesses the basis of income creation is the sales volume, which is not considered to be of prime importance but it is a consequence of previously mentioned income generating sources. Satisfied customer becomes a loyal customer with multiple positive effects that reflect themselves upon the enterprise's profitability. It is exactly this tendency, to establish permanent customers and not just making another sale, that characterize 80% of surveyed tourism businesses.

Is the Marketing Concept Reality of Albanian Tourism Economy or just a myth?

Finally, the marketing concept can be really applicable or adopted only on conceptual level. The surveyed population assess that marketing concept is fully adopted in 14% of tourism businesses, in 20% tourism businesses to a greater extent, in 31% of tourism businesses partially and in 33% of tourism businesses insufficiently. Although, the real level of enterprise's market orientation tends to be extremely difficult to determine objectively and precisely, based on the above results of survey, we think that the responses from the surveyed population regarding the level of enterprise's market orientation can be accepted.

Internal factors affecting the adoption of marketing concept

Despite unfavorable business conditions, the real market orientation of tourism businesses is contingent upon attitudes and behavior of their employees. In this instance, the relevant groups of internal factors affecting the adoption of marketing concept are considered to be:

- top management,
- interdepartmental dynamics and
- organizational system.

Top Management plays a crucial role in creation of such organizational culture in which employees of all business functions share their thoughts about delivering value to the customer as a primary goal of doing business. It is therefore expected that top management make market orientation a priority and to clearly communicate the idea of market orientation to the lower levels. According to the results of performed research, in 42% of surveyed tourism businesses top management believes that customer satisfaction constitutes a major business mission. In 13% of surveyed tourism businesses the answer to the same question was negative, while in 45% of them customer satisfaction in consideration but do not give it a priority. Although the strategic commitment of top management to customer satisfaction does not have to be in writing, it improves communication of managerial vision and gives clear direction for actions by the lower organizational levels.

The spirit of market orientation embedded in the mission statement is presently found in 28% of tourism businesses, i.e. 71% of those who responded to have adopted marketing concept in full or to greater extent. Based on the results of the survey, the idea of market orientation is clearly communicated by the top management in 46% of surveyed tourism businesses. Important role of top management arises from its innovative behavior, which is a precondition for the adjustment of offer to market demands. According to the research findings in 68% of surveyed tourism businesses top management is inclined to introducing innovative offer, in 8% of tourism businesses this is not the case and in 24% of tourism businesses top management exhibits certain resistance to changes.

Interdepartmental Dynamics plays an extremely important role in its implementation if market information is considered as gathering and disseminating of information about marketing environment and functioning of the entire organization, then consistent with this realization, the interdepartmental dynamics. The interdepartmental dynamics is achieved through the network of formal and informal relations between organizational departments. Those relations may take form of conflict or cooperation.

With respect to the first one it is important to review conflict as it relates to the marketing function and like a conflict between marketing and other business functions. In effect, the execution of integral marketing may be slowed by the existence of only a few marketing functions or administrative structures of several marketing functions by the organizations with more developed marketing activities.

According to the research results in 42% of surveyed tourism businesses there are outdated organizational structures of marketing activities in place (sales, commercial activities and the combination of those two functions), which by their nature affect the achievement of short-term sales goals. In 35% of tourism businesses marketing and some of the mentioned departments simultaneously exist, which causes long and short-term tensions, while in 20% of the tourism businesses' marketing functions are unified. Execution of marketing activities in other departments (3%) practically denies the market orientation.

This finding indicates how the change of individual attitudes and managerial activities consistent with the market orientation (psychology of organization) is still not appropriately implemented in the formal organization of marketing function (anatomy). Accordingly, the communication between marketing personnel is critical for the implementation of marketing activities (philosophy of marketing functions).

Related to the conflict between marketing and other business functions, in view of the surveyed population, in 40% of the tourism businesses these appear to be no tensions between various departments obstructing the dissemination of market information. In 25% of tourism businesses it is believed that there is a conflict between the departments, while 35% of examines claim there are conflicts that arise occasionally. The conflicts between individual business functions emerge due to the incompatibility between their goals and the struggle for, in our circumstances, modest financial resources.

Given that besides top management, marketing function plays a major role in advocating market orientation of the enterprise, affirmed marketing function headed by the marketing manager contributes to the reduction of conflict and adoption of marketing concept. In this concept it is necessary to review two essential questions: the competence of marketing function and the attitude of top management and other managers towards necessary investments into the marketing function. The question of competence of marketing function arises from this is very nature.

In fact, professional marketing requires the development of truly professional marketing personnel and marketing information system. This is considered to be a long-term investment with effects that become evident in the long-term. So budgeting for these investments puts the marketing function in direct conflict with other management functions for scarce financial resources or is directly opposed to the short-term profit orientation of the enterprise.

In surveyed tourism businesses prevails the opinion that investment in marketing function do not appear as too high when they are compared with potential returns (41% of tourism businesses), 27% thinks positive, while 32% of surveyed population thinks that financial requirements appear to be high, but not exaggerated.

Although only 18% of all tourism businesses managed to establish an integrated marketing informational system, it is positive that, especially those tourism businesses that started developing market orientation before the transitional period, invest in domestic and international personnel training. In general, 50% of surveyed population expressed their satisfaction with the respect to the contribution of marketing function towards the achievement of business goals, 42% considers it less competent and only 8% of surveyed population expressed their dissatisfaction. The Manager's personality received the best rating, so that in 67% of tourism businesses marketing manager enjoys confidence by other managers.

Direct contacts between employees from various functions contribute to the market orientation, which is achieved through dissemination of market information and better mutual cooperation. According to the research result, in 52% of tourism businesses organizational units are well connected via managerial meetings or in some different manner, in 6% of tourism businesses personal contacts are evaluated as weak and in 42% of the tourism businesses this cooperation is considered mediocre. Of total number of tourism businesses who claimed to be adoptive of marketing concept in full or to a greater extent (47%), in 74% of them there is a good connection between individual functional areas, i.e. 77% believes that co-ordination between marketing and other business functions is appropriate. This finding indicates that good communications within the enterprise may have a positive impact on market orientation of enterprise.

Organizational System is third category of internal factors of market orientation is made up of the organizational system.

Relevant factors making up the category are centralization and reward system. From the performed research on the sample of Albanian tourism businesses a conclusion can be drawn that in 42% of organizations dominates centralized decision-making. This is especially true with respect to the strategic issues. In 44% of tourism businesses the smaller management team makes decision, while in 14% of tourism businesses decisions are made on a decentralized basis. The business conditions are generally marked by big and rapid changes, world globalization and increasingly wider interactively, which bring about turbulence, complex situations and unpredictable movements and behaviors, to which in Albania additionally contribute significant changes related to the process of transition.

Thereby, Albanian tourism businesses are faced with a challenge of decision making under uncertain conditions where flexibility becomes the most important feature like "ability of enterprise to react to the newly created changes in environment".

The decision making, which is moved closer to centralized manner in surveyed tourism businesses, according to the opinion of surveyed population is adequate for business conditions in time of transition and although it negatively impacts the flows of information, to a larger extent (75% if surveyed population) it contributes to the enterprise flexibility and market prosperity even in the case of greater business systems. Factor which strongly affects the employee behavior and with it the adoption of market orientation is the reward system.

According to the research results in 6% of tourism businesses the employee reward system is based on the achieved customer satisfaction, while in 38% of tourism businesses apply compensation based on share in sales. This leads to a conclusion that relatively high level of marketing concept adoption in the context of employee awareness and organizational processes are still inadequate implemented in organizational structure.

External factors affecting the adoption of marketing concept

The state of external environment an enterprise operates in has a significant impact on the execution of marketing activities and their results. Social and Economic reality of Albania is characterized by the insufficient level of production, high unemployment and the drop in living and social standards in general. In addition, the rate of unemployment in 2004 accounted for 14.3%. While nominal net Salaries index increased by 480 times in the period between 1990 to 2004, the price index increased by 584 times. This indicates an increase in the cost of living and consequential lowering of the living standards of population. For this reason, Albanian economy is rated near the bottom on scale measuring the level of development of transitional European countries. Likewise, a drop in investments and capital expenditures still remains with all of the negative consequences of divert investment and deepening of the technological gap in comparison to developed countries of the world.

Economic circumstances are considered to be major adversary to the market orientation of enterprise (75% of surveyed population), while technological advancement was rated as stimulating (82% of surveyed population), when it is possible for tourism businesses to keep a pace with it. In fact, in addition to their acknowledgement of market demands, several of the surveyed tourism businesses contribute their success to the effective adoption of new technology.

Despite noted adjustments of Albanian legislation to the western legal systems, the overall legal environment is assessed as non-stimulating (72% of surveyed population). High uniform Value Added Tax (VAT) rate is considered especially inappropriate.

Organization and co-ordination of marketing activities

Naturally, marketing activities have to be appropriately structured. Advocating the customers' interests is the prime task of marketing function. Often investigated, although it does not have to be real measure of the market orientation of the enterprise is the existence of marketing department. In the surveyed tourism businesses marketing functions takes a variety of organizational forms. So, in 22% of tourism businesses those activities are concentrated in marketing department, while in 48% of tourism businesses there are simultaneously marketing and sales department in existence and in 30% of tourism businesses Marketing and Sales Department perform marketing activities.

Of remaining tourism businesses, in 38% of tourism businesses there is Sales Department, Commercial Department or a combination of those two and in 35% of tourism businesses there are other organizational forms in place. The finding which indicates that in 27% of all tourism businesses there is a Marketing Department, leads to conclusion that surveyed tourism businesses have at least formally adopted marketing concept to a greater extent.

The implementation of integrated marketing assumes appropriate co-ordination and cooperation with other functional areas, which are assessed as predominately successful in 38% of tourism businesses, moderately successful in 44% of tourism businesses and weak in 18% of tourism businesses. The cooperation of Marketing with Human Resource function is considered to be the weakest, which points to the problem of recruitment of personnel trained for performing marketing activities.

Consistent with the contemporary understanding of the marketing concept, i.e., the term market information as marketing concept application, providing value to the customer is a result of intertwining of all functional areas with the awareness about the priority of meeting customer needs. According to the assessment of surveyed population, in 72% of all tourism businesses providing value to customers is part of their corporate culture. However, all employees are oriented at creating satisfied customer in 52% of surveyed tourism businesses.

Conclusion

The application of the marketing concept is one way of overcoming the economic difficulties Albania is faced with during its transitional period. Marketing concept has proven to be an effective exchange regulatory instrument in the developed countries of the world. Building on the results of previously conducted research, which lead to a conclusion that the marketing concept has not been adequately affirmed in Albania, this research was aimed at determining the degree of marketing concept adoption. Furthermore, the research was specifically aimed at the factors of its adoption under transitional conditions on the sample of 100 most profitable Albanian tourism businesses. The importance of these tourism businesses to the Albanian economy is tremendous.

The results of empirical research essentially confirm the hypothesis of work, which states more profitable tourism businesses tend to be more market oriented than the average of the Albanian economy as a whole. The sources of profit generation are in 52% of cases achieved customer satisfaction and quality of offer, which points out to the acceptance of basic hypotheses of marketing concept. Formal adoption of marketing concept in form of the existence of marketing department is present by 42% of tourism businesses. The previous findings are confirmed by the assessment of the surveyed population that in 34% of tourism businesses marketing concept is adopted in full or to the greater extent, which we consider to be objective.

From the research results it can be concluded that marketing function relatively successfully fulfils its role of expertise in market events, the role of supplying the decision-makers with necessary information and by its competency in promoting market orientation. The difficulty is mainly due to inadequate marketing system and high turbulence of environmental surrounding. For these reasons achieving strategic market determination is even more difficult.

Although still inadequate, tourism businesses pay great attention to offer innovation and to efforts towards the application of target marketing. The degree of market orientation can be greatly influenced by several external and internal factors. The economic and legal environment and high cost of capital are considered to be a major limiting external factor. It is imperative to design and consistently execute realistic development strategy of Albania and to consolidate tourism businesses in all aspects in order to achieve priority goals of stimulating growth and development by boosting manufacturing and employment.

With respect to this, on enterprise level there are three major factors that affect the market-oriented activity: top management, interdepartmental dynamics and organizational system. The research has shown that in Albanian tourism businesses there appears to be awareness about a special importance of top management in adopting market orientation, the activities of which are prominent but still insufficient. The innovative behavior of top management received the highest grade, while the smallest improvements were achieved in strategic component of the mission statement design.

Formal and informal relations between the departments, which affect the spread of market information and which might have a feature of conflict or cooperation, are assessed a good overall. From the research of the activities' features and relations and ties within the marketing function the conclusion can be derived that market orientation still has not found an appropriate expression in formal organization of marketing function. Nevertheless, positively assessed ability of marketing manager and of marketing function contributes to the market orientation in general.

The finding about interdepartmental dynamics points out to the fact that tourism businesses that are of the Albanian economy should improve the way they establish their marketing functions, improve interdepartmental relations and put in more effort on building integrated marketing information system.

As far as the organizational system is concerned, it was established that in the researched tourism businesses predominates centralized decision making. This way of decision-making appears to be suitable for the business conditions of economies in transition. Although this type of decision-making has a negative effect on the flow of information, it contributes more to flexibility and market prosperity even in the context of larger business systems. A reward system as a very significant factor of influence is based on marketing standards only in smaller number of tourism businesses. Therefore there is a need for decentralizing those decisions which stimulate internal entrepreneurship and the adoption of reward system which will be based on long-term market performance criteria.

Some of the thinking and empirical research about the application of marketing concept in Albanian economy lead to a conclusion that, Marketing, that is marketing logic and marketing way of thinking tend to be extremely limited, regardless of how business and non-business spheres of life and organized. Marketing is not adequately established. The reason for this can be prescribed to the surrounding conditions, as well as to subjective weaknesses. This indicates that the acceptance of marketing still remains in its infancy.

2.5. MARKETING RESEARCH UTILISATION IN TOURISM: THE CASE OF ALBANIAN TRAVEL AGENCIES

Liljana Elmazi

Abstract

The main question which this paper attempts to answer is: what are the factors that determine marketing research orientation in a tourism organisation?

The study makes an understanding of the role that marketing research information plays in management of tourism organisation. Our paper provide a cros sectional view of the status-quo of marketing research in Albania.

The questionnare is used to determine the perceptions of respondents of the level of control exercised by airlines and wholesalers; the level of research activity performed by airlines and wholesalers and the cost and usefulness of marketing research.

The initial questionnaire was pretested with 20 marketing executives. The final questionnaire, after two stages of refinement, was administered during personal interviews.

The final sample used in analysis consisted of 91 travel agencies. The sampling selection procedure in this study was not strictly probability- based, and the sampling propotion was probably about 10% of the relevant local population.

Keywords: marketing research; tourism organisation; travel agencies; respondents.

Introduction

The main question which this paper attempts to answer is: what are the factors that determine marketing research orientation in a tourism organisation?

The study makes an understanding of the role that marketing research information plays in management of tourism organisation.

Our paper provide a cros sectional view of the status-quo of marketing research in Albania.

The questionnare is used to determine the perceptions of respondents of the level of control exercised by airlines and wholesalers; the level of research activity performed by airlines and wholesalers and the cost and usefulness of marketing research.

The initial questionnaire was pretested with 20 marketing executives. The final questionnaire, after two stages of refinement, was administered during personal interviews .

The final sample used in analysis consisted of 91 travel agencies. The sampling selection procedure in this study was not strictly probability- based, and the sampling propotion was probably about 10% of the relevant local population.

The variables derived from the questionnaire tended to be rather global, and mainly of value for broad comparisons. While there may seem to be a lot of detail inherent in a list of 38 types of marketing research activities, simply knowing that most organisations claim to perform advertising effectiveness research, actually said very little.

In order to characterise the marketing research orientation of small travel agents, the following research questions were raised:

1. What are the marketing research activities of, and techniques used by, small travel agents?
2. What are therelationship between the organisational characteristics of small travel agents and their marketing research orientation?
3. What was the relationship between the individual characteristics of decision makers in small travel agencies (such as their age, formal education and business specialisation) and the marketing research orientation of the agencies?
4. What were the perceptions of decision- makers in small travel agencies with regard to the cost and complexity of marketing research?
5. What were the perceptions of decision-makers in small travel agencies with regard to airline/wholesaler over their product, and the amount of marketing research performed by airlines/wholesalers?

In our paper we will discusse various hypotheses to be tested, and the techniques used in analyses of the data.

At the last, the paper presents the findings and discusses their relevance in terms of academic theory and managerial practice. Directions for further research are indicated.

The Travel Agents Study

Participation of small to medium sized organisations in our study was limited, and travel agencies were not specifically identified in its findings. A review of the existing academic literature revealed a number of facts: *a)* although there were a number of studies of the planning and scanning practices of small businesses, none of them specifically concentrated on marketing research practices; *b)* a limited number of studies into the marketing research practices of businesses in general existed, but none of them focused on small businesses; and c) there was little written on travel agencies. None of the existing studies was specifically concerned with small travel agents. Resultingly, an exploratory study was undertaken to profile and analyse the marketing research practices of small travel agents.

In order to characterise the marketing research orientation of small travel agents, the following research questions were raised:

1. What were the marketing research activities of, and techniques used by, small travel agents?
2. What was the relationship between the organisational characteristics of small travel agents and their marketing research orientation?
3. What was the relationship between the individual characteristics of decision makers in small travel agencies (such as their age, formal education, and business specialisation) and the marketing research orientation of the agencies?
4. What were the perceptions of decision-makers in small travel agencies with regard to the cost and complexity of marketing research?
5. What were the perceptions of decision-makers in small travel agencies with regard to airline/wholesaler control over their product, and the amount of marketing research performed by airlines/ wholesalers?

The sample in this research study was limited to businesses with fewer than 20 employees. Other guidelines for the definition of a small travel agent were the annual gross turnover of the agency (less than $25m), and the following common management or organisational characteristics which are traditionally associated with a "small" business: *a)* independently owned; *b)* closely controlled by the owner/ manager; and *c)* the operations of which are usually locally based, although its markets might not be.

In this study, the questionnaire was an instrument to profile the general characteristics and marketing research orientation of small travel agencies. Sections of the questionnaire on marketing research activities and techniques were shortened to make them more relevant to small businesses.

Otherwise, these sections were used without alteration to enable comparative analyses. Questions were added to identify various characteristics of the decision makers of small travel agencies, such as their age, education, area of specialisation, and their management orientation. Finally, a section of three questions was included to determine the perceptions of respondents of the level of control exercised by airlines and wholesalers; the level of research activity performed by airlines and wholesalers; and the cost and usefulness of marketing research. The initial draft was pretested with 20 marketing executives (mostly from the travel and hospitality fields).

The final questionnaire, after two stages of refinement, was administered during personal interviews conducted by the final year undergraduate marketing research students of a major Melbourne university. A non-probability sample (Churchill, 1995) using a combination of judgement and convenience, was utilised, with the students each being asked to choose five travel agencies within the greater Tirana area.

Necessary guidelines were provided to prevent duplication and to ensure a sample distribution profile with required characteristics according to the judgement component of the research design, i.e., students' choices were restricted to those agencies that conformed to the selection criteria provided.

The majority of respondents interviewed within each agency comprised the primary decision-makers. In other cases, the respondent was nominated by the decision-maker as the person with an intimate knowledge of the organisation. The interviews were conducted at the place of business of the respondent. Respondents were provided with a copy of the questionnaire at the beginning of the interview to try to ensure that misunderstandings did not occur because of the technical nature of questions relating to research activities and techniques.

A total of 104 respondents from as many travel agencies was interviewed. Four agencies were excluded later from the analysis because their location fell outside the boundaries of the Tirana area. Three travel agencies were excluded because they had more than 20 employees. A further six questionnaires were excluded because the names of respondents were not disclosed. Although an assurance of full confidentiality was given to all agencies, the name and location of each respondent were considered a necessary prerequisite to ensure that duplication did not occur, and that the results were not contaminated because of an inclusion of an agency representative without the authority to act on behalf of the decision-maker.

The final sample used in the analysis consisted of 91 travel agencies. Attempts were made to quantify the relevant population of the study.

In keeping with the exploratory nature of the study, the variables and their relationships were analysed within the boundaries of the five research questions listed earlier. For the purposes of simplifying and clarifying the initial analyses, variables were collapsed by recoding the data either into two categories based on high or low value split at the median level, or in three categories split at the 33 and 67 percentiles approximately.

In summary, the study provided the following answers to the research questions (for a discussion of the full results, see Yaman and Shaw 1998b): A general understanding of the marketing research activities of, and techniques used by, small travel agents was established. Most organisational characteristics were not related to marketing research participation, although greater devotion of resources to marketing research was reflected in more comprehensive usage of marketing research, and a more positive attitude to the cost-effectiveness of marketing research in small organisations. The desirability of travel agents considering seriously the role of marketing research in assisting in clarifying the future options for the sector was noted.

As in the second question, most individual characteristics of the decision-makers of small travel agencies were not related to the marketing research orientation of the agency. The lack of a significant relationship between the education level of respondents and the marketing research activities of, and techniques used by, the agency was of interest. It would have been expected that respondents who were formally educated in a business discipline would be more familiar with the various techniques and activities.

This study confirmed the that managers of small businesses harbour certain "myths" about marketing research. One of these myths is that marketing research is too expensive to conduct for small enterprises. Results indicated that small travel agents, in general, believed that enough research was conducted by airlines/wholesalers to determine customer needs. However, further research was needed to ensure that these perceptions are in keeping with the reality.

Do such Trends Exist in the Albanian Travel Market?

The sampling selection procedure in this study was not strictly probability-based, and the sampling proportion was probably about 10 per cent of the relevant local population. Therefore, the results could not be projected to the nominal population unreservedly. Rather, the scope of the study was exploratory, with the intention of providing some useful and suggestive base case data. In this respect, the study was successful. A basis has been provided for a comparison of the travel agency sector with other elements of the tourism system, particularly in terms of the indicative activity levels regarding marketing research. Further, differences were observed within the travel agency sample which deserved research, e.g., are differences in marketing research usage based on reflective managerial judgments, or are they incidental to the genuine lack of familiarity of managers with the field? Regardless of this answer, it is clear that there is widespread unfamiliarity with MR techniques, and hence the opportunity to remedy that situation profitably—for both the educator and the travel agency.

Another limitation of this study was the suspicion or perception of some interviewers that some of the travel agent respondents were providing invalid or unreliable responses. That is, on occasion, some interviewers found it difficult to accept some of the answers, on various grounds. For example, respondents may have stated that they frequently used Likert scales, and other techniques, but the interviewer may have detected a general lack of sophistication in most aspects of a small suburban agency.

Whether social desirability, pride, or other factors such as the desire to conclude the interview quickly, were operating, is unclear but not unimportant in determining the confidence that may be placed in the data. This difficulty in obtaining reliable data from studies of small firms is "traditional" according to Smeltzer, Fann, and Nikolaisen (1988). Dollinger (1985) noted that structured personal interviews, as in this case, might well be preferable to mail surveys in this context because, although more time consuming and consequently usually being restricted to smaller sample sizes, they yield more reliable data.

Dissemination of Results of the Exploratory Studies

From a theoretical perspective, the answers provided by the results of the exploratory studies of marketing research use in tourism contributed to the development of positive theories of the marketing research system. They also confirmed the need for, and furnished the basis of, the more rigorous study that is the subject of this thesis. The contact with tourism decision-makers initiated by the studies has shown that most managers were interested in the development of normative theories of marketing research use, including the development of decision support models which address issues such as the optimal design of marketing research for specific types of organisations and purposes.

Research Instrument

In both surveys, questionnaires with closed, structured queries, mostly on Likert-type scales, were used. For the first survey (Tourism 95), a first draft of the questionnaire, which was a combination of the Kinnear questionnaire and the USER instrument, with only the minimum alterations to make it industry and culture specific (i.e., for the Albanian hospitality and tourism industry), was prepared. This draft was then discussed with several close industry contacts of the author in informal but structured interviews. The contacts were chosen from among the senior operational managers of the tourism industry and they broadly represented various sectors of the industry as categorised in the instrument. The managers were asked to evaluate the questionnaire with a view to: (1) assessing the relevance of its conceptualisation of marketing research utilisation, (2) appraising the suitability of the terminology to specific sectors, (3) identifying any other potential marketing research uses that are not covered by the proposed questionnaire, and (4) making other suggestions, criticisms and comments on the questionnaire and its facets. Based on this pretest, necessary revisions were made to the instrument to ensure its relevance to the hospitality and tourism industry within a specific (Albanian) culture. In total 20 managers were approached, although only 13 of them were ultimately interviewed.

Their feedback was recorded and analysed and necessary alterations to the instrument were made with the proviso that the altered instrument was sufficiently similar to the original instruments that it was based on, to enable comparative studies. The first section of the questionnaire began with the preliminary questions regarding sector identification, organisational demographics, and marketing research department structure and budget. Then, a list of marketing research activities, divided into six sectors of questionnaire, was presented and respondents were asked to indicate whether the type of research was conducted by their organisation and, if it were, whether it was conducted by their marketing research department, another department in the organisation, or an outside organisation. In section two of the questionnaire, respondents were asked to focus on a recent marketing research project related to their organisation with which they had been associated. The use of one critical incident, rather than general questions about research, was chosen so as to obtain responses that are relatively less affected by attitudinal bias. This approach is in keeping with work on marketing research that preceded the present investigation (e.g., Deshpandè and Zaltman 1982, Menon and Wilcox 1994).

However, given the mode of data collection, all measurement was based on respondent perceptions rather than observed behaviour. Since there are methodological problems associated with self-reports (Malhotra 1996), the use of a recently conducted project as the research incident of focus was in order to avoid an unduly large positive utilisation bias on the part of the respondents. It was also thought that short-term memory being more reliable than long-term memory, the discussion of a recently conducted research project could provide more meaningful responses. Another perceived advantage of using this critical incident approach is the avoidance of non-recursiveness in the model to be tested. Since this thesis conceptualises utilisation as a cyclical process, the aggregative impact of experience makes causal model testing unreliable. By imposing a critical incident focus on one recent research project, sequential activities in the research process can be analytically separated and handled in a consecutive order.

The questions in section two of the questionnaire were largely similar to those in the USER instrument discussed earlier. The items were grouped in similar fashion to USER, with the exception that group headings were removed to avoid undue prompting that may lead to response bias. A six-point (rather than five or seven-point). Likert-type scale format was also kept in the belief that an even numbered rating may minimise the possibility of respondents taking the middle ground out of a desire to complete the questionnaire quickly or to avoid thinking carefully on issues. The questionnaire ended with a space for respondent name and position title, and the name and address of the organisation. To reinforce the assurance of total confidentiality, the completion of respondent details was made voluntary. A copy of the research results was promised to respondents who completed the respondent details section. This was the only incentive offered for the response.

The results of the survey indicated the need for a number of revisions of the initial questionnaire. In the first section, some questions on organisational demographics (revenue, number of personnel, and the age of the organisation) were moved towards the end of the questionnaire. This was principally because it was found that a number of respondents viewed the questions as commercially sensitive and their reaction influenced their decision to continue with the questionnaire. The questions on marketing research budget and marketing research department structure were simplified and left in the beginning of the questionnaire. Four questions from the questionnaire were discarded because they did not produce meaningful responses or they replicated information that could be deduced from other questions.

The question on research activities was condensed in content but expanded in the choice of answers to include the parties who developed the research, and those who analysed the data ('mainly this organisation', 'mainly outside organisation', 'both this and outside organisation'). A new, 46-part question on research techniques was added to this section inquiring whether the respondent recognised the technique and, if so, whether the technique was used at all and how often.

The 39 items in section two of t questionnaire were kept, with the main modification of converting all statements to positive ones as a result of an exploratory factor analysis carried to assess the USER instrument (Yaman and Shaw 1998a). Another 44 items were added to measure respondent perceptions of the cost-benefit of marketing research, the information culture of the organisation, environmental factors, organisational structure, and the effect of marketing research on financial and other performance. Outside of two open questions that measured respondent perception of research priority needs of their organisation, all items were closed, Likert-type rating scales. The final instrument contained 90 main questions and a total of 142 answerable items.

Hypotheses and Reliability

The theoretical concepts that have been discussed in earlier sections, and relevant literature citations that have already been developed, along with some others the relevance of which is confined to the composition of hypotheses, are brought together in this section in an attempt to answer the central question that was posed at the outset of this thesis: What are the factors that influence the use and consequences of marketing research information in tourism? Firstly, the empirical hypotheses to be tested are presented and tested. Secondly, a discussion of the methods of analysis that are employed is presented. Thirdly, reliability and validity issues in the research design and its operationalisation are presented.

Hypotheses

The diverse variables that have been suggested earlier as influencing the utilisation of marketing research information in particular, and marketing research orientation in general, in tourism organisations can be drawn together into a network of testable hypotheses. These hypotheses are detailed in this section with a brief rationale for their articulation. Most of these hypotheses are grounded in earlier literature (either in marketing, management, tourism theory, or organisational theory). This section will be followed by the analysis of research results through a number of subsets of the final model. Then these subsets will be elaborated into the complete model presented earlier in the thesis. The general model will be tested for causal implications in the last sections of this section.

The Statistical Packages Used in the Analyses

The data was edited and coded, and the preliminary analysis and the descriptive analysis presented upper, were conducted through SPSS (version 8). A computer statistical package named AMOS (version 3.61) was used for the structuring and analysis of the general model and its subsets in this study. Apart from being the latest, and therefore presumably the most advanced, software program on the subject, Amos was chosen for its relative ease of use. AMOS 3.61 has the facility to read data from SPSS1.

The Method

A questionnaire was developed, based on the previous studies by the author and other work in the area, and tested with a select group of industry executives. The questionnaire was refined and restructured as a result of these pilot interviews. The final questionnaire was used to survey a judgmental sample of executives in the largest tourism organisations in Albania. The executives surveyed were those in charge of marketing research or, in the absence of such position, those in charge of marketing operations of their organisations.

Unlike the previous studies into marketing research

utilisation, this study employed a strict definition of marketing research to prevent any possible confusion or conflation with other, more informal, forms information acquisition, such as market intelligence, which is defined as an informal, ongoing information acquisition process. Similarly, to preserve the rigour of the study, close definitions of other crucial concepts, tourism and its sectors, were provided. Most of the survey was conducted through person-to-person structured interviews, which adhered strictly to the questionnaire.

Summary and Interpretation of Results

Apart from two exploratory studies, which were also conducted by the author, this was the first study to investigate the knowledge acquisition and utilisation through marketing research activity in tourism. It was also the first to investigate the consequences of marketing research in terms of organisational performance anywhere. Because of this inaugural nature of the study, it was thought useful to present a status report before a more empirical form of statistical analysis was conducted. This consisted of a mainly descriptive presentation of data that were collected during the survey. The main objective of this presentation was to convey an understanding of the role that marketing research plays in the management of tourism organisations in Albania. The descriptive results showed that tourism organisations devoted large sums to marketing research and conducted many different types of research. Of the studies conducted, the majority was on buyer behaviour and promotion studies. Around half of the organisations surveyed used outside consultants to conduct the studies and/or analyse the results.

The results presented in the status report also showed that the majority of executive were satisfied with the quality and outcomes of marketing research activity in their organisations and thought that marketing research was cost-effective. The majority of the executives thought that the decision-confirmatory value of marketing research (instrumental use) was its most useful quality. They were a little more reserved on the issue of the educational value of marketing research (knowledge-enhancing use) although they gave some credence to this quality. On the other hand, only a small minority of executives believed that marketing research was used solely for the sake of appearance only (affective use), although many of them acknowledged the political aspect of research.

The results of the status report showed that the majority of tourism marketing executives viewed their organisations as highly centralised and the operational procedures highly formalised. There were some differences of opinion among the different sectors of the industry. The majority of executives in general perceived their businesses' external environment as a reasonably turbulent market where the competition was highly "cut-throat". The technology was changing very rapidly with the technological changes are providing new opportunities. Around half the organisations surveyed evaluated their marketing research activity on a formalised basis. However, majority of them had a positive view of the effect of marketing research on organisation's financial performance. The majority of executives believed that employee morale in their organisation was high and there was a positive team spirit.

Summary and Interpretation of Empirical Findings

Statistical analyses were conducted to test how well the model fit to data. Specific findings are reported in the sections below. Findings that relate to antecedents and consequences of innovativeness, as defined by the level of marketing research activity conducted and the number and complexity of marketing research techniques applied. In order to avoid unnecessary repetition the concept of 'innovativeness as defined by marketing research activities conducted and marketing research techniques utilised' will be referred as 'marketing research activity' from this point onwards.

The Significance of Findings for Management

Outside the theoretical and methodological issues, this thesis has a number of implications for the marketing research management in tourism. These are summarised below:

> The more careful and objective the evaluation of marketing research is in an organisation the higher the understanding of its effect on financial performance. Despite that, less than half the organisations that invest resources in marketing research have formalised evaluation procedures in place. Managers should realise intuitive responses to research processes might end up in the waste or misallocation of valuable resources. Despite the considerable attention directed to marketing research and the high level of formal qualifications among them, the managers who are expected to be experts in the field of marketing and marketing research are generally not well informed about research techniques. Taking into account the fact that the majority of executives surveyed had qualifications in business, it is assumed that they undertook courses in research techniques and statistics. The findings have implications for the efficacy of the technical teaching in our colleges and universities.

One of the guiding assumptions of this study is that knowledge, if applied properly and wisely, is power. Therefore, using research is a good thing because it is essentially acquisition and utilisation of new knowledge. The responses received from the industry executives (including those who are employed by organisations that choose not to do much research) reaffirm this assumption. There is strong belief that positive financial outcomes emanate from research use. These findings provide support for a number of recent studies that asserted the growing importance of "managing intellectual capital for superior performance" (Menon and Wilcox 1994, and see also Kohli and Jaworski 1990, Glazer 1991, Menon and Wilcox 1994, Yaman and Shaw 1998b). Tourism managers must note that the evidence increasingly leads to the proposition that intensified research use (where it improves decision-making quality and managerial confidence) leads to better market performance. In the future, market-driven organisations in tourism will be tantamount to knowledge-driven organisations.

2.6. DESTINATION MARKETING: CASE OF BUTRINT IN ALBANIA

Liljana Elmazi

Introduction

Albania is considered as a new cultural destination in the tourism marketplace, as a Balkan country of dramatic natural beauty, with a wealth of historic buildings and ancient archaeological sites that can compare, for interest and variety with any in the Mediterranean world. Analyzing Albania as a new destination in the tourism marketplace one can easily bring into light a series of disadvantages (i.e. poor quality of service such as electricity, water supply, and the perception of the country as an unstable and potentially dangerous destination). There are however many advantages (i.e. undiscovered natural beauty, proximity to established or growing markets) that increase the chances for Albania to attract visitors interested in a new destination and a new cultural experience. Attempts to project the country to the outside world began in the 1970s using classical heritage as an element of national identify. Thus heritage is represented today in Greek, Roman and later Byzantine archaeological wealth generated by Albanian lands due to its favorable geographical position in the Balkan in classical times as a key area for trade, agriculture and minerals. After a long period of instability, Albanian heritage is again being projected as an integral component of the country's reconstruction.

Case Study of Butrint—Albanian's Major Heritage Visitor Attraction

Albania comprises an important amount of splendid archeological sites. Ottoman heritage, as well as a number of national parks bearing an outstanding natural beauty. Among others, it is worth mentioning the archaeological site a museum of Apollonia, which together with Dyrrachium makes two most important ancient Greek settlements in Albania. The citadels of Gjirokastra and Berat, characteristic of which are the beautiful mosques and churches that can be seen, whereas the domestic architecture of these two town are considered the best preserved examples of Ottoman towns of their period that have survived anywhere in the ex-imperial territories. The national parks (Divjaka National Park, Lura National Park, Llogara National Park, etc.) established mainly after the World War II are in remote forest areas and comprise a remarkable variety of plants and some of the last refugees of rare animals and birds that have disappeared from other regions of Balkans.

Sitting in the south of Albania within region of Saranda, just across the straits of Corfu, the WHS of Butrint of Butrint National Park, is Albania's main cultural and natural heritage site. The importance of the site was recognized both nationally and internationally. This has been proved by the fact that the at times the site has received several designations which have significantly built up its image and attracted more visitors and specialists in the area. A collage of several evaluations made by the academia and public media prove not only the perception of the place by the people and the impression that the site leaves, but of the grandiose dimensions of the values that the site carries. Of the great classical sites of the Mediterranean, Butrint is the least known, the least frequented and the least spoiled. Visiting it today must be like visiting Ephesus or Baalbek a hundred years ago: nor car parks, no souvenir stalls, no sound but the sound of birds and the ever-buxy crickets. If you yearn to lose yourself in romantic meditation, alone among the ruins of a once-great city, then Butrint in the place for "Butrint is a magical place. In special atmosphere is created by a combination of archaeology and nature not found elsewhere in the Mediterranean. This is one of the great, largely unknown archaeological sites of Albania and of the whole Balkan Peninsula.

The Park is now the single most important tourist asset for the Saranda region and arguably for Albania as a whole. It has been recognized as a site of international and national importance for its wetlands, as an historic landscape important for the caliber of the archeology and as a focus for national and regional cultural identify. In addition, the Park has been identified as a place of national importance for education (over 25,000-school children visit the site each year) and an important local resource for farming and fishing activities".

Table 1: Chronological list of national and international designation for Butrint

1948	"Cultural Monument", designed under the first Albanian Cultural Monuments Act.
1981	"Protected woodland", designated under the first Albanian Law on the "Protection of sites of environment importance".
1992	UNESCO WHS, inscription by the WH Committee based on the cultural criterion.
1997	Inscription on the List of World Heritage in Danger by the World Heritage Committee.
1999	Butrint National Park was established by the Ministry of Culture
2000	Confirmation of the enlargement of the WHS site to 29 km^2.
2001	An application for RAMSAR status was prepared in winter 2001.

An observation of the above "trophies" shows that international recognition has increased significantly during the last decade. That is certainly a result of the opening of the country.

Visitors at Butrint

It is fact that Butrint makes Albania's major visitor attraction. Since late 1980s, day visitors from Corfu were taken to the site and soon made half of all Albania's foreign tourists in numerical terms.

The upward trend in visitor numbers dates back to early 90s when the fall of communism, the visitor numbers stated to increase steadily. In 1996 the site attracted 20,000 visitors. Apart from a serious drop in numbers as a result of the civil unrest and the turbulent events in Albania and Balkans during 1997 and 1998, the visitor numbers built up again 23,000 by September 2001. In 2002 visitorship has surpassed 40,000, an increase of about 50% over 2001 and in 2005 visitorship has surpassed 100,000. It has only the last two years that data on the different types of visitor group using the Park has been gathered at its ticket office.

Five visitor groups have been identified:

- Independent visitors (domestic)
- School and college groups (domestic),
- Coach parties (domestic),
- Day-trip groups from Corfu (foreign) and

- Independent visitors (foreign).

Each group has different visiting patterns and demands different things from the Park (Martin 2002). From a careful observation of the percentage of each group against the total number of visitors one noticed that although the visitor number doubled from 2001 to 2002, the rapport of each group with the total number of visitors changed too. It is obvious that the school groups' number increased by less 5% of the total in relation to last year whereas the domestic visitors lave increased by 2% more. There is a drop in foreign groups by 2% while, independent foreign visitors as well as undetermined (free) have increased by respectively (1+2) from 2001 to 2002 it still remains the dominating part of the market share. The identification of visitor's types for the WHS of Butrint is an important step towards the shaping and implementation of a strategic marketing plan and a marketing strategy option that the site might adopt in the future. It specifically relates to the process of market research as an initial operation undertaken by the marketing sector of every attraction organization.

Table 2: Visitor types (percentage against the total number of visitors 2004, 2005)

Nr.	*Visitor Types*	*% of total visitors (2004)*	*% of total visitors (2005)*
1.	School groups	9	14
2.	Domestic Groups	48	46
3.	Foreign Groups	27	29
4.	Foreign independent	3	2
5.	Undetermined (free)	13	9

Marketing for the WHS of Butrint

The following part of this section consists of the preparation of a long-term strategic marketing plan for the WHS of Butrint based on the information available. The whole process goes through the stages explained earlier in the research.

The plan prepared at this section is used as the subject around which in-depth interviews are developed and the primary information is collected.

Identifying the Needs for the Adoption of a Strategic Marketing Plan for the WHS of Butrint—An Environmental Analysis

Among fifteen important objectives that the site management ha identified in its Management Plan it is important to distinguish those of the Regional Development. A prior short-term action for the regional development objectives is the devising of a Marketing Strategy for the region. In fact, a marketing strategy is a toll that helps attractions achieve their goals and objectives set in a long-term strategic marketing plan therefore, the process of devising the marketing strategy remains a crucial phase of this plan and depends on the preparation of such a plan for the WHS of Butrint. However, this should not be considered as the only reason.

Observing the site's situation carefully or, conducting an environmental analysis provides a more complete answer that justifies the adoption of the plan for Butrint.

The SWOT analysis prepared for the site helps to identify the main needs for the adoption of a strategic marketing plan for Butrint. Beginning with the analysis of the external environment, we must say that the site should not be considered as an isolated unit (attraction) within the region, the external environment has always influenced the developments in the site. During the 10 years, political instability has reigned in the country and the region of Saranda. This has been major generator of threats for the site. While the site itself is being developed slowly, cautiously and sensitively not the same can be said about the southern region of Saranda. There has been an absence of planned and managed urban development and uncontrolled tourism development especially in Ksamili and Saranda region. The development policy for the region intends to generate revenue based on tourism, which increases the dependency of the region on tourism.

There are in fact more opportunities for parallel development of other resources in the region. Under communism, Saranda encompassed a rich agricultural land that gave it district advantages over other districts. State-owned farms and agricultural cooperatives accounted for above 80%

of the district's total production and that was heavily supported by the agro processing of the fish, canned food, a salt mine and a manufacturing base consisting primarily on handcrafts and carpet production. This uncontrolled development has bought uncontrolled demographic movements. The situation in Ksamili has been exacerbated by a further unflux of economic refugees from the north of Albania (Holland and Antonopoulos 1999). This has been perceived as a major threat to the preservation of the ecological and archaeological resources of the area. The long isolation of the country from the rest of Europe and the World has cut the site off mass tourism and its negative impacts. At the same time, improvement of infrastructure and communication can bring this threat forward (see app. 2).

At the same time the fact that Saranda, therefore Butrint too, is adjacent to well established regional markets, especially. Northern Greek destination such as Corfu and Epirus (inland Greece) with a mixed tourism product contributes to increased competition for the site as an attraction. In long-term a broader development of the Heritage Trail concept as part of a Partnership Programme will reduce this threat. At an organizational level, or else in the internal environment analysis it is important to consider that despite the wealthy resources that the site encompasses within its borders, only a limited number of products are sold for the moment. The valuable contribution of the foreign and national experts in management and marketing issues of the site accompanied by a lack in local capacity building. More specifically, although a local office, responsible for the safeguarding of the Park was created there is still a lack in visitor management skills and tools. This threat has become more evident since the increase in visitor numbers.

Despite of the "soft" promoting policy adapted by the Butrint Foundation members at an international level, little has been done at regional and local level. The increase in foreign visitorship emphasizes the high dependency on foreign (mainly Greek) intermediaries indicating at the same time the lack of local tour operators and of a marketing strategy. Consequently, there is a lack encouraging direct selling or control over the intermediaries.

Setting the Aim, Goals and Objectives of the Strategic Marketing Plan

Prior to setting the aim, goals and objectives it is necessary to stress that they have to be turned in with the principal aims of the site development and management. Butrint Management Plan aims.

To preserve the character and qualities of Butrint for future generations.

To promote sustainable forms of agricultural, educational use and tourism in and around the Park and thereby contribute to the regional economy and the community.

To unite the local communities and interest groups involved with the park behind a single programme of action.

To meet the needs of the existing visitors to the Park and bring the local communities into the process of development, by focusing facilities in their villages.

From the viewpoint of modern (societal) marketing the strategic marketing plan will contribute to a sustainable use of the resources, increased capacity, healthy local economy and happy visitors. Relying on the above aims the mission for the proposed plan can be: Support the development of cultural tourism as a form of sustainable tourism in order to assist in building a socially harmonious local economy.

Main goals that derive from this mission range as follows:

- Increase numbers of cultural visitors in the site.
- Minimize marketing costs by increasing the numbers of repeated visitors.
- Generate income from for the WHS of Butrint and the region.
- Regenerate culture and arts a crucial element that provide competitive advantage.
- Support local initiatives that provide authentic cultural products/experiences.
- Improve the set of communication tools especially interpretation and education.

The above goals can be converted into more detailed objectives that may be:

- Set up a regular daily basis inventory of the site visitors based on ticket counting.
- Involve staff at the entrance (a visitor information unit) aiming to identify the visitor types on basic of motivation, their requirements, their impressions and suggestions.
- Undertake a regional market research in order to identify potential cultural visitors and the product offered by other regional attractions.
- Identify authentic cultural assets (resources) in the surrounding area of Butrint.
- Formulate new products by allocating these assets in culturally unique experiences/products.
- Apply for financial support that would help start any local initiative for the creation of Park's exclusive products or services (i.e. souvenir productions with Park's logo, etc).
- Design a variety of locally based tours that would include a night stay in local houses.
- Increase the number of cultural tourists at the site through the promotion of these cultural experiences/ products (i.e. local events celebrated in the area) within and out of the park area especially to potential domestic market.
- Improve the use of communication tools that could reach targeted cultural customers (i.e. marketing, education, interpretation).
- Use communication tools for the locals, locking at them as important recipient and transmitters of these messages.
- Increase the awareness of the locals about the cultural and natural wealth and uniqueness of the area.

However, the possession of the assets is not enough. It requires organized efforts made by professional people to recognize the cultural visitors and their requirements, design the appropriate products (experiences) that meet these requirements and approach them using the most efficient communication tools.

Devising the Marketing Strategy Model

In a customer led marketing area knowing more about the customers (visitors) helps market sites more efficiently.

The above aim, goals and objectives chosen in harmony with the wider goals and objectives of Butrint dictate at the same time the adoption of this strategic option. The marketing strategy option proposed will not aim at selling the site products (activities) but will try to approach 'niche' markets proactively by using special products that will meet demands of global tourists search for the authentic experience.

Therefore, this strategy will develop in three main directions:

- Identify market segments among the existing visitors at Butrint that are motivated by culture in their traveling decisions.
- Create unique cultural experiences by integrating products and services based on local resources that would provide Butrint a competitive advantage as a cultural destination in the Mediterranean.
- Prepare an educational and interpretative set of communication tools that would help the site promote its activities towards the targeted visitors and at the same time improve awareness of the locals.

It is clear that the strategic option selected involved the locals in the implementation process not only by appreciating the products they offer but, considering them an important target whereto the management can send its messages, be they of conservational or promoting nature in relation to Butrint properties. Therefore, a major conclusion drawn at this point is that the implementation of the strategy will heavily depend on two very important elements of the mix, promotion and people.

Why a Visitor-Led Marketing Strategy?

The changing nature of customers has placed increased demand upon destinations. The new tourist is no larger satisfied with a passive experience. He is seeking instead authenticity at destinations with a view to understanding the indigenous culture, history and environment, how local people live and work. Such a strategic option for the WHS of Butrint not only considers the trends in the successful management of the site but also encourages the involvement of visitors and locals in the process of product formulation and delivery.

As said above the marketing strategy chosen does not aim primarily at selling Butrint or its products/experiences to visitors but formulate a product after having discovered what visitors would like to experience through it.

Cultural tourists defined as people that intend to visit a cultural tourism attraction; art gallery; museum or historic site; attend a performance or festival; or participate in a wide range of other activities at any time during the trip; regardless of their main reason of traveling (McKercher 2002), has nowadays become the focal segment for many attractions. Although the WHS of Butrint may attract culturally motivated visitors due to the possession of the necessary recourses, this is not enough to develop cultural tourism at the site successfully.

The reasons of adopting a proactive visitors led strategy are many however, it is worth mentioning the fact that:

1) The development of high prestige cultural tourism can be only achieved by maintaining a highly satisfactory visitor experience.
2) The competition in the marketplace is won only after choosing the right ways of approaching the visitors.

Less price sensitive segment require a special experience and this is initially achieved by the adoption of a visitors led strategic approach which if successful provides high income levels; increased awareness about preservation and conservation; repeated visits and once defined this visitors are easily targeted therefore the marketing cost for this market reduces.

Concentration of the management efforts in the specific strategic direction will certainly prove more productive and will help coordinate their actions.

The Criteria of Evaluating the Implementation of the Strategic Marketing Plan for the Management of the WHS of Butrint

It is important to understand that the implementation of the long-term plan will be made only after converting it in short tactical one-year plans each of them will fulfill some of the goals and objectives set earlier. However, management should not start immediately implementing it. Even in cases when the management is convinced that the plan provides the way to success, there is still a very important phase to be considered, that of the evaluation of the implementation of this plan. Within this frame, a set of criteria on basis of which each attraction makes the evaluation is set. In the case of Butrint it would be recommendable to make this assessment by looking at main constraints and implications that derive from the resources needed to implement the strategic marketing plan.

As with any other organization, these resources are divided in financial, human and physical and are related to the organizational performance of Butrint. However, the management considers other criteria related to the external environment. One of them is the flexibility of the plan to adapt to sudden changes in the business environment.

Taking the above-motioned criteria separately we can convert the financial resources into the budget available to implement the plan.

The human resources into the strength and weaknesses of the marketing staff including their training, experience and attitude. It is important to understand that this criterion encompasses staff from all the levels of the managerial hierarchy, marketing managers dealing managers dealing with decision-making and those that deal with day-to-day marketing.

The physical resources usually consist of the equipment and building required (i.e. visitor information units set in and out of the park area, office, souvenir display units within the site, etc).

The set of criteria is wider than what we offer so as additional ones we can mention:

- The size of WHS of Butrint as an attraction organization.
- The time of the implementation of this plan.
- The actions of competitors.
- Elements of the mix used to implement the strategy selected.

We can explain that the size of the attraction reflects its marketing organization and consequently the performance in terms of implementing e plan. Strategic marketing plans cover a long-term period stretching in a time length of 5 years. These plans usually apply for large attraction organizations. A long-term plan for the management; therefore, the size of the organization and the timescale of the plan are important for the evaluation of the implementation of this plan. External environment criteria are also the actions of competitors as a source of benefits or implications for this plan. Other elements of the mix such as price, product, promotion etc, are considered in the evaluation process.

Conclusions

Albania as a country that has recently opened to the world is considering tourism an important activity that will contribute to the country's reconstruction. In this frame, Albanian heritage has been projected as an integral part of the country's reconstruction. Butrint is considered the most important among other attractions of Albania and its values have been recognized in a national and international level.

Apart from the political instability that the country has experienced during the last decade, Butrint has attracted a dominant number of visitors compared to the total of visitors that have entered Albania. This was dedicated to the cultural and natural resources that gave the site a series of designations, its favorable geographic location and the job done to project it in the marketplace.

The designations mentioned carry as many responsibilities for the management of Butrint, as prestige for the site. One of the primary needs that derive from this point is the formulation of a management plan that will guide the sustainable development of the Butrint. Consequently, the preparation of strategic plans for all the management aspects will be the next step toward success for the site. The Strategic Marketing Plan presented in our case carries the mission, goals and objectives for the marketing management of Butrint.

Although the plan may be well prepared, that is, its mission goals and objectives may be chosen in harmony with the main objectives of the site, an environmental analysis may have been conducted, a marketing strategy may have been selected, a monitoring system may have been installed, there is still a very important phase that the management always considers. This phase is the assessment of the implementation of this plan made by the management of attractions prior to adopting it. The chapter provides the assessment criteria that are used in these cases usually divided in criteria related to the sites as organizations and criteria related to their external environment.

On basis of these criteria, the researcher has structured the interviews conducted with the management of Butrint as well as other experts in the field, in order to collect the required information. This data is presented in the following chapter, let us look at it.

2.7. THE ROLE OF INFORMATION TECHNOLOGY IN ALBANIAN TOURISM INDUSTRY: THE CASE OF TISCOVER

Liljana Elmazi

Overview

Information technology has been playing a fundamental role in tourism industry for a long time. The Internet particularly is increasingly emerging as a perfect platform to bring tourism products direct to the customer. Web-based tourism information systems, however, are required not only to offer online brochures but also to provide both value and service. The Albanian tourism information system, TIScover, meets this challenge by focusing on three crucial points. First high-quality access is provided. Second, the content is of high quality that is achieved by enabling tourism information providers to mantain their products directly, as well as by integrating external tourism information sources. Finally, the system is designed in such a way that is easy to customize. This paper focuses on the crucial aspects of Albanian tourism information systems as they are implemented in TIScover. For this, first, an overview of the whole architecture of TIScover, including a short description of the manner in which the system may be customized, is given. E-commerce transactions in the context of TIScover are discussed and different access paradigms supporting the information phase are emphasized. Afterward, the paper deals with mobile access to TIScover by means of cellular phones and presents mechanisms used in TIScover to achieve interoperability. The paper concludes with the outlook for future work.

Introduction

Despite the fundamental role of IT in the tourism industry, when developing tourism information systems today, one has to keep in mind that only publishing online brochures is by no means enough. Three crucial aspects can be identified that seem to be essential for the success of tourism information systems; these are quality of access, quality of content, and ability to customize the whole system.

First, the acceptance of tourism information system particularly depends on comfortable and powerful access capabilities. To succeed in this, one prerequisite is that the system supports all phases of an e-commerce transaction, from the information phase via the negotation phase to the settlement phase. The information phase especially requires detailed consideration to provide the tourist with powerful navigation and search capabilities so the desired tourism information or product can be found conveniently and efficiently. Another prerequisite is that access tourism information and products on arrival at the destination or to provide mobile access, that is, access independent of location and need for a laptop.

Second, since information has been identified as one of the most important quality parameters for efficient service a tourism information system has to focus on the content aspect by providing comprehensive, detailed, accurate, and topical tourism information. The dynamic nature of some tourism information, for example, rates, schedules, events, opening hours, and weather forecasts changing with the days, weeks, months and seasons, makes this a challenging task. One possibility to achieve a high-quality content is to allow its maintenance directly by the tourism information providers. However, it is not feasible to store all the information a tourist might be interested in at one Web site, neither in terms of storage costs nor, more important, in terms of maintenance overheads. Another way to provide comprehensive contents supporting interoperability. Integrating this information automatically would enable the tourist to collect all tourism information at one place, no matter what is desired, be it information about weather and traffic conditions, schedules of trains, planes and buses, or current events.

The third crucial point is that a tourism information system should represent a generic platform allowing the presentation of arbitrary destinations, as well as integrating different kinds of tourism information providers. One problem in this respect is the complexity and hetergeneity of tourism information and products depending on both the kind of provider and the destination being presented Another problem is that tourism information providers, regions, and countries should differ from each other, since especially in the tourism industry, uniqueness is the main attraction. Consequently, the system should be easy to customize with respect to different tourism information providers, regions, and countries while preserving the individuality of their presentation.

The Case of Albanian Information System—TIScover

The Albanian tourism information system has faced these crucial points. It has adopted the TIScover. The aim of TIScover is two-fold:

First, tourists should be supplied with comprehensive, accurate, and up-to-date tourism information on countries, regions, villages, and all destination facilities they offer, such as hotels, museums, or other sights. Second, it aims to attract the tourist to buy certain tourism products either offline or, if possible, online. TIScover was developed in 1996 based on the experiences of the pioneering systems TIS and TIS & Web (Burger et al. 1997).

E-Commerce Transactions in TIScover

Today's tourism information systems are required to fully support an e-commercetransaction. The interaction processes between the participants of an e-commerce transaction can be grouped into three phases: the information phase, the negotiation phase, and the settlement phase. In the following section, the concepts and mechanism employed by TIScover to support these phases are described in more detail. Where the support of e-commerce transactions is concerned, a visionary approach would be to allow the tourist not just to book accommodation by means of TIScover and contact Web sites, for example, of car rental companies or airlines individually, but rather to allow the tourist to assemble a whole holiday package and to book the package at once.

The Information Phase. In this phase, customers, that is, tourists, acquire a market overview by gathering information about potential market partners: tourism information providers, as well as their products and services. To provide a comfortable information access, TIScover supports three paradigms for finding tourism information and products.

- First is the hypertext paradigm for navigating through information by using hypertext links. This is realized by means of the Atlas module.
- Second, the database query paradigm for a precisely structured search on the basis of a common database schema is provided by the Scout module.
- Third is the classical information retrieval paradigm, providing a full text search as it is done by most search engines on the Web.

The Atlas module allows the customer to browse through all kinds of tourism information by navigating through a geographical level offers those pieces of tourism information and products that are important at this level. Both the kind of information and the content gets more detailed the deeper one navigates into the hierarchy. Accommodations—for example, hotels—are placed at the village level and represent the starting point for online booking. To prevent tourists from following links with products that cannot be booked online, the booking button is only visible if there are products within a village and at least one of them is available for online booking.

Furthemore, the Atlas does not have to access the database during navigation but can work fully on Web pages, which as already mentioned, are generated from the database every time the underlying data changes.

The Scout module represents the second way offered by TIScover to find tourism information and products. In contrast to Atlas, Scout makes navigation completely superfluous in that it realizes a precisely structured search within the TIScover database by allowing the specification of various search criteria, which are represented by attributes of the common database schema. These criteria include location, name, and facilities of the accommodation, type of room, type of board, price limits, and arrival and departure dates. In general, the Scout module is especially appropriate for the single-minded tourist who already has a clear idea of what he or she wants. A major benefit of Scout is that products available at the required time. Note that this is different from Atlas, where the tourist has to navigate down to the lowest geographical level, namely, villages, before there is any posibility to check the availability of products.

Finally, TIScover allows a tourist to start a full text search, at any geographical level, to find all Web pages containing an arbitrary keyword, for example, all pages containing the keyword "carving". This approach is comparable to well-known Internet search engines, stemming from traditional information retrieval. One advantage of this approach is that the customer is free to choose the search keywords.

This is in contrast to a structured search, in thus, part of the common database schema. Another advantage is that unlike the structured search, in which the result set of a query can only be empty or non-empty, the results of a full text search are ranked. However, there are also some limitations. First, the tourists has no guidance in using the right keywords; thus, it is quite hard to find words matching the index of the Web pages. For example, one will obviously not succees by using synoniyms that are not part of the index. Second, there is a considerable system overhead every time the robot is started to index the pages again. And third, the less often the robot is started, the higher the probability that the search is processed on an index that is outdated.

It is important to note that the three access paradigms implemented by TIScover are not isolated from each other. Instead, they are seamlessly integrated so that a tourist can arbitrarily switch in-between and the system automatically preserves all necessary context information. When, for example, browsing on the Tyrolean level of Atlas, a switch to Scout or to full text search implies that the following search is done automatically in the context for browsing is automatically the village the product is related to.

The Negotation Phase. In this phase, the conditions of the e-commerce transaction are negotiated. The conditions for tourism products are, for example, facilities at the accommodation, type of board, duration of stay, price, and terms of payment. In the simplest case, these conditions are predefined in full, and the customer cannot tailor certain product to his or her individual needs. A more sophisticated negotation phase would be based on some negotation protocol, in which one or both participant(s) are able to negotiate the final terms. In TIScover, the tourism information provider is responsible for defining the negotation protocol for tourism products in that he or she specifies the conditions according to which he or she is willing to sell them. There can be products that are fully predefined (e.g., a last-minute offer) but also products where the tourism information provider specifies the product's conditions but the customer is able to tailor the product to his individual needs. TIScover allows the same tourism product to be offered with different conditions. For example, different types of board or different seasons imply a price reduction or increase. With the time conditios, it can be specified that a tourism product is only available during a certain season and valid on weekdays only.

Finally, it can be ascertained whether credit cards are accepted and which ones, and whether payment by bank transfer is possible. If a customer searches for a tourism product via the Scout module, the information phase and the negotation phase overlap, since to carry out a search, the customer has to define the criteria according to which he is willing to book a product. Depending on how precisely these criteria have been specified and whether the product has been fully predefined by the tourism information provider, the results list contains products that allow no further customization and can be booked directly or products that can be further adapted to individual needs, for example, by choosing the type of board. It has to be emphasized that each modification of the conditions implies an immediate recalculation of the price.

The Settlement Phase. In this phase, both parties fulfil the terms agreed in the negotation phase. As is the case with many products sold electronically, only part of the settlement phase can be supported by the system for tourism products since there is a difference between the time of booking and the time of consuming. Existing tourism information systems often do not really support the settlement phase. Some offer only a telephone number, others offer only an e-mail address, without checking availability or dealing with a proper actualization of the inventory. To book products in TIScover tourists have to enter their personal data; their credit card numbers, if payment by credit card has been chosen; and confirmation that they accept the booking conditions. If tourists decide to pay by bank transfer, they get an automatically generated e-mail with the request to confirm the booking by forwarding this e-mail to the provider. The internal booking process comprises several steps. First, the personal data of the tourist and all data concerning the product booked are stored in the database. Second, the inventory of the product is actualized. Third the tourism information provider is notified of the booking by an automatically sent fax and e-mail. Finally, the tourist is sent a voucher confirming his or her booking. All data transferred during the booking process are encoded via the Secure Sockets layer protocol.

Mobile Access To Discover

With the rapid growth of wireless telecommunication on one hand and the exponential expansion of the Internet on the other hand, the convergence of these two mainstreams is predictable. Mobile access to Internet content and services by means of mobile devices, such as cellular phones, is needed becoming an interesting possibility, both for the tourism information provider to reach new customers and for tourists on the move. Mobile services are not replacing pure Web applications or interactive television services, but they complement them in that for example, topical information is accessible both at home and whereever is most convenient for the tourist. The market for this new application area seems to be ready. According to the latest TIA travel poll of 5.200 U.S. adults, 58% of business travelers and 49% of the pleasure travelers over the past year said they took their cellular phone with them on a trip (TIA 2004). furthemore, there will be more than 830 million owners of cellular phones by the year 2004, and a substantial proportion of the phones will allow Internet access.

To stay abreast of these promising changes, TIScover already provides three different mobile services, namely, weather forecasts, avalanche conditions, and snow reports. This kind of tourism information is also available via the traditional Web, but it is especially well suited to mobile access. This is because it represents a hot spot within the TIScover database, being subject to a particularly high update frequency. At the same time, the value of this information depends on its topically and, therefore, on the ability of the tourist to access this information at any time, independent of location. In the following section, the basic technology for realizing mobile access and its usage in TIScover is described in more detail.

To use the mobile services provided by TIScover, the

tourist has to connect to TIScover by simply entering the respective unified resource locator (URL) into his or her cellular phone. After the connection has been established, the TIScover logo is shown, and the tourist can select one of the services displayed, that is, "snow reports", a list of all Albanian regions is shown, and the tourist has to select one option. Now, the tourist is able to enter the first letter, but preferably the full name, of the village or skiing area desired. If the name is misspelled, TIScover uses a phonetic search to find names within the database that sound similar. If the results list contains more than one entry, the tourist can scroll up and down and select one of the entries or can navigate back and start another search. As soon as an entry has been selected, the snow report is displayed, comprising name of the village/skiing area, date, snow level, and snow quality for mountin, valley and village. Furthermore, direct links to both weather forecasts and avalanche conditions of this geographical area are provided.

Interoperability of TIScover

Although quality of access is a major prerequisite for a successful tourism information system, as already mentioned, quality of content is equally, if not more, important. To fulfill this requirement, it is of course infeasible to store all information a tourist might be interested in at one Web site, both in terms of storage costs and, more important, in terms of maintenance overhead. A more promising idea would be to take advantage of the huge amount of other relevant tourism information that is already distributed throughout the Web. However, most of current Web sites do not allow for the integration of multiple data sources beyond simple links between them. TIScover has been extended with an External data Source Layer to federate multiple structured and semistructured tourism information sources on the Web. These sources comprise different in-house databases employed in the various tourism offices, Excel files used for managerial purposes, and finally, HTML pages of other Web sites.

Conclusions

Foreseen can be a further specialization, focusing on different services, but also an integration of the various players and products by a common technological infrastructure. This development is similar to that which has already occurred in the industry with the appearance of the CRS/GDS. They provided a common platform to reach the market, i.e., at that time only the travel agents.

Future competition in the (electronic) tourism market place will be characterized by the efforts of the players to exploit technology to facilitate organizational responsiveness and learning as well as customer relationship management by:

- using the infrastructure for enforced marketing efforts, generating user interest by specific services;
- being able to move in the quickly changing industry network, finding the balance between cooperation and competition;
- developing a strategy for knowledge management and permanent learning;
- permanently adopting to and using technological developments;
- maintaining customer relationships, based on sophisticated user and interface tools; and
- monitoring ongoing trends and relying on advanced tools for product development and innovation.

Recommendations

Recomendations are given with respect to all three areas described in this article, that is, e-commerce transaction support, mobile access, and interoperability.

1. Where the support of e-commerce transactions is concerned, a visionary approach would be to allow the tourist not just to book accommodation by means of TIScover and contact Web sites, for example, of car rental companies or airlines individually, but rather to allow the tourist to assemble a whole holiday

package and to book the package at once. Two scenarios of varying complexity can be distinguished. First, the Web sites, whose products can be selected to assemble the package, could be predefined. This is similar to electronic shopping malls where the shops participating are known in advance. Second and more visionary would be for the user to navigate from TIScover to arbitrary Web sites offering products, and some runtime engine checks whether the web site is capable of participating in a global booking process.

2. Mobile access poses several interesting possibilities for future developments. With respect to e-commerce transactions, W@P provides the proper technology to allow secure online transactions. This means that it will be possible in the near future for a tourist to book tourism products anywhere via cellular phones. Furthemore, W@P will define a "push mechanism", enabling any Web server to send information to the client, that is, the cellular phone, without having to wait for information requests. This function would alert sucsribers when time-sensitive information changes. For example, immediate information about a predictedfall in temperature would be of great value for an alphinist. Finally, W@P also provides location information, meaning that the mobile services can vary depending on where one uses them. An interesting application scenario would be a location-dependent tourist guide for city visitors, where the visitors are provided with context-sensitive information, such as where to find the best restaurant, when the next bus leaves from the bus stop, or what the current waiting times at local attractions are.
3. Concerning interoperability, recomendation will be done primarily to enhance the components and tools developed in the course of MIRO-Web to be able to collect and disseminate knowledge instead of just data. Through a rule-based XML-wrapper, tourism information from corporate databases, HTML files,

and office applications will be collected in data warehouses. Using classical data mining tools, knowledge will be extracted from the warehouses in the form of derived tourism information and rules. Through XML-based query tools, users will be able to subscribe and receive personalized tourism information in an appropriate format on various devices including computers, cellular phones, and faxes.

2.8. INTERNAL MARKETING AND SERVICE QUALITY: THE CASE STUDY OF ALBANIAN SEA-SIDE HOTELS

Liljana Elmazi

Introduction

Quality is the main topic and issue of modern economy and market change.

So, service quality has been increasingly identified as a key factor in differentiating service products and building a competitive advantage in tourism. The process by which customers evaluate a purchase, thereby determining satisfaction and likelihood of repurchase, is important to all marketers but especially to services marketers because, unlike their manufacturing counterparts, they have fewer objective measures of quality by which to judge their production.

The concept of service quality includes service to customer (providing what is required and being "nice" to the customer), delivery/operations, relationships with customers, and internal relationships between employees and management. The study done in the field of quality (explanation, classification, evaluation and modeling) have try to identify the critical dimensions need to consider a service to be of a good quality.

The quality evaluation is done by the customer on the basis of their own viewpoint and expectations that are formed before consumption (personal sources, its own experience, communication of tourism firm with external customers), however their experience lives within service supply and after analyzing the final result. If their expectations were fulfilled it is considered that the quality is satisfactory, it his prospects went beyond, the quality is ideal, and if his prospects are not fulfilled, the quality is deficient.

First Part of the Study. Methodology and Results

This part intends to investigate the correspondence between operational quality which is linked to the performer of the service, and perceived quality which is linked to consumer of the service respectively.

Taking into consideration the elements of services quality theoretical known, I choose to apply two type questionnaire and to survey the services supplied by 30 hotels on the Ionian and Adriatic coast in Vlora Prefecture. In order to investigate upon quality of service I came up with a questionnaire for the personnel (employees and managers) in the 30 different hotels and their clients in the period July–August 2005.

There were 300 questionnaires were for clients (and they had a response rate 70%) and 100 questionnaire were conceived for suppliers (with a response rate of 80%). The results are:

1. The majority of tourists are for the first time in the observed hotel (92.5% - there is hardly a fidelity towards the provider), the personnel was working for the first time in the hotel (a majority of 70%) out of which half are working for the first time in a tourism based unit. Their lack of experience might be a possible problem. I consider that getting to know the values of the organization which employed them, as well as a good training might be hard to accomplish due to the length of the high season which makes the employees instable relating to their workplace.
2. The majority of clients (82%) are base-services consumers (meaning that they are only interested in accommodation and meals) whilst the supplementary and the complementary services are less demeaned.

In the "other services" category, parking is intense and frequently asked for. Clients have also complained about the lack of entertainment services. Supplementary services such as washing and cleaning are resolved by the hotel's employees by hand, manually.

3. Analyzing the criteria which are to be considered in a basic quality evaluation, I have come across a normal situation also anticipated by the specialist.

Table 1: The comparison between the importance of evaluation criteria of service quality from client's and service provider's point of view (in general)

Evaluation criteria of services	*Importance in the client's perspective (maximal is 100%)*	*Imortance in the provider's perspective (maximal is 100%)*
Inferior and exterior aspect	67,36	72,5
Modern equipment facilities	61,05	90
Ambient	65,78	95
Modernity of the building	60	70
Using computer-based systems for registering tourist	79,47	90
Cleaning state	87,36	95
Well trained personnel	66,31	100
Personnel's availability to serve	76,31	97,5
Communication skills	83,68	95
Promptness in the serving clients	87,36	97,5
Enthusiasm and good- humored	76,31	92,5
Capacity of task fulfilling	68,42	97,5
Capacity of dealing and solving problems	72,1	95
Kindness	88,42	95

As seen from the table, the most important criterion of client's perspective is the kindness of personnel. The role of relating is here obvious: clients look for "human side" of the service.

Second in place is the cleaning state which is hot spot of Albanian tourism, being permanently brought into light by the local mass-media. The last criterion is the modernity of the building, even though from the provider's point of view is the most used "excuse" for poor accomplishment. On the other hand, the provider's consider that their strongest point in ensuring quality is personnel training, followed by promptness, availability, etc. this is a classic mistake, when the main focus is on training and not on the behavior. Clients have ranked personnel training only on the 6th position as for them it's of no relevance how well trained the employees are, but how this reflects of the customer–provider relationship.

4. When asked of the reason that made them choose these facilities, the majority of respondents indicate that it was what their traveler agent recommended (24%), next being that it was their worker's union offer (20%) featuring good prices, friends and family recommendation (19%), good prices and nice surroundings in the resort (12%) each). When bound to make a decision, the consumers are mostly influenced by selling forces and personnel sources of informing oneself. The Albanian tourist is mainly interested in saving advantages, which is the main reason for which they choose hotel's facilities. It is obvious, that given situation, the tourist's choices are limited.
5. Analyzing how the quality of services provided by the observed units is appreciated we have come across a spectacular result. We are able to identify a positive appreciation from the client's point of view, their evaluation being even more "soft" than that of providers. The criteria mostly taken into consideration by the consumers are personnel kindness and cleaning state, which were very well appreciated in the observed hotels. The most unimportant characteristics for clients are the ones less appreciated. Is this the sign that the needs of the consumers are met by the provider's offer? One might explain the results using the fact that it might be possible for the client's needs

to be lowered by the past bad experiences, out of which, by comparison, the actual situation seemed satisfying.

6. Comparing client's and provider's appreciation, I clearly observe that providers treat all criteria more severe than their clients, which is something to be appreciated. Only when asked about their capacity of solving and dealing with problems the providers' awarded themselves with more credit.

Table 2: Comparison between appreciating the criteria of service quality evaluation out of client's and provider's point of view (in the observed hotels)

Evaluation criteria of services	*Importance in the client's perspective (out of a maximam possible of 100)*	*Imortance in the provider's perspe-ctive (out of a maximum possible of 100)*
Inferior and exterior aspect	59,47	77,5
Modern equipment facilities	50,52	75
Ambient	57,36	85
Modernity of the building	56,84	72,5
Using computer-based systems for registering tourist	60,52	95
Cleaning state	81,05	90
Well trained personnel	73,68	90
Personnel's availability to serve	67,36	92,5
Communication skills	77,36	95
Promptness in the serving clients	64,21	92,5
Enthusiasm and good- humored	75,26	90
Capacity of task fulfilling	58,42	92,5
Capacity of dealing and solving problems	84,73	92,5
Kindness	84,73	92,5

7. When asked about increasing service's quality, the providers' agreed that clients suggestions might be useful (89,48%) but don't know whether the clients' would be willing to offer feedback (63,15%). This

response suggests that providers might not be interested in acting in such a manner. When dealing the satisfaction of the clients with eh service provided, we observe that 73,68% of the responses suggest that the consumers were satisfied and very satisfied with their accommodation, while nobody declared to be not all satisfied. In some aspects of the evaluation, clients' declared nothing so the percentage of 100% couldn't be reached.

8. When asked about the satisfaction produced by the quality of meals, a great majority of 73,67% declared that they are greatly/on a certain amount/less satisfied which was because some of the guests were required to purchase meals in a restaurant situated 500meters from the hotel.
9. The typical client's profile is coming from an urban society, married, with an monthly income which varies between 600-1200 EURO, higher education, aged between 35-55, which is interested in spending an average 10-15 days.

Second Part of the Study: Methodology and Results

Second part of the study presents the role of triangle marketing in improvement of tourist quality service. Triangle marketing directly and indirectly serves to narrow the gaps in service quality. Delivery of quality service in tourism requires cooperation from employees, management and customers. Our hypothesis which will be tested is: Triangle marketing directly and indirectly serves to narrow the gaps in tourism and hospitality service quality.

This part represents: How these relationships narrow the gaps in service quality? Finally, several guidelines applicable to the development and maintenance of these relationships suggested.

To achieve high-quality services in tourism and hospitality industry is to:

- Understand tourists' expectations,
- Set quality specifications based on tourists' expectations,

- Verify that delivery of the service conforms to quality specifications,
- Not promise more than it can deliver and therefore create very high expectations,
- Constantly monitor tourists perceived services to verify that they are not lower than their expectations.

The primary data were collected through a self-completed questionnaire. The sample consists of individuals working i the observed hotels. The study is based on primary and secondary research. National statistics, previous contributions in this field, internet sources, etc., served as secondary data. Survey methods served as the source of the primary data, which have been processed by SPSS. We made factor analysis using the correlation matrix to try to determine which sets of variables cluster together in a reasonable manner. The major contribution of the factor analysis to the research is that it supports the existence of hypotheses.

The Marketing and Service Quality

Relationship marketing is a process of strengthening ties between the organization and its customers, intermediaries, suppliers and employees. According to Service Quality Gap Model exist five gaps:

> Gap 1 represents the difference between customer expectations of service and company perceptions of customer expectations of service and company perceptions of customer expectations. Effective internal marketing includes gathering customer information from employees whose boundary-spanning roles allow them to tap into customer expectations.

It establishes clear lines of communication up the chain of command.

Hypothesis 1: Effective relationship marketing to external customers means knowing what they expect. All of these activities directly impact the extent of the gap and executed, serve to narrow it.

Gap 2 created when company perception of customer expectations is translated into service designs and standards. The service is custom designed to the needs of a client. When systems are devised in this manner, no guessing is involved , there is less error in the translation than in a hit –or-miss approach.

*Hypothesis 2: The building solid cust*omer relationships at the structural level narrows ties gap.

Gap 3 involves the transfer of service design to service delivery. The gap is potentially created by several employee-related problems and issues. The strong relationships with customers at the social and structural levels diffuse the reliance on price for leveling fluctuating demand. Finally, close management of the advertising function can ensure that customers are informed of their roles in the delivery transaction.

Hypothesis 3: Effective internal marketing, training and empowerment all encourage effective delivery of service and reduce the performance gap.

Gap 4 is the difference between service delivery and communication about service to customers . The causes for this gap include ineffective communication among internal and external markets and overpromising. Advertising should be used to communicate roles of customers as well as employees, not only to themselves, but to educate each of them about the roles of other. Key to this communication is avoidance of the natural tendency to make unreasonable promises. When these rules are followed as part of relationship management and marketing, this gap is significantly reduced.

Hypothesis 4: Key to the communication is avoidance of the natural tendency to make unreasonable promises. When these rules are followed as part of relationship management and marketing, this gap is significantly reduced.

Gap 5 is defined as difference between perceived and expected service. Since this gap is a function of the first four gaps, it is indirectly affected by the implementation of strategies to reduce the preceding gaps.

Hypothesis 5: Customized service strategies directly

narrow this gap, as they represent the opportunity to exceed customer expectations.

The 50 questionnaires were randomly distributed to workers within the sample areas, and the response rate was 62%. The resulted content of the sample was 72 females (46.8%) and 82 males (53.2%).

In the sample, 25-35 year old respondents make 31.8% of the total, which is the dominant part, and until 25 year old represent 26.6%. The main reason is that the younger tend to be more mobile than older people.

The respondents for question "How long have you been working for a bank or financial institution" answer: 6% of respondents had less than one year, , 12% of them had 1 – 2 years, 21% of them had 3–5 years, 13% had 6–10 years, 3% had 10-15 years and 4% had over 15 years. This related with the trends of tourism business for employment of the younger.

As part of the assessment of human capital, the study used education classification based on four levels. It shows that the majority of respondents (57.8%) have higher educational level. This is a characteristic that comes by high rate of unemployment in Albania, and it is good for the quality of the tourism development.

Question: "Do you supervise other people? Only 18% of respondents answer Yes, others (82%) answer No. In tourism and hospitality services there are not too many levels of management between customer-contact personnel and top management.

Question: "How much of your average work day is spent in direct contact with customers?" 60% of their spent 71% of work day in contact direct with customers, 16% of their spent 10-30%, 19% of their spent 31-70%, and only 5% of their spent less than 10%.

In the questionnaire there is a table including 24 statements related to the possible motives for taking up a job in hotel industry. The respondents were asked to rate, on a 7-point Likert scale (0–strongly agree, 3-neither agree nor disagree, 6- strongly disagree), the degree of their agreement or disagreement for 24 statements. Factor analysis was applied

Table 3: Total Variance Explained and Extraction Method: Principal Component Analysis.

	Initial Eigen values			*Extraction Sums of Squared Loadings*			*Rotation Sums of Squared Loadings*		
Component	*Total*	*% of Variance*	*Cumul-ative*	*Total*	*% of Variance*	*Cumul-ative %*	*total*	*% of Varian*	*Cumul-ative %*
1. Internal marketing and gap 2	7.124	29.685	29.685	7.124	29.685	29.685	5.957	24.821	24.821
2. Internal Marketing and gap 1	5.026	20.943	50.628	5.026	20.943	50.628	3.988	16.618	41.439
3. Internal Marketing and gap 2	4.365	18.187	68.815	4.365	18.187	68.815	3.699	15.412	56.851
4. Interactive Marketing and gap 3	2.523	10.513	79.328	2.523	10.513	79.328	3.547	14.777	71.629
5. External Marketing and gap 4	1.711	7.130	86.458	1.711	7.130	86.458	2.994	12.475	84.103
6. Internal Marketing and gap 3	1.432	5.966	92.424	1.432	5.966	92.424	1.997	8.321	92.424

to the data. The approach to factor analysis according to the main study objectives was based on above five hypotheses.

The "Total Variance Explained" table following shows the eigenvalues, which are the proportion of total variance in all the variables which is accounted for by that factor. A factor's eigenvalue may be computed as the sum of its squared factor loadings for all the variables. A factor's eigenvalue divided by the number of variables (which equals the sum of variances because the variance of a standardized variable equals 1) is the percent of variance in all the variables which it explains. The ratio of eigenvalues is the ratio of explanatory importance of the factors with respect to the variables. If a factor has a low eigenvalue, then it is contributing little to the explanation of variances in the variables and may be ignored as redundant with more important factors. Only six are extracted for analysis because, under the Extraction options, SPSS was told to extract only factors with eigenvalues of 1.0 or higher.

The "Rotation Sums of Squared Loadings" give the eigenvalues after rotation improves the interpretability of the factors (we used Varimax rotation, which minimizes the number of variables which have high loadings on each given factor). The six factors solution satisfies both Kaiser's criterion of selection. Note that the total percent of variance explained is 92.424% (see the cumulative value for factor 6). That is, after rotation each extracted factor counts for a different percentage of variance explained, even though the total variance explained is the same.

Also, each factor is named in accordance with the meaning of the correlated variables as well as in line with the five hypotheses. The five hypothesis of the research are true.

Conclusions and Recommendations

It is time now to (re)present the arguments and issues covered in the previews paragraphs, and advance some conclusions and recommendations related to the topic.

Referring the first part of the study, despite the positive appreciation, I must point out that most of guests were only surprised about the services' quality, and not impressed.

Nevertheless, as the theory suggests no value of 100% is not satisfying for Total Quality Management.

Even though I have take into account this aspect, there is no such thing as an effort to determine the clients returning the following year.

The offer includes no "added value" which would help increase towards the ideal quality. The questioned personnel, although young and enthusiastic, seemed pretty confused when asked about the necessary training required. The increase of competition on the Ionian –Adriatic seacoast in Albania is a real quality booster, but there are still many aspects which need improving.

To improve and achieve high-quality services in hotel industry is to:

- Understand tourists' expectations,
- Set quality specifications based on tourists' expectations,
- Verify that delivery of the service conforms to quality specifications,
- Not promise more than it can deliver and therefore create very high expectations,
- Constantly monitor tourists perceived services to verify that they are not lower than their expectations.

In their boundary-spanning roles hotel service employees are the connection between organization and the customers. Customer evaluation of the service and the organization are based on interactions with service employees.

A staff of trained, paid, motivated employees is likely to generate satisfied customers. Building, maintaining and retaining the workforce requires a competent management and marketing effort. The recruiting, job training methods, and offering a benefit package to employees can build relationships with employees. These strategies are based on triangle marketing, that directly and indirectly serves to narrow the gaps in tourism and hospitality service quality.

A better cooperation between the tourism and hotel industry and the universities in order to let them know what we offer, and for us to know better what the industry really needs. This would help, firstly, in developing better curricula and syllabus, in a better marketing of the knowledge's of our graduates, and secondly, in the quality of the service of this industry. In line with that our research could be more valuable to the local and national development of tourism.

2.9. MANAGEMENT TOOL FOR STRATEGIC DECISION—MAKING IN TOURISM MARKETING

Liljana Elmazi

2.9.1. The Problem

The destination managers of the Albanian tourism regions face new challenges in developing their offers and marketing activities due to corporate changes and increasing international competition. Nowadays, knowing the guests and their needs thoroughly provides a decisive competitive edge.

The tourism regions must clarify a number of issues:

1. What image do the guests have of the region? How satisfied are your guests with the price-performance ratio, the opening hours, the offers, etc.? What are the strengths and weaknesses of the region?
2. Who are the guests of a particular tourism region (guest structure, information gathering and booking behavior, activities, daily expenditures, etc.)?

2.9.2. Solution

2.9.2.1 Tourism Monitor Albania

The guest survey tool called Tourism MONITOR Albania was developed by the Albanian National Tourist Office within the Tourism, Culture, Youth and Sports Ministry in conjunction with the commercial provider MANOVA as well as the input of all six Albanian provinces in order to provide the Albanian tourism regions with answers to these questions.

T-Monitor Albania is a solid basis through which the existing targeted offers in the respective regions can be improved and tailored towards the needs of the customers.

As many as 30,000 holiday-makers in Albania were interviewed in the first two years alone. The close cooperation with all the participants has made this success possible. In addition to the Albanian National Tourist Office and the six Albanian provincial tourism organizations, a number of regions and destinations take part in T-Monitor as well.

2.9.2.2 What information does T- Monitor Albania provide?

T-Monitor records extensive information on the guests of a region or destination. Regular face-to-face interviews (duration approx. 20 minutes) are conducted in all six Albanian provinces and a number of Albanian regions.

- The guest structure—where do our guests come from?
- The information gathering and decision-making behavior
- How the journey is conducted (duration of stay, arrival data, travel companions)
- The stay (accommodation, type of holiday, holiday activities)
- The expenditure breakdown
- Destinations image
- Satisfaction and intention of recommendation
- Guest typology
- Strengths/weaknesses analyses
- And much more

All T-Monitor participants use the same questionnaire.

2.9.2.2.1 Who is interviewed?

The survey is directed at holiday-makers in Albania (the interviewee must be at least 14 years of age), The survey is NOT directed at business travelers (the journey must be for private reasons only). The person must overnight at least once (in gratuitous or non-gratuitous accommodations).

- Minimum age: 14 years

- Holiday for private purposes
- At least 1 overnight stay

2.9.2.3 What Is Special About T-Monitor Albania?

2.9.2.3.1 Benchmarking

"Normal" guest surveys are conducted quite often. The disadvantage of such guest surveys is that there are no benchmarks for the results and these are then difficult to evaluate. T-Monitor Albania features benchmarking possibilities among its participants: each participant can view their own as well as the anonymized data of the other participants in the online database.

2.9.2.3.2 Online Evaluation

The conducted interviews are collated as quickly as possible via the Internet in a joint data base and are made available to the participants—immediately accessible ONLINE in graphics and charts with the click of a button.

2.9.2.3.3 Simple Categorization

T-MONA is a revolutionary system that is self-explanatory and easy to use: the results can be easily broken down (interactive tables) e.g. by nationality, age, gender, booked hotel category, travel motive and much more.

2.9.2.4 How To Participate in T-Monitor Albania

ANTO conducts n=2800 interviews per year. Provinces, larger cities, regions that want detailed evaluations for their region must incorporate their own interviews (at their own expense) into T-MONA. T- Monitor Albania participants commission a local market research institute to conduct the interviews.

ANTO

- provides the questionnaire (uniform for all users),
- calculates the quota (based on indications regarding countries of origin and types of accommodation the guests selected)

- makes the online system available (with all analysis and benchmarking possibilities)

2.9.3 Cultural Tourists

The number of interviews enables the Albanian National Tourist Office to analyze virtually any target group and any country of origin. This helps gather detailed information on the cultural tourist, whereby the most significant or characteristic results for the target group cultural tourist (in benchmarking for the summer guest in general) are presented.

2.9.3.1 Size of the target group and countries of origin

20% of summer guests in Albania are cultural tourists.

Where did the cultural tourists come from? The relative majority of cultural tourists come from Kosovo and Macedonia (51%). Domestic guests enjoy holidaying in Albania as well: 25% of the cultural tourists come from Albania themselves. In comparison to Kosovo and Macedonia and Albania, other countries of origin play a smaller role in Albanian cultural tourism: Italy follows with 7%, the Netherlands with 6%, Great Britain with 5% and the USA and Switzerland with 3% each.

Cultural tourists have a higher educational level and consequentially a higher net income than summer tourists. The average cultural tourist is 46 years old, whereby, as expected, the percentage of under 30-year-olds (16%) is comparably low.

2.9.3.2 Socio-demographic data

Cultural tourists have a higher educational level and consequentially a higher net income than summer tourists. The average cultural tourist is 46 years old, whereby, as expected, the percentage of under 30-year-olds (16%) is comparably low.

2.9.3.3 Travel Companions

Do cultural tourists tend to travel alone, with a partner or in groups? Just like Albanian summer guests in general, cultural tourists prefer traveling with their own partner as well:

43% of cultural tourists travel with their own partner (compared to 42% of Albanian summer guests). Cultural tourists clearly travel less frequently as a family than summer guests in general: 14% of cultural tourists travel with their family with children under 14 years old (compared to 20% of summer guests in general). 8% of cultural tourists travel as part of a group (compared to 4% of summer guests in general). Thus cultural tourists travel less often with their families and more often in a group.

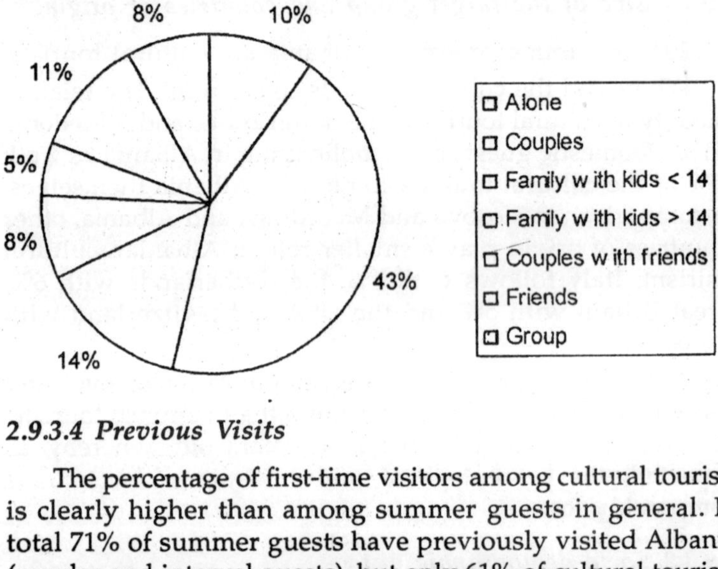

2.9.3.4 Previous Visits

The percentage of first-time visitors among cultural tourists is clearly higher than among summer guests in general. In total 71% of summer guests have previously visited Albania (regular and interval guests), but only 61% of cultural tourists have traveled to Albania before.

2.9.3.5 Information gathering behavior

How did the cultural tourists gather the information they needed about the destination of their choice?

As expected, the percentage of summer guests who do not require any holiday information (32%) is clearly higher than that of cultural tourists—this can be attributed to the higher percentage of regular guests among the summer guests.

Cultural tourists, on the other hand, gather information significantly more often than summer guests in general from travel guides and literature, catalogues of tour operators, from the Internet or consult travel agencies in their country of origin.

2.9.3.6. *Expenditures*

Euro 100 – per person and day

In comparison: the average summer guests spends 80 – euro per person and day.

2.9.3.7 *Activities*

Walks	84%
Dining in restaurants (outside the accommodation)	81%
Going to coffeehouses	78%
Sightseeing	76%
Enjoying and/or buying typical regional food/drink	71%
Museums, exhibitions	70%
Shopping	68%
Visiting natural attractions	59%
Individual excursions from the holiday resort	56%
Hiking tours	41%

The portfolio of top activities of cultural tourists differs from the Albanian holiday-maker in general as follows: The cultural tourist visits museums and exhibitions more often, goes sightseeing more often, and goes to restaurants and coffeehouses more often. What is remarkable is that cultural tourists also visit natural attractions more often than summer guests in general.

2.9.3.8 *Marketing Tips for Attracting the "Cultural Tourist"*

- Provide attractive offers for couples and groups
- Don't neglect the importance of an informative Internet representation;
- Consultation in travel agencies play an important role for cultural tourists—seek cooperation with travel

agencies (inform them of insider's tips, up-to-date events and information)

- Stronger promotion of museums/exhibitions and sights in connection with indulgence opportunities—e.g. walks that include visits to restaurants/bars/taverns
- Focus on recreation for "cultural tourists" as well: inform about "natural attractions"—also in urban areas
- Promote the charming, cultivated sides of Albania—show them that Albania loves its guests

2.9.4. Further Development of T-Monitor Albania

2.9.4.1 Integration of the Country Studies

Besides surveying the guests who are already in Albania, the Albanian National Tourist Office annually conducts surveys in two to three of Albania's source markets on the travel, information gathering and booking behavior of foreign guests as well as foreign guests with an affinity to Albania (persons who have previously spent holidays in Albania or are planning to). The survey includes questions on the image of holiday land Albania as well as the reasons speaking for or against holidaying in Albania.

The results of these country studies are also stored in T-Monitor Albania. The great advantage is that this target group of foreign holiday-makers (not visitors of Albania) can be viewed online. The guest survey offers information online on those guests who have already visited Albania, and the stored data of the country studies can deliver information online on the travel behavior of the foreign guest as well as of those who have principally demonstrated an interest in Albania.

2.9.4.2 Integration of the Results of the Source Market Analysis

In the Source Market Analysis (QMA) are evaluated systematically on the basis of approx. 60 tourist and economic indicators. The development dynamism in the source markets as well as the current and medium-term market chances of a destination country (e.g. Albania,) are analyzed.

The result is a ranking of the source markets according to chances of success for the destination country based on a model indicating the budget resource allocation/distribution among individual source markets.

The indicators of the Source Market Analysis will be available online in T-MONA at the end of 2007.

The integration of the guest survey with the results of the country studies and the Source Market Analysis has turned T-Monitor Albania into an essential and indispensable management tool for strategic decision-making in tourism.

REFERENCES

Anderson, C., J. Ciarlo, and S. Brodie (1981), 'Measuring Evaluation-Induced Change in Mental Health Programs' in J. Ciarlo (ed.) *Utilising Evaluation: Concepts and Measurement Techniques,* Sage Publications, Beverly Hills, California, 97-124.

Andreasen, A.R. (1983), 'Cost-Conscious Marketing Research', *Harvard Business Review,* (July-August), 74-79.

Arbuckle, J. L. (1997), Amos User's Guide: Version 3.6, SPSS, Chicago.

Assael, H., and J. Keon (1982), 'Nonsampling vs. Sampling Errors in Survey Research', *Journal of Marketing,* Vol. 46 (Spring), 114-123.

Athiyaman, A., and R. W. Robertson (1995), 'Strategic Planning in Large Tourism Firms: An Empirical Analysis', *Tourism Management* 16, 199-205.

Baker, K., G. Hozier, Jr., and R. Rogers (1994), 'Marketing Research Theory and Methodology and the Tourism Industry: A Nontechnical Discussion', *Journal of Travel Research,* Winter, 3-7.

Barabba, V. P. and G. Zaltman (1991), *Hearing the Voice of the Market: Competitive Advantage Through Creative Use of Market Information,* Harvard Business School Press, Boston.

Boomsma, A. (1987), 'The Robustness of Maximum Likelihood Estimation in Structural Equation Models' in Currance P. and R. Ecob (eds.) *Structural Modelling by Example: Applications in Educational, Sociological, and Behavioral Research,* Cambridge University Press, 160-188. Bourgeois, L.J. (1980), 'Strategy and Environment: A Conceptual Integration', *Academy of Management Review,* 5 (January), 25-39.

Bracker, J.S., B.W. Keats, and J.N. Pearson (1988), 'Planning and Financial Performance in a Growth Industry', *Strategic Management Journal* 9, 591-603.

Browne, M. W., and R. Cudeck (1993), 'Single Sample Cross-Validation Indices for Covariance Structures', *Multivariate Behavioral Research*, 24, 445-455.

Burns, P.M. and A. Holden (1995), *Tourism: A New Perspective*, Prentice Hall, London.

Campbell, D.T. and D.W. Fiske (1959), 'Convergent and Discriminant Validation by the Multitrait-Multimethod Matrix', *Psychological Bulletin*, 56, 81-105.

Greenberg, B. A., J.L. Goldstucker, and D. N. Bellenger (1977), 'What Techniques are Used by Marketing Researchers in Business?', *Journal of Marketing*, 41, No. 2, 62-68.

Hair, J.E., R.E. Anderson, R.L. Tatham, and W.C. Black (1995), *Multivariate Data Analysis with Readings* (fourth edition), Prentice Hall, Englewood Hills, New Jersey.

Hall, G., A.G., and W. Rutherford (1979), Measuring Stages of Concern About the Innovation: A Manual for Use of the SoC Questionnaire, Research and Development Centre for Teacher Education, Austin, Texas.

Kinnear, T.C., and A.R. Root (1995), Survey of Marketing Research, American Marketing Association, Chicago.

Kinnear, T., and J. Taylor (1996), Marketing Research: An Applied Approach (fifth edition), McGraw Hill, New York.

Kinnear, T., J. Taylor, L. Johnson, and R. Armstrong (1993), *Australian Marketing Research*, McGraw-Hill, Sydney.

Knorr, K. D. (1977), 'Policymakers' Use of Social Science Knowledge: Symbolic or Instrumental?' in C. H. Weiss (ed.) *Using Social Research in Public Policy Making*, Lexington Books, Lexington, Massachusetts, 165-182.

Kohli, A., and B. Jaworski (1990), 'Market Orientation: The Construct, Research Propositions, and Managerial Implications', *Journal of Marketing*, 54 (April), 1-18.

Barlett, CA., & Guoshal, S. (1998). Matrix management: not a structure, a frame of mind. *Harvard Business Review* paperback, 90082, 108-109.

Calantone, R.J and Mazanec, A.: Marketing Management and Tourism. *Annals of Tourism Research*, 18(1), 101-119, 2001.

Deshpande, R.J., Farley, J.U., & Webster, F.E., Jr. (1999). Corporate culture, customer orientation, and innovativeness in Japanese firms: A quadrat analysis. *Journal of Marketing*, 1.23-27.

Drucker, P. (1969). The practice of Marketing. Heinemann: London.

Heath, E. and Wall, G.: *Marketing Tourism Destination*, John Wiley and Sons, Inc., Toronto 1992.

Jaworski, B., & Kohli, A. (1993). Market orientation: antecendents and consequences. *Journal of Marketing*, 7, 53-70.

Kohli, K., & Jaworski, B. (1990). Market orientation: the construct, research propositions, and managerial implications. *Journal of Marketing*, 4, 1-18.

Lumsdom, L.: *Marketing for Tourism*, McMillan, London, 1999.

Medlik, S.: *Managing Tourism*, Butterworth and Heinemann, London, 2001.

Meler, M.: Marketing Approach to the Tourism Product Conceptualization in a Globalization Condition, 16th International Conference, Association for Global Business, Cancun, November 18-21, 2004.

Narver, J., & Slater, S. (1991). The effect of a market orientation on business profitability. *Journal of Marketing*, 3, 20-35.

3

Strategic Tourism Marketing in Kenya: Reflections on the Nyanza/Western Region

*Dr. Roselyne N. Okech**

Introduction

The tourism and hospitality industry today faces a set of new challenges arising from changing consumers and environment. In Kenya, only wildlife and beaches have often been promoted as attractions as well as the Maasai communities. Promotions and marketing of other regions in the country have been slack. One such area is the Western Kenya Tourism Region which is one of the most beautiful places in Kenya. The tourism region here comprises of Nyanza and the Western Provinces and part of the Rift Valley Province. The present focus is on the diversification of the tourism product from the traditional beach and wildlife to suit the changing taste of the modern traveler. Opening up this region completely as a unique destination therefore will among other benefits encourage economic development and help in alleviation of poverty. This can be done by developing a

* PhD, Memorial University of Newfoundland, Canada.

marketing strategy which will specify long-term goals and objectives, identifying opportunities and the scope of activities needed to realize the full potential of tourism in this area. This contribution highlights the two major attractions - Lake Victoria and Kakamega Forest that can be strategically marketed and promoted not only to the international visitors but also to the locals as well.

A successful tourism destination is, among others, evaluated by the positive revelations of visitors to the area, the amount of money spent per capita and prospects of repeat visits to the destination. In this regard it is argued that visitors consume the products of a destination: therefore the products must be something the visitor wants and needs. The tourism and hospitality industry today faces a set of new challenges arising from changing consumers and environment. It is estimated that only those operators who recognize the changes occurring in the marketplace and proactively respond to these challenges will continue to be successful in the future. Thus, for the Nyanza/Western region in Kenya, strategies are necessary in order to address the more demanding needs to be more forward thinking than ever before. It is suggested that strategic marketing decision-making is the management process responsible for coordinating an organization's marketing activity. Kenya lies a long the East coast of Africa covering an area of 586,350 sq.km. with an estimated population of 30 million. Agriculture is the mainstay of the economy. Kenya is in the process of establishing a firm industrial base with import substitution and processing industries having been firmly established.

The country aims at joining the newly industrialized nations status by the year 2020. Tourism is currently the second largest contributor to the economy after agriculture. Tourism in Kenya dates back to pre-independence days and history has it recorded that as early as the 1930's, overseas visitors and explorers had started coming to Kenya mainly for big-game hunting expeditions while others came in search of solitude.

These expeditions were locally referred to by the Swahili word "Safari" thus bequeathing to the travel world literature with a new vocabulary. Among the early visitors were

Statesmen, Royalties and celebrities such as Theodore Rosevelt, Her Majesty Queen Elizabeth II, and Ernest Hemingway respectively. At that time, there was already a relatively well developed but limited tourism infrastructure. The available accommodation was spartan but ideal for both the visitors as well as the settler community in Kenya. However soon after independence, the Kenya Government realized the enormous potential of the nascent tourism industry and hence undertook to upgrade the existing infrastructure and superstructure as well as investing in additional facilities.

To achieve its goal, the Government encouraged local and foreign entrepreneurs to invest in the tourism and hospitality industries thus paving the way for the future development of the sector. In spite of increased competition from other destinations, Kenya is still one of the foremost tourist destinations in Africa. Tourism in Kenya is mainly based on natural attractions which include wildlife in its natural habitats as well as idyllic beaches. Approximately 10% of the country has been set aside for conservation of wildlife and biodiversity. Game viewing is a very popular pursuit since most visitors to Kenya are predominantly interested in seeing "the big five" namely the Elephant, Rhino, Lion, Buffalo, and the Leopard, not to mention other lesser and unique game of the Africa's savanna and forests. A Safari is such a popular product that has enabled the country to continue recording remarkable growth in the volume of visitors. Kenya registered well over 1,000,000 visitors' arrivals in 2002 while the bed capacity rose to over 73,000 beds in classified hotels. The sector is a major employer as it currently employs approximately over 219,000. This figure represents about 11% of the total workforce in the country.

3.1. Role of Tourism in the National Economy

The impact of tourism in the economy is felt mainly through forward and backward linkages expressed as demand for goods and services in the agricultural, textiles, beverage, transport and entertainment sectors. Hence the tourist dollar has such multiplier effects that its absence would affect the general government revenue collection.

Employment in the Tourism Sector

Since tourism is essentially a service industry, it provides relatively more jobs than any other economic sector. The industry is labour intensive and hence its expansion generates more job opportunities than an equivalent expansion in other sectors of the economy. Besides, allied improvements in tourism infrastructure also catalyses other economic activities. It is estimated that well over 219,000 people are currently deriving their livelihood from tourism.

Tourism earnings, contributions to exports and the Gross Domestic Product (GDP)

Foreign exchange earnings have been increasing steadily over the past ten years representing an appreciable growth rate. While tourism is sensitive to the level of economic activity in the tourist generating countries, it provides higher and stable earnings than those from primary products. Tourism earnings have tended to increase at a higher rate than earnings from other export commodities in a number of countries. The earnings incurred are in turn used to offset shortfalls on the visible trading account, and hence are of critical importance in the financial reckoning. Tourism contributes greatly to Government Revenue through license fees, customs and exercise duty, VAT on tourism services, landing fees, passenger service charge, entry fees to game parks as well as income tax levied on employees in the tourism industry. The generated revenues play a pivotal role in the overall development of the economy.

Tourism and Development of Infrastructure

The benefits accruing from investments in such infrastructure and superstructure as airports, hotels and restaurants, road network, communications, power and water supply as well as other related public utilities are widely shared with other sectors of the economy. Their development enhances the overall development at the local level and also encourages greater economic diversification. It has been argued that tourism has a larger multiplier effects than any other sector since every unit of tourist expenditure goes through several rounds of income creation and expenditure before its effect is exhausted. For instance, money spent by a tourist on hotel accommodation, food and beverages, shopping, entertainment and transport, does not stagnate but provides an income to hotel staff, taxi operators, shopkeepers and suppliers of goods and services. They in turn spend part of this income on their daily requirements of goods and services. Hence money accruing from tourism circulates through numerous segments of the economy through the multiplier process.

Tourism and Regional Development

Tourism has been cited as a major promoter of international goodwill and understanding as well a prime means of developing social and cultural understanding on the local level. Accordingly foreign visitors are considered to be the best ambassadors of their respective countries. In view of the fact that we are living in a global village, thanks to advances in communication technology, the industry contributes significantly to international commerce and good relations among nations. It is worth noting also that the development of tourism may serve as an important vehicle in promoting economic advancement of less developed areas that are not endowed with alternative resources. In this regard such developments play an important part in redressing regional developments and income distribution imbalances. The essence of this contribution is that all the regions of Kenya are potential tourism markets and therefore efforts should be taken to promote the same.

3.2. Environment Analysis and Assessment

To be successful in the hospitality and tourism markets, businesses must be able to interpret the needs of their customers, identify appropriate ways of segmenting the markets in which they compete, develop and launch appropriate products and effectively communicate with potential consumers. These issues are closely interrelated as they form the basis of marketing interface between the organization and its business and market environment.

Tourism takes place in a complex, dynamic and constantly changing environment that must be monitored and adapted to by all tourism and hospitality enterprises. The industry today faces a set of new and increasing challenges arising from changing tourist behaviour and environment conditions. These challenges include:

- The reconciliation of the need to consolidate the industry's service offerings to the consumer and maintain a market position with the need to remain flexible enough to respond to changes in its operational environment
- To design and properly deliver products and services corresponding to the needs of the various markets.

It is estimated that only those businesses that recognize the changes occurring in the marketplace and proactively respond to these challenges will continue to be successful in the future. These tasks require a strategic marketing approach, as well as more reliable information through proper long-term strategic and decision-making. Both the general and market environments create opportunities and pose threat to the tourism and hospitality businesses. Within a perspective of strategic marketing planning formulation, the first major task is a situation analysis, which consists of two analyses: environmental and resources:

- In the environmental analysis, an assessment of the major environments—macroeconomic, competitive and market—is emphasized in order to identify opportunities and threats
- The purpose of a resource analysis is to identify the strengths and the weaknesses in the tourism and hospitality industry.

These analyses should be followed by business's goal and strategy formulation. These steps form the foundation for the development of an enterprise's marketing strategy. It should be noted that information is the basis of planning an decision-making, and is needed in order to develop meaningful and effective strategies. The importance of monitoring and analyzing the tourism and hospitality environments has been documented by several authors.

Scanning the environment for trends that dictate strategic postures is a necessary and vital part of strategic marketing. The one certainty of the future is that change will continue and those tourism businesses and destinations which are both are of economic, social and technological changes, and develop effective responses to them, will achieve longer-term viability. Predictions are that the industry will continue to be volatile, consolidation will continue, consumer satisfaction will become even more important and technology will play an increasingly more important role. Therefore, environment and resource analysis and assessment are essential to the organizations in order to identify and respond to changes incurring in any field and to undertake the appropriate marketing actions.

3.3. Strategy Formulation and Implementation

Nyanza/Western Kenya tourism-promoting organizations need a new vision in the 21st century in order to address the development needs of the local people, to avoid increasing damage to favourite destinations, to achieve maximum potential in tourism and to reduce conflict between local people and parks. The two provinces in this study need to offer diversity in tourism through a blend of wildlife and cultural tourism. This can dispense tourist impacts more broadly hence minimize overcrowding and damage often experienced when attractions are limited to type and place. It will further facilitate the redistribution of wealth in order to benefit the local people and stem the erosion of traditional skills through the homogenization of culture. In order to help conserve African heritage and also boost tourism, plans are underway to set up a museum on self-help, harambee basis at Mukango trading center, approximately 5 kilometres from the Kakamega forest. This will improve the livelihood opportunities of the local communities. The Nyanza/Western regions in Kenya will have to adopt strategic marketing approach that involves the appropriate choices in the following major fields:

- Setting marketing goals and objectives;
- Selecting market trends, based on marketing objectives;

- Formulating the marketing strategy, including positioning and marketing mix strategies; and
- Preparing the promotion/communication plan, the strategic choices take form of a marketing action plan

Hence, marketing strategy is based upon and reflects the environmental analysis, resource analysis, and goal formulation stages. As for implementation, it is worth noting that:

- In order to implement a strategic marketing approach effectively, appropriate marketing systems—information, planning, and evaluation—are required
- One aspect of strategy implementation is resource planning, at both the organizational and operational levels
- There is need to develop and implement action plans in all related fields, such as human resources and quality

The following section provides an overview of two major attractions that can be marketed effectively for the benefit of the nation, region and the local community. They are Lake Victoria to cater for the Nyanza with Kisumu city being a direct beneficiary of the activities thereof and Kakamega Forest Reserve as a case study for the Western area with Kakamega town being the beneficiary of tourism activities.

3.4. Case Study One: Lake Victoria

Lake Victoria (See Map 1) is the second largest freshwater Lake in the world and has a surface area of approximately 69,500 sq km with adjoining catchments area measuring 184,000 sq km. The Lake is not part of the rift valley system and, at only 100 meters deep, is very wide and shallow compared to other bodies of water. Lake Victoria acts as a boundary between Tanzania and Uganda and Kenya, yet international water travel between the countries is no longer possible. The only Lake excursions available occur between Kisumu and ports further south. Kenya actually owns only a tiny 3,785 sq km corner of the Lake. The Lake attracted great interest from Europeans after its discovery. In 1858, John Hanning Speke was the first European to cite the vast

Lake as the source of the White Nile. Kisumu city situated in the Nyanza region of Kenya had been a busy port town since its early days, but the break up of the East African Community in 1977 coupled with the cessation of international ferry services on the Lake substantially slowed the city's once bustling pace.

Kisumu whose main occupants are of the Luo tribe, boasts some interesting sites in addition to Lake Victoria; Impala park is a game sanctuary and animal orphanage and home to the rare sitatunga antelope. Hippo point is famed as an exceptional vantage point for viewing hippos, not to mention Lake Victoria's spectacular sunsets. Also of interest is the Kisumu museum, which features a display of local traditional customs and crafts. The Kisumu market, one of the busiest and largest in Kenya provides a fascinating glimpse into

MAP 1

the day-to-day existence of the peoples of Nyanza region. There are numerous small villages around Lake Victoria of interest to the traveler. Dunga Beach, a fishing village near Kisumu, is a wonderful place to experience the traditional lifestyle of the Lake fishermen. Local villagers can be hired to provide canoe tours through the papyrus reeds beds to see hippos and birds.

Mfangano Island has some obscure rock paintings and a small fishing village, but is now most popular as an upscale fishing camp. Ndere National Park, a 4.2km island game park features snakes, hippos, crocodiles, sitatunga and numerous species of water bird. Near the small town of Homa bay is the volcano shaped Mt. Homa and Ruma National Park. This 120 sq km encloses the Lambwe Valley. Most of the animals found here have been imported, including Kenya's only herd of roan antelope. Rusinga Island is home to an exclusive fishing camp and the tomb of Tom Mboya (1930-1969), the nationalist leader assassinated in Nairobi during the political unrest of the late 1960s. Mary Leakey first put this tiny island on the map with her discovery of a 3 million year old skull belonging to Proconsul Africanus. Additional fossils were also found dating back 17 million years.

Economic Impacts of The Lake

The region is endowed with abundant natural and human resources. The natural resources include the rich soils of Kisii highlands as well as ample rainfall which supports agriculture and livestock. Lake Victoria has about 54,000 fishermen operating 11,235 fishing boats. Over 90% of the country's total output of fish and products come from Lake Victoria. A number of major rivers traverse the province and drain towards Lake Victoria for example River Nyando, Sondu Miriu, Yala among others. Most of these rivers have potential for irrigation. Lake Victoria multi-species fisheries are an important economic resource in the region. The agro bases industries are tea processing, coffee, sugarcane industries and tobacco. Great potential for tourist attractions, include many historical sites such as Ruma National Park, recreational sailing Islands and Kisumu museum.

Employment

Lake Victoria being the major attraction site in the Nyanza province has generated employment to the host community. As people go to the Lake they have their cars washed at the Lakeside. They also go to eat in the kiosks by the Lake, which is a major feature of Kisumu city. Most tourists frequent these kiosks to have the taste of fish Tilapia, which has been well prepared. Most tourists take rides on the boats at the Lakeside paying the boat owners in return. The Lake has stimulated domestic industries. These industries include the fishing industry at the Dunga beach.

It has also led to the development of the hospitality industry in Kisumu. Hotels like Kisumu, Sunset and Imperial have emerged to provide accommodation to the increasing number of tourists in this region. The Lake has led to the creation of employment opportunities in the business communities. Most people get employed in food kiosk at the Lakeside, others get involved in the transportation business and others are also employed in the few hospitality organizations around Kisumu. As a result of increased entrepreneurial opportunities goods and services that are not readily available in the community are made available. Goods such as the Kisii soapstone carvings, curios and also Masai's regalia for example (outfit, necklace, bangles, anklet). Services such as tour and travel have emerged as a result of increased number of tourist in the region.

Improved Infrastructure

From colonial time the presence of the Lake led to the construction of the Mombasa-Kisumu railway. At that time rail was the most used means of transport. With industrialization roads have been improved and constructed connecting Kisumu town to other major towns. The Lake has seen the construction of the Kisumu airport, which receives local flights from Nairobi and Eldoret. Amenities such as hospitals have also been developed greatly. Kisumu also boasts of having a University on its environs to be the only one so far situated on the equator.

Cultural Impacts

The Lake has assisted in enhancing local cultural awareness but may distort it later. Domestic tourist tends to appreciate their culture when they find out that international tourists are interested in their culture. The locals uphold their culture for the same reason. Many of the locals still do not appreciate the Lake as required hence the promotion of culture in this area will be necessary to enhance the livelihoods of the local community. Sharing of the cultural knowledge and experience can be beneficial to both the guest and host community. Tourism also enhances the local communities esteem and it also provides a forum for greater understanding and communication among the people of diverse background.

3.5. Case Study Two: Kakamega Forest Reserve

The Kakamega National Reserve is a 36 km2 reserve, situated at the north end of the Kakamega Forest, in Western Province, Kenya, at an elevation of about 1560 m, along the northeastern edge of the Lake Victoria basin. Along its eastern edge rises the partially forested Nandi Escarpment which runs along the western edge of the Rift Valley. The Kakamega Forest (Map 1) is generally considered the eastern-most remnant of the lowland Congolean rainforest of Central Africa. Faunally and florally, Kakamega is dominated by central African lowland species, but due to its elevation (predominantly between 1500 m and 1600 m) and proximity to the formerly contiguous Nandi Forests it also contains highland elements and is thus unique. The forest boundary (including the reserves) encloses about 238 km2, of which less than half is still indigenous forest.

Throughout the forest are a series of grassy glades, ranging in size from about 1 to 50 ha, with a few larger clearings. The origins of the glades are uncertain. Some are certainly recent clearings, but others predate recent records. These may have originated from past human activity such as cattle grazing or may be the result of herbivory and movements by large mammals such as buffalo and elephants (both now extirpated from the region). The glades vary a great deal in structure, some being open grass and others having a considerable number of trees or shrubs. A number of streams and small creeks run through the reserve. The larger creeks are usually bordered by a few to tens of meters of forest on either side which divide the glades, while the smallest creeks flow through open grasslands, often forming small marshy patches.

Climate

The Kakamega Forest is very wet, with an average of 2.08 meters of rain per year. Rainfall is heaviest in April and May ("long rains"), with a slightly drier June and a second peak roughly in August to September ("short rains"). January and February are the driest months. Temperature is fairly constant throughout the year, with mean daily minimums of about 11⁰C and mean daily maximums of about 26⁰C.

Flora and Fauna

No complete floristic studies have been done at Kakamega. The forest hosts about 160 tree and shrub species, many of Congolean lowland forest affinities, including 380 plant species, including Croton, Celtis, Trema and Antiaris. Mama Mutere *(Maesopsis eminii)*, the tallest tree in the whole of Kakamega forest and a number of endemic plant species, mostly ferns and orchids. The flora of the open areas and glades has not been well studied. The glades often have small trees *(Combretum molle, Psidium guajava, Maesa lanceolata, Harungana madagascariensis and Chaetacme aristata)*. Conspicuous flowering plants include flame lilies and Gladiolus. The forest edge is lined by dense thickets of Acanthus pubescens , a shrub with sharply spined, thistle-like leaves. Marshy patches are dominated by sedges and the grass Echinocloa pyramidalis. The forest is best known for its diversity of birds: 367 species have been recorded including the magnificent Great Blue Turaco. The avifauna is a mix of lowland and highland species, but lowland elements dominate. 400 butterfly species. It is the home of 40% of all Kenyan butterflies.

Nine of the species that occur at Kakamega are found nowhere else in Kenya, and two of its species, Turner's

Eremomela *(Eremomela turneri)* and Chapins' Flycatcher *(Muscicapa lendu)*, are threatened. Insects are abundant and some are quite spectacular, such as giant Goliath beetles *(Goliathus goliathus)*, pink and green African flower mantids *(Pseudocreobotra wahlbergi)*, and numerous colorful butterflies. Particularly well represented groups are ants (Formicidae), Lepidopterans, Orthopterans, and beetles. Gastropod mollusks, millipedes and spiders are also common. Kakamega is also known for its diverse snake fauna, with over 40 species, including the rare Gold's Cobra, Jameson's Mamba and the Rhinoceros-horned viper. Lizards are more in evidence, with various skinks (*Mabouya spp.*), chameleons (*Chamaeleo spp.*), and agamas (*Agama spp.*) the most common. Amphibians are represented by a number of anuran species, the most common being Bufo and Phrynobatrachus toads and Ptychadena (Rana) mascariensis frogs. Except for the monkeys (*Colobus guereza, Cercopithecus mitis, C. ascanius,* and *Papio anubis*) and squirrels (*Protozerus strangeri* and *Heliosciurus rufobranchium*), large mammals are not much in evidence.

Today only smaller antelope (primarily various duikers) and bush pig (*Potamochoerus porcus*) are present. Small carnivores, such as Egyptian mongooses (*Herpestes ichneumon*), African civets (*Viverra civetta*), servals (*Felis serval*), genets (*Genetta tigrina*), and palm civets (*Nandinia binotata*) are common; some larger carnivores, including jackals (*Canis adustus*), spotted hyaenas (*Crocuta crocuta*), and leopards (*Panthera pardus*) also occur there. Although rodents, insectivores, and bats are clearly present, they have been little studied at Kakamega.

Economic Impacts

Pottery

At Ilesi trading Centre, the home of the Weeping Stone, 3kms from Kakamega town, are observed varieties of beautiful ceramic items lined up along the roadside of Kakamega/ Kisumu highway (Wishitemi & Shitemi, 2002). The clay-modelled articles include cooking pots, flower vases, sugar dishes, ashtrays, water jugs and other ornamental earthenware sculptures. They come in different shades, sizes and types.

The potters are very creative and they emerge with a variety of artwork. Traditional kilns are in use hence their environment friendly vocations. In this regard self help groups have emerged. They constitute of those culturally endowed with the art and others who learn it as a means of income-generation. For example, the thirty members of Machina Pottery Group is a group, which specializes in pottery and modeling.

Unfortunately, they lack adequate funds to purchase a modern kiln and also lack adequate marketing machinery. Though potters are capable of producing 5000 or more articles per month which they sell at varying prices depending on the type and size, they have not been able to get a ready market. They also modern modeling equipment and transportation facilities that can help them increase their productions and economic empowerment. Major tourist hotels along the Kenyan coast, several kilometers away, have benefited from these items. They form part of the decorative adornments in these hotels giving them an African look and sight. The potters however are often at disadvantage in the exchange.

Basketry

In the same area, is also found the art and trade of basketry. Vilivi, cane chairs, cane doors Lwichi, mats, Majiambi, of various sizes and types are woven from raffia obtained from the swamps. From along the Kakamega forest stretch, raffia and capping plant materials are harvested for basketry. Such material alongside timber, clay and other natural vegetation was significant in the preparation of most of the equipment used in homes. Currently, however even the potters and basketry weavers are also using these materials to weave modern items for both primary use and decoration. From the forests are also found natural very nutritious foods and fruits. These include Mmbalakaya, the fig Mukhuyu, and Manuna. Most of the trees have consumable fruits and seeds that can be eaten fresh or when boiled. From within the same area therefore are many tourist attractions that not only mesmerize the eye, as with the wildlife, but also are associated with its cultural heritage, crafts and tradition.

Cultural Impacts

Tourism development around the Kakamega Forest has the following potential cultural impacts:

Cultural heritage sites

Sacred groves (Kavunyondes) where Tiriki initiation ceremonies for young boys are held abound on the Tiriki section of the forest around Kaimosi. These sites are not only used for circumcision ceremonies but also for housing the initiates. These groves together with the nearby Maragoli hills, and the granite rocks along Kisumu-Kakamega-Webuye road can be an inspiration to the tourists. Other sites that could be inspiring include the weeping stone (Ikhongo Murwii) near Ilesi, Kakamega and Isiukhu falls. The site below the waterfalls has traditionally been used by the Isukha as a cleansing ground to ward off any evil or omen that could befall the community should one of the clan members be involved in crimes as murder and incest.

Historic Ruins and Landscapes

The ruins of the gold mines and buildings at Rosterman around Kakamega offer unique experiences typical of the cultural and architectural ruins of the west.

Sites associated with historical events and people

The Maragoli who inhabit the area bordering Maragoli Hills have a myth linking these hills to their story of migration and settlement. This myth together with the view that the hills have from colonial times acted as a refuge in times of war or calamities could be promoted as a cultural resource. Other features that have been associated with refuge during tribal wars, cattle rustling and other calamities are the caves of Lirhanda Hills.

Musical instruments

Luhya musical instruments including drums, horns, flutes and traditional stringed instruments are comparable to modern guitars and holds a lot of potential for cultural tourism in this area. Isikuti—the famous Isukha drum together with Lidungu and Ubukhana should be promoted and marketed as a unique tourist product. Isikuti drum and dance are so famous that the drum is played in numerous national ceremonies in Kenya.

Traditional Arts and Crafts

The Luhya traditional arts and crafts industry is so well developed that its products are sold beyond the forest borders. Handicrafts made using palm (Lishundu) leaves from the forest and along riverbanks include baskets, tablemats, traditional granaries (Madele) and trays. These together with other products like walking sticks, serving sticks and spoons, and ropes should be promoted as unique products. Besides this, the skill acquired by women in making pottery products such as cooking pots and flowerpots should be promoted and marketed. In addition, belts and other articles made from wildlife skins and twines, bracelets, earrings and necklaces, and also products such hoes, axes, slashers and sickles made by blacksmiths hold a lot of potential.

Traditional Clothing and Regalia (Ubucheka)

Traditional ceremonial clothes made from leopard and the white and black colobus monkey skins and worn by chiefs during installation ceremonies among the Isukha hold a lot of potential for cultural tourism. This together with the accompanying regalia composed of the three legged traditional stool, spear and shield for defense, walking stick and the fly whisk should be marketed as an important resource base.

Traditional Food and Drinks

The Luyha traditional food like ugali accompanied by traditional vegetables such as cowpeas constitute an important resource. Other foods that should be promoted include the Isukha delicacy of smoked primate derived meat, mushenye (mixture of pounded maize, sweet potatoes and beans). Other elements which could be promoted within the culture include: traditional cooking stove; traditional houses; indigenous wildlife; traditional medicine; traditional utensils; festivals and ceremonies; folkmedia; farming practices; food processing and storage techniques; herbalism and herbal practice

3.6. Specific Strategic Issues For Nyanza/Western Kenya

This section provides a brief overview of some issues of special interest in strategic marketing for the two provinces in Kenya. They include destination marketing, customer relationship marketing and information and communication technologies.

Destination Marketing

Tourism destination marketing involves many stakeholders and a complex product offer. The strategic marketing approach makes the coordinated marketing of all actors involved feasible. This includes inter-relating the tourist attractions, activities, facilities and services and the various and increasingly fragmented tourist markets. Given the variety of businesses operating from a particular destination, and the geographic dispersion of source markets, cooperative marketing arrangements are quite common and offer clear advantages. There is an increased demand in destination marketing due to rising customer expectations and growing competition between destinations. The destination marketing partnerships are important because most destinations have to compete at a global level.

Recent studies stress the crucial role that knowledge management and information and communication technology (ICT) could play for these partnerships and other joint schemes in the field of destination marketing. Virtual marketplace is an ideal tool for all destination management organizations that can implement marketing facilitation strategies, by using Websites simultaneously for information, promotion, distribution, relationship marketing and marketing research. These strategies are particularly valuable for both smaller-sized and medium-sized companies that lack the resources to undertake marketing activities.

Customer Relationship Marketing

Customer Relationship Marketing (CRM) is essentially

about getting and keeping customers. There are many reasons why a tourism and hospitality business wishes to identify, deal differently and generally from relationships with its loyal customers. The marketing of services aged orientation from a product management to a customer relationship management has changed orientation from product management to customer relationship management. Once again relationships with customers are brought to the forefront of marketing activities. CRM strives to create a competitive advantage for the organization. This goal can be reached by implementing the appropriate strategies, such as loyalty, indirect competition, cooperation network and creation of value for the customer. The network of relationships between customers and markets requires a strategic focus. One key issue in the concept of strategy is the delivery of value to the customer. CRM essentially offers a broader view of marketing and offers a framework that operates more openly and builds inter-functional customer and value chain-based links.

Information and Communication Technology

The rapid advancement of information technology (ICT), notably the Internet and the World Wide Web, has created challenges and opportunities for the tourism and hospitality industry. ICT developments permeate every aspect of tourism marketing. A rapidly changing business environment, largely brought about by the internet, requires companies to quickly implement new networks and alliances, and be creative in their marketing. It is obvious that marketing in the digital age requires dynamic and innovative strategies. Therefore, there is an imperative need for tourism and hotel businesses to actively select between business models that can best support an effective online marketing strategy. Apart from the formulation of a strategy and organizational planning, the development of a business presence on the Internet requires appropriate actions in order to ensure its quality, thereby contributing to the general marketing strategy's effectiveness.

3.7. Conclusions and Recommendations

Tourism has long played an important role in the economy of Kenya, representing the second highest single source of foreign exchange after tea. Therefore, tourism marketing represents the systematic, coherent and consistent effort of hospitality and tourism businesses to develop, formulate, and implement their strategies in order to achieve their main goal: making the tourism product a successful experience for their guests/visitors. In a strategic approach, tourism marketing has taken on new dimensions which increasingly reflect the perspective of tourists and those hosting them. There are several important benefits to undertaking a strategic approach to marketing. These advantages include: establishing the overall objectives and strategies, providing a rational basis for decision-making on marketing and laying the foundation for effective implementation of the marketing plan. The strategic approach to marketing at the business and destinations levels is now widely adopted as a principle, although implementation of the action plans is still weak in some instances.

The following strategies could be put forward to hospitality and tourism operations in order to effectively formulate and implement strategic marketing:

- Marketing strategy is based on a careful analysis and assessment of the marketplace and depends on the use of appropriate marketing information. Relevant and accurate information is required in order to carry out effective strategic marketing plans
- In order to implement a strategic, marketing approach effectively, appropriate management support is required
- In order to ensure that marketing objectives, strategies and tools are optimally adapted to the dynamic environment, an evaluation system should be developed

Destinations in Africa enjoy a privileged position in relation to the major tourist generating markets due mainly to their unique features, history as well as a wide range of products on offer. The strong awareness for conservation of the environment and the demand for exoticism by potential travellers translates into increasing demand by an ever growing number of foreign visitors. Accordingly there is need for destinations in Kenya to co-operate more closely in areas of product development, research, manpower development and training as well as exchange of tourism experts and tourism information. It is also necessary to harmonise travel within the regions so as to encourage free flow of visitors both local and international and maximisation of benefits accruing from tourism interactions within the regions.

In the development, promotion and marketing of our respective destinations we should always bear in mind the complementary nature of our products within the region. Most of Kenya's Eco-system still remain intact and unspoiled thus providing a strong basis for a sustainable tourism development. All that is required proper planning and management of the available resources. It should be born in mind that sustainable tourism cannot thrive if we do not take care of our fragile environment. In this context, therefore, we should always remember the cardinal point that we all have a duty to practice responsible tourism so that at the end of the day we shall be able to conserve our fragile environment and biodiversity for the benefit of mankind.

To this end there is therefore, an urgent need to put the necessary legislations and codes of conduct in place so as to ensure balanced development of tourism in Kenyan tourist destinations. Exchange of information and experience among Kenyan nationals would also be vital in achieving the requisite results for the development of sustainable tourism in conservation of the environment. In the final analysis, the government of Kenya should do the following to promote tourism in the Nyanza/Western region:

- Contribute to the conservation of any habitat of flora and fauna affected by tourism;
- Encourage relevant authorities to identify areas worthy of conservation and to determine the level of development, if any, that would be compatible in or adjacent to those areas;

- Include enhancement and corrective actions at tourism sites to conserve wildlife and natural ecosystems;
- Ensure that community attitudes, local customs and cultural values, and the role of women and children, are understood in the planning an implementation of all tourism related projects;
- Provide opportunities for the wider community to take part in discussions on tourism planning issues where these affect the tourism industry and the community;
- Encourage relevant authorities to identify cultural heritage worthy of conservation and to determine the level of development if any which would be compatible in or adjacent to those areas;
- Contribute to the identity and pride of local communities through providing quality tourism products and services sensitive to those communities;
- Maintain environmental management systems;
- Conserve and reduce energy, waste and pollutants;
- Educate and inform others about local environments and cultures; and
- Cooperate with other individuals and organizations to advance environmental improvements and sustainable development practices, including establishing indicators and monitoring.

REFERENCES

Calver, S. (1994) Strategic Marketing Communication. In R. Teare, J. Mazanec, S. Crawford-Welch and S. Calver (eds.) *Marketing in Hospitality and Tourism: A Consumer Focus*. London: Cassell, 213-311.

Chon, K.S. and Singh, A. (1995) Marketing Resorts to 2000: Review of Trends in the USA. *Tourism Management* 16(6), 463-469.

Christopher, M., Payne, A. and Ballantyne, D. (1991) *Relationship Marketing*. Oxford: Butterworth-Heinemann, 3-28.

Crawford-Welch, S. (1996) International Marketing in the Hospitality Industry. In R. Teare and A. Boer (eds.) *Strategic Hospitality Management: Theory and Practice for the 1990s* (4th edn). London: Cassell, 166-193.

Du Rand, G.E., Heath, E. and Alberts, N. (2003) The Role of Local and Regional Food in Destination Marketing: A South African Situational Analysis. In: C.M.Hall (ed.) *Wine, Food and Tourism Marketing*. The Haworth Hospitality Press. pp 97-112.

Gummesson, E. (2002) *Total Relationship Marketing*. Oxford. Butterworth Heinemann.

Ipara, H. (2002) Towards Cultural Tourism Development around the Kakamega Forest Reserve in Western Kenya. In: J. Akama and P. Sterry (eds.) Cultural Tourism in Africa: Strategies for the New Millennium. Proceedings of the ATLAS Africa International Conference December 2000 Kenya.

Knowles, T. (1996) *Corporate Strategy for Hospitality*. Essex: Longman.

Matovic, D. and McCleary, K. (2003) Marketing in the Next Decade: A Qualitative Study of the U.S. Hotel Industry. *Journal of Travel & Tourism Marketing* 14(2), 47-65.

Middleton, V.T.C. (2001) *Marketing in Travel and Tourism* (3rd edn.). Oxford: Butterworth-Heinemann.

Mistilis, N. and Daniele, R. (2005) Challenges for Competitive Strategy in Public and Private Sector Partnerships in Electronic National Tourist Destination Marketing Systems. *Journal of Travel & Tourism Marketing* 17(4), 63-73.

Moscardo, G., Faulkner, B. and Laws, E. (2000) Introduction: Moving Ahead and Looking Back. In: B. Faulkner, G. Moscardo and E. Laws (eds.) *Tourism in the Twenty-first Century: Lessons from Experience*. London: Continuum, xviii–xxxii.

O'Connor, P. (1999) *Electronic Information Distribution in Tourism and Hospitality*. Oxford: CAB International.

Okech, R. (2006) The Impact of Ecotourism Development in Kenya: Environmental Issues of Planning and Management In: S. Dixit (ed.) *Promises and Perils in Hospitality and Tourism Management*. Aman Publications, New Delhi, India.

Porter, M. (1995) *Competitive Advantage: Creating and Sustaining Superior Performance*. New York: Free Press.

Riege, A., Perry, C. and Go, F.M. (2002) Partnerships in International Travel and Tourism Marketing: A Systems-Oriented Approach between Australia, New Zealand, Germany and the United Kingdom. *Journal of Travel & Tourism Marketing* 11(1), 59-77.

Scott, N., Parfitt, N. and Laws, E. (2000) Destination Management: Cooperative Marketing, a Case Study of the Port Douglas Brand. In: B. Faulkner, G. Moscardo and E. Laws (eds.) *Tourism in the Twenty-first Century: Lessons from Experience*. London: Continuum, 198-221.

Soteriades, M.D. (2006) The Application of Marketing Strategy in the Tourism and Hospitality Industry. In: S. Dixit (ed.) *Promises and Perils in Hospitality and Tourism Management*. Aman Publications, New Delhi, India.

Teare, R. and Calver, S. (1996) *Consumer Marketing: A Resource-Based Approach for the Hospitality and Tourism Industries*. London: Cassell.

Varvaressos, S. and Soteriades, M. (2005) Tourism Services Marketing Evaluation Approaches to the Parameters Market, Quality and Price. *Review of Economic Sciences* 8 (forthcoming).

Wishitemi, B. and Shitemi, N. (2002) Cultural Tourism: Strategies Towards Sustainable Rural Development for Western Kenya. In: J. Akama and P. Sterry (eds.) Cultural Tourism in Africa: Strategies for the New Millennium. *Proceedings of the ATLAS Africa International Conference*, December 2000, Kenya.

Witt, S. and Moutinho, L. (eds.) (1995) *Tourism Marketing and Management Handbook*. Hertfordshire: Prentice-Hall Europe.

World Tourism Organization, Business Council (1999) *Marketing Tourism Destinations Online: Strategies for the Information Age*. Madrid: WTO.

You, X., O'Leary, J. and Fesenmaier, D. (2000) Knowledge Management through the Web: A New Marketing Paradigm for Tourism Organizations. In: B. Faulkner, G. Moscardo and E. Laws (eds.) *Tourism in the Twenty-first Century: Lessons from Experience*. London: Continuum, 181-197.

4

Marketing Management of Serbian Tourism

*Slobodan Čerović**

4.1. Introduction

The evaluation of expected effects of future development of tourism in Serbia and its influence on the whole economy and regional development must be begun from its qualitative basis. It encompasses analyzed, solid resources, positive tendencies in international and domestic tourist environment, further development of these segments in the field of foreign tourism, which are distinguished by quality in terms of demand for suitable contents and in terms of readiness for needed expenses as well as other elements. However, intensification of development means large positive changes in the domestic economic environment of Serbia and its surroundings. Only with significant changes which would overcome existing barriers, Serbia could increase its foreign and domestic tourist traffic, foreign exchange income as well as foreign tourist consumption. This all could be done with the use of existing capacities and with available domestic tourist product.[1] Thus, with the change in the international

* Ph.D., Singidunum University, Serbia.

position of Serbia, as well as with the change of market structures possibilities could be opened for faster economic development on the basis of property transformation and attached activities in securing domestic and foreign capital. Dynamic role of tourism in the economic development of Serbia, as well as its known multiplying effects would generate increased levels of basic and supplementary employment, especially in the underdeveloped areas. This would contribute to increase in tourist and complementary activities and widen markets (including multiplying effects of spill over of consumption from abroad) for the investment of domestic products and services in all sectors. Therefore, in the overall economic development of Serbia, it is necessary to determine development priorities of Serbia. These are tourism, agriculture and communications.

4.1. General Characteristics of Development of Tourism of Serbia and Implementation of Marketing up to 2005

Development of tourism in the said period has been generally looked upon as one of the socio-economic priorities of development. The basis for such an approach was in availability of resources, as well as in characteristics of international and domestic tourist demand. However, in the said period development goals of tourism have never been realized. As main indicator of that situation could be unavailability of respective social and economic ambient in which all resources and market advantages available for tourist development could be utilized. By this it is meant inadequate social and economic system which did not favor expression of creative possibilities of business and tourist entrepreneurs. Hampering of market activities over a long period of time had adverse effect on tourism, as a synthetic indicator of success of economy and society as a whole. From this basic factor stems a specific one in relation to tourism, which have significantly influenced on the utilization of market concept in tourism, and relates to political and economic factors. This complex includes:

a) long-term non-existence of basic development document concerning tourism;

b) inadequate measure of economic policy with constant factor of change and inconsistency

c) inconsistent aerial plans and disrespect of main presumptions on which those plans were based;

d) inadequate coordination at the level of tourist policy;

e) unfavorable relation towards private sector, which in majority of tourist developed states represents backbone of tourist development;

As a result of all these factors, tourist economy of Serbia realized its activities in the conditions which brought about following significant consequences:

a) inadequate structure of lodging and other capacities from the aspect of demand, wishes and needs of potential tourists;

b) Unfavorable economic status of companies of tourist economy, with restrictive possibilities for enlarged reproduction.

Systematic hampering of market economy has significantly influenced inadequate implementation of market principles in tourism. Stemming from this situation arose certain defects in connection with the utilization of marketing instruments such as:

a) stereotype and old fashion behavior; undiversified tourist product in regard to potential tourist demands;

b) implementation of inadequate methods of formulating and inadequate differentiation of tourist costs;

c) inadequate utilization of purchasing channels as well as organization of tourist trips;

d) inadequate organization of leading promotional activities with inadequate scope of financial resources and lack of coordination with factors in charge of tourist activities at the level of other tourist destinations;

e) Insufficient and weak exploration of markets, small scope of computerization of internal and external options, as well as inclusion into contemporary tourist information systems.

It is evident that marketing activities were not adequately used as incentive factor of the development of tourism of Serbia, which additionally was highlighted by development in the last decade of the XX century.

4.2. Characteristic of Development of Tourism of Serbia and Implementation of Marketing Principles in the Period 1989-2005

Conditions in which tourist companies in Serbia did their business in the period 1989-2000 could be evaluated as specific in regard to the world wide tourist business dealings during the same period. Long-term downfall of tourist traffic, especially foreign, as well as inadequate foreign currency inflow of tourism, is evident index of cause and effect of the situation in which tourist economy of Serbia found itself. It is sufficient to say that in between 1989 and 2000, mainly due to the internal and external factors outside the sphere of tourism, it was registered reduction of the number of lodging for 35,6%, out which domestic for 30,1% and foreign for 71,6%. Reduction of the total number of tourist arrivals in the same period totaled 47,9%, out of which domestic for 37,8% and foreign 82,4%. Tourist foreign income inflow in the period between 1990 and 2000 was reduced by 93,6%. In order to highlight the scope of falling behind it should be noted that in between 1989 and 2000 world tourist traffic, measured by the number of arrivals, was augmented by 73,1%, and income by 127%.

The participation of tourism of Serbia in gross domestic product has remained the same in the same period and averaged 2% while the participation of the number of employees has risen from 3% to 4%, which is the consequence of work intensive character of tourism as a major economic branch and structural changes in the economy of Serbia caused mainly by sanctions. It is also necessary to state that at the same time the fall in the participation of tourism in investment from 2.3% to 0,5%, as well as in overall foreign income revenue from 5,8% to 1,7%.

The basis for return of Serbia to international tourist market has been achieved by return of FR of Yugoslavia into international institutions and by normalization of relationship with key international factors, as well as by democratic changes initiated in 2000. It is understood that these consequences have influenced domestic tourism also, especially by influencing its scope and structure.

Independently from the present positive tendencies, if we were to incorporate into the actual condition also indicators from previous period regarding structural changes, caused by outside factors, the overall appraisal would show deep and comprehensive disturbances in the tourist economy of Serbia.

When speaking about utilization of market principles, special attention should be given to the formulation of a long term strategic approach of return of Serbia to the international tourist market, renewal of all tourist facilities and activities as a basis for tourist business dealing. In this framework, one could consider that key factor would be strategic marketing beginning of new tourist era, as well as definition of basis for repositioning of Serbia as tourist destination.

Advantages of development of tourism could be achieved only if consistent process of planning is implemented, as a concept of observing and formulating future activities and confronting anticipated consequences of those activities. Key factor in strategic planning is a vision about what the future would look like in order to define phases of action as well as strategy which would enable tourist destination to realize its vision.

In order that this vision be established, it is necessary to define situation, as well as consequences of long-term trends in this field. All relevant indicators show that, as in other countries, tourism in Serbia represents a missed opportunity. It could be said that the tourist economy of Serbia in the mentioned period was heavily protected—especially from foreign competition, because of restricted policy of foreign investment in tourist capacities of Serbia. This was done in order to alleviate the tourist economy of Serbia from stronger influence of tourist demand, because of absence of long-term sources of stable demand, as well as to protect it from domestic competition, because of business dealings with, in advance, known and restricted demand.

Those are the reasons because of which have not been realized preconditions for development of entrepreneurship in the field of tourism, for development of new tourist product and for the advancement of other sectors of economy.[2]

Basic factors which hamper or stimulate development of tourism, or which determine actual situation in the field of development of tourism of Serbia, could be defined in the following manner:

— Long-term absence from international tourist market because due to sanctions and measures of isolation of international community, as well as self-isolation measures;

— Inadequate market knowledge of Serbia, as tourist destination, as well as inadequate profiled image or negative image which stems from the influence of non-tourist factors;

— Long-term underestimation by official institutions who are in charge of formulating conditions for the development of tourism, of real development possibilities as well as consequences of inadequate investment of development of tourism and promotion of this branch of economy;

— Inadequate involvement and integration of local authorities and certain social groups in development of tourism;

— Lack of tourist infrastructure, general and special, especially in the economically undeveloped areas;

— Backwardness in the sphere of education of tourist human resources in relationship towards world tendencies (international accreditation, licenses, etc);

— Absence of adequate national, regional and local development structures of managing and promoting tourism;

— Long-term decline of quality of tourist services;

— Inadequate management of the protection of environment in the function of tourism.

The main factors which act as an incentive in the development of tourism could be defined in the following manner:

— existence of tourist products which have been tested at the international tourist market (Beograd, mt. Kopaonik, monasteries) and for which exist belief that it is possible to find out adequate tourist segments;

— suitable outside conditions which favor return of Serbia onto tourist market;

— beginning of process of privatization and presence of renowned international hotels ("Hyatt", "Intercontinental", "Best Western");

— tourist factors, as well as other, generally viewed, which in this moment benefit the return of Serbia onto tourist market.

There are four factors of fundamental importance which benefit future development of tourism in Serbia:

— diversity of tourist product (mountains, spa's, lakes, rivers, urban centres, village centres, hunting tourism, "advanterous" tourism);

— well preserved environment;

— richness of cultural heritage;

— hospitality of population;

Marketing mix of tourism in Serbia consists of the following standard points which could be analyzed in the following manner:

— Product—basically general, made up in the manner to logistically exploit natural resources and attractions (culture, mountains, villages, spa's, Danube, etc). Contemporary concept of the product is inadequately based on the whole scale chain of values where, for example, information about villages is available in limited scope. However, there is no information where certain product can be bought. Information is available about lodging, which is supplementary activities, etc.

— Price—price factor is momentarily in line with the concept of the product and it could be stated that there exists a solid relationship between price and value which is returned for the invested money. Other content alongside main product (gastronomy, activities, shopping) also gives good values in relationship to price.

— Promotion—system of promotion creates numerous materials, but due to nonexistence of strategic marketing and media plan, result which promotion give are very modest (taking into account relationship between invested resources and increased number of lodging of international visitors).
— Distribution—weakest chain in the mix, where there exists numerous inconsistencies.
— Distribution by traditional channels (tour-operators, agencies, etc) is not adequate because of lack of existence of images of tourist destinations which cannot be inserted into brochures and programs of tour-operators and agencies.

Taking into account these facts, one of the crucial questions which can be asked in regard to strategic plan of return of Serbia and its companies to international tourist market whether there were similar cases, i.e. whether there were countries which were in similar position like Serbia.

4.3. Competition Defects of Tourism in Serbia

Identification of competition defects and its level of presence have been analyzed by several participants of a workshop, as well as by team of consultants of Horwath Consulting Zagreb and Economy Faculty in Beograd. First approach to competition defects was presented in the sphere of diagnosys of actual situation of the strategy of development of tourism in Serbia. So the the identified defects will be basis for definition of program of competition which need to be implemented in order to enhance current situation and augment level of tourist competition of Serbia.

Rewiew 1: List of Identified Shortcomings and their Priorities[3]

Shortcomings identified	*Competitiveness programmes*	*Priority*
	Tourist companies and rivalry	
The majority of accommodation capacities is low,medium-low or medium category (1, 2 and 3*)	TCR.1. Improvement and development of the acco-mmodation system	Very high
Shortage of international hotel chains	TCR. 1. Improvement and development of the accom-modation system	Very high
Low level of development of - accommodation capacitiesin rural environments	TCR. 1. Improvement and development of the acco-mmodation system	high
Lack of cooperation in the accommodation sector	TCR. 1. Improvement and development of the acco-mmodation system	high
Absence of a control system for the accommodationcapacities	TCR.2. Tourist quality system	high
Absence of specialised quality marks foraccommodation capacities	TCR.2. Tourist quality system	high
Tourist demand based on dom-estic market	TCR.2. Tourist quality system	high
Low level of sophistication of the clients	TCR.2. Tourist quality system	high
	State of Demand	
Absence of legislation regarding the protection of thebasic rights of consumers in tourism	SD.1. Consumer protection programme	high
Absence of an image and posi-tioning, as well as of an overall branding strategy for the country	SD.2. Development of the tourist information system	Very high
Low performance level of tourist information centres	SD.2. Development of the tourist information system	Very high
Low level of diversification and quality of tourist products in brochures	SD.2. Development of the tourist information system	Very high

	Support/supply sector	
Lack of a strong management organization in Serbia. Local tourist organizations work individually, without mutual coordination and cooperation	SS.1. Destination management and implementation	Very high
Lack of specialized destination management companies (DMC), as organizers of tourist products, activities andpackages	SS.1. Destination management and implementation	Very high
Culture and natural resources have not been used forcreating tourist products	SS.1. Destination management and implementation	high
Low level of performance of specialization of localtravel agencies	SS.2. Development of complementary tourist offer (trade, gastronomy, catering, activities, etc.)	high
Lack of local products, souvenirs, handicrafts and their marketing in tourism in Serbia.	SS.2. Development of complementary tourist offer (trade, gastronomy, catering, activities, etc.)	high
Low level of diversification and specialization ofsupplementary tourist products, activities and services	SS.2. Development of complementary tourist offer (trade, gastronomy, catering, activities, etc.)	high
Lack of specialization in the catering sector	SS.2. Development of complementary tourist offer (trade, gastronomy, catering, activities, etc.)	high
The catering sector mainly provides a low, medium-lowor medium quality offer	SS.2. Development of complementary tourist offer (trade, gastronomy, catering, activities, etc.)	high
	Production factors	
Low level of service performance in public transportand taxi services	PF.1. Accessibility (air, land, water)	Very high
Low level of Utilization of alternative energy sources:wind, sun, etc.: as well as an absence of a materialrecycling and waste management system	PF.2. Improvement of public services (power and water supply, effluent water, waste, recycling)	high

Absence of a tourist marking system (resources, attractions, services and activities, etc.)	PF.3. Road information and marking system	Very high
Lack of river berths on major rivers in Serbia	PF.4. Plans for improving and maintaining rivers and lakes	Very high
Absence of a system for the protection and conservation of the culture and natural heritage	PF.5. City/municipal plans relating to: the environment, aesthetics,attractions, equipment, etc.	high
Absence of a local awareness about the importance of the preservation and the conservation of the naturalenvironment	PF.5. City/municipal plans relating to: the environment, aesthetics,attractions, equipment, etc.	Very high
Lack of professionalism among human resources, particularly outside the area of major towns	PF.6. Education and advanced training programmes	Very high
Low level of complementary activities for tourists	PF.7. Development of small and medium-sized entrepreneurship intourism	high
Low level of small and medium-sized enterpreneushipin tourism	PF.7. Development of small andmedium-sized entrepreneurship intourism	Very high
High level of bureaucratization and low level of supportand subsidies for tourist development	PF.8. System of development facilities and incentives	Very high
Absence of interpretation centres for tourists	PF.8. System of development facilities and incentives	high
Absence of strategic guidelines for the development of accommodation capacities, particularly in the hotel sector of Serbia	PF.8. System of development facilities and incentives	Very high
Low level of investment in the improvement anddevelopment of accommodation capacities	PF.8. System of development facilities and incentives	Very high
High interest rates on tourist investment loans	PF.8. System of development facilities and incentives	Very high
Absence of guidelines for strategic development of theoverall tourist sector in Serbia	PF.9. Creation of a Tourist Development Agency	Very high

Note: TCR = tourist company and rivalry, SD = State of demand, SS = support sector, PF = production factors, with numerical markings next to the abbreviations representing the sequence of the programmes as listed in the Competitiveness Action Plan.

Source: Horwath Consulting Zagreb and workshop participants.

4.4. Strategic Bases for Development of Serbia as a Tourist Destination

4.4.1. Available resources and the effects of the tourist development

4.4.1.1. Natural attractions and social factors in favor of the tourist development

No doubt that Serbia has quality and diversified/various bases for tourist development. Natural attractions as well as the attained level of accommodation and other capacities show that there are possibilities for development of the numerous aspects of tourism specially if taken into consideration the geographic diversity of the natural resources. They offer the possibility for taking up different sport activities, both in the winter and the summer period, further on for spa and thalassotherapy, hunt and fishing and various other activities linked to the stay in the particular region of Serbia. Also, Serbia has a very attractive position situated in the important transit region. However, Serbia is at its beginnings when it comes to creating the internationally concurrent tourist industry on the basis of the identified structure of the attractions and tourist products able to be commercialized on middle and long term basis. The frame for the development of the marketing system was set by evaluating realistic commercial and industrial potential of Serbian tourism in the coming period of 10 years. In this period Serbia should significantly increase its tourist performance by reaching 20 million tourist lodgings among which 50% would represent the foreign lodgings as well as to increase the incomes coming from tourism up to 1,2 to 1,5 billion of euros.

The geographic situation as well as the transport situation, hydrographic characteristics, fleur and fauna, climate and other characteristics of the nature in Serbia can be good basis for the tourist development and also good basis for Serbia for becoming a part of the most important international tourist industry[4]. However, based on the strategically determined factors, a big part of the natural attractions is still about to be included in the modern tourist offer. The first step would be the selective and market oriented strategic development. One of the priorities could be national parks

(Djerdap, Tara, Kopaonik, Golija, Fruska Gora and the Sar Mountain) huge areas of protected nature, spread on the territory of 18 communes, because they contain high quality resources for tourism. Further on, there are 20 regional parks and 120 natural parks as well as the numerous rare and protected plants and animal species.

Socially favorable aspects for development of tourism in Serbia are numerous. Among the most important factors contained in the social advantages are the anthropogenic factors - the resources incorporated in the bases of available tourist values of Serbia (that is why they are in front of the other social factors important for the development of tourism). The anthropogenic diversity comprises not only the extremely valuable cultural-historical monuments, but the contents connected to the life and customs of the people. Moreover, there are notable and original types of settlements and architecture, folklore and other.[5]

Besides that, the opening up of commerce and industry, culture, science and education, and development of the sport and social activities in general, and the direct contacts with the citizens of the other countries, represent at the same time important tourist resources (e.g. for carrying out the business visits and foreign and domestic conferences and meetings).

The social aspects, not exploited enough in the past period should be developed, built up and entertained. In order to optimize tourism and successfully use the geographic, anthropologic, demographic and other conditions of life in Serbia together with its cultural heritage many events were established, among which the biggest ones have already traditional character. Many of these events take place on the protected areas and that is why they contribute to sustainable development of tourism—the economic, ecologic, demographic, and all the other sustainable tourism in certain area.

Generally, the important social aspect for development of tourism is overall opening to the world of Serbian industry and commerce. In all development strategies, tourist industry was one of the priorities of the social development. In reality, this point was not put into practice enough.

The protection of the environment is a very important element in the strategic development of the tourism in Serbia. That is why it is essential for the future development to stress out the protection and the maintenance of the quality of the environment. In that way the role of tourism should be to generate the entire development of the region in combination with the market and selective approach in developing of tourism. Therefore, applying the concept of sustainable development of tourism should be together with the market and economy condition equally important condition for developing of tourism.

Nevertheless, geographic area of Serbia is exposed to the influence of different degradation processes which are by intensity and character as well as by space differentiated. All those processes influence the degradation of the environment and reduce the territory favorable for tourism exploitation[6]. That is why, many ecological issues demand taking the different measures for protection of the environment. By their systematical carrying out it is necessary to maintain the quality and value of the environment and primarily of the one that is of crucial importance for development of tourism. Until now, putting in force of the protection of the environment protection was not complete, adequate nor systematic enough. In order to establish compatible relation between natural environment, specially its most valuable elements and tourism, it is essential to bear in mind that a tourist complex if placed, concealed or used inadequately can also have a degrading effect. That is why it is important to neutralize this potential degrading impact of tourism development. Natural attractions and social element favorable for tourism development in Serbia together with protection of the environment are one. On the same territory could be found along with the natural attractions the quality anthropogenic resources as well as the cultural and historic monuments. Thus, their protection, revitalization and adequate implementation into the tourist system is also very important demand of Serbian tourism.

4.4.1.2. Tourist Offer and Its Rebuilding

The development of the tourist economy mainly depends

on the level and the state of development of the entire economy of one country. One can say that the development of tourist economy is bound to the other branches of economy. Consequently, the overall state of economy and society has absolutely great impact on the level of development of tourism and tourist economy (in economy, in general, the great non-economic changes and serious narrowing of the market in 1990s had a negative impact on the relatively solid tourist capacities developed for much wider market at that time).

Commerce, transportation, craft industry, public utility services, agriculture and various industrial sectors, together with catering, hotel business and travel agencies find themselves in a very difficult position being exposed to numerous economic and non-economic factors.

That is why rebuilding tourist economy is bound to number of economic and non-economic factors and activities in another word bound to the society in general. The transportation is the branch of economy directly connected to tourism. Meanwhile, there are visible defects when it comes to transportation infrastructure and transport capacities notably insufficient development and out-of-date transportation network and capacities.

Considering the predispositions of Serbia for the quality transportation we are of the opinion that the extensive development and the modernization are two parallel directions of tourism development.[7] On the other hand, commerce, its network, retailing and wholesale trade capacities were always considered to be an important component of efficient supply for tourist destinations and their overall offer. At the same time, they were an important item in the structure of consumption of domestic and foreign visitors.

a) Bed Supply and Their Structure

The level of utilization of bed supply is under great influence of the season in the tourist economy, since the highest percentage of their capacity is used during the summer period. Apart from the low utilization rate of bed supply, the major problem of the tourist offer of Serbia is generally on the poor level when it comes to quantity and quality.

The biggest number of tourist constructions was built before 1976 and thus demands huge reconstructions, renovations and adapting. In that process the European regulations which set the strict criteria of categorization of tourist complexes should be also taken into account. Beside the technical equipment these regulations attach the importance to the sport and recreational activities entertainment and other activities that the gests prefer.

Organization, equipment and the quality of services are the must for getting certain category while the location, appearance of the complex and the inside space and various facilities provided to the guest are considered as a facultative element in determining the category of a tourist complex.

In last decade in Serbia there was almost no investment in building a new accommodation offer. In spite of this, globally seen, the existing structure of the basic and the complementary accommodation facilities is favorable as it is in developed tourist countries. The number of the basic accommodation facilities is especially important, since it shows the possibilities of a country in regard to the international market.[8]

Using comparative analysis, development of bed supply in Serbia can throw more light on its position in the international tourist market, taking into account the tourist statistics of OECD and data available for 1995. This is especially true when using data of European states of the OECD which are similar to Serbia in terms of population and territory as contained in table 13 (in 2000 data slightly changed but that does not alter the main thrust of this paper). For example, the total number of beds in Serbia was 91.687,and of this number there was 46.200,in basic facilities which make 50.4% of all beds (Source: Tourism Organization of Serbia).

Table 1: Share of Basic Facilities Providing Beds in the total Number of Beds in 1995 (in thousands)

Country	*Total number of beds*	*Total number of beds in basic*	*Share of basic capacities in%*
Austria	1.135,2	646,1	57
Czech	233,9	131,2	56
Hungary	253,6	131,8	52
Portugal	469,1	204,1	44
Switzerland	270,0	264,4	98
Serbia and Montenegro*	212,6	85,6	43
- Serbia	120	49,2	45
- Montenegro	92,6	36,4	39

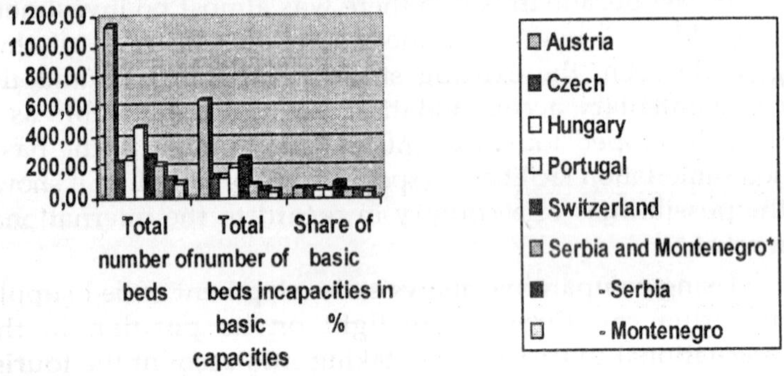

Source: Strategic Development of Tourism in Serbia, Belgrade, 1999. pp. 9
* Data given for 2005.

The above shown overview shows that the similar countries have a higher number of beds from Serbia when it comes to overall and basic accommodation facilities. That is why it is important to evaluate the potential of a basic accommodation facilities offer in regard to the market needs, in other words to determine the level of its sufficiency in the present and future development of tourism. When answering this complex question, few different indicators can be used. Very indicative is the so called tourist density—which represents potential of accommodation facilities seen as a relation of basic facilities accommodation with the number of inhabitants from one side and the surface area of the specific destination from the other side. Based on the 1994 data, this indicator shows the developed tourist economy of Serbia in regard to the similar countries in Europe (similar in the surface and number of the inhabitants) and an average in regard to the countries members of the European Union. Taking into account all the methodological differences and imperfections in using this indicators, they show that development of tourist economy in Serbia is way under the level of the EU countries and the similar neighboring countries.[9]

Table 2: Lodging Potential's in Certain Countries

Countries	*Basic lodging capacities on 000*	*Number of inhabitants in milion*	*Territory in square km*	*Basic capacity in relationship to inhabitants 000*	*Basic capacity in square km*
Greece	508.4	10.4	131.900	48.89	3.85
Austria	650.0	8.0	83.853	81.25	7.75
Portugal	202.4	9.9	92.389	20.45	2.19
EU as a whole	8.363,4	370.4	3.234.100	22.58	2.59
Czech	93.8	10.3	78.864	9.11	1.19
Hungary	126.3	10.2	93.932	12.38	1.36
Switzerland	264.0	7.1	41.293	37.18	6.39
FR Yugoslavia	86	10.5	102.173	798	0.82
Serbia	52	9.9	88.361	5.01	0.56
Montenegro	34	0.6	13.812	57.07	2.48

Source: "Strategic Development of Tourism in Serbia", Belgrade, 1999 and TOS.

However, from the aspect of overall tourist offer, Serbia has enough possibilities for further extensive development of lodging offer in comparison of the size of its territory. Thus, Serbia has at its disposal undiscovered potential but that does not mean that it has to concentrate on extensive development (especially having in mind that even existing ones are not used enough). Therefore it is necessary to carefully determine what that would mean from the aspect of endangering existing space. It would also mean accepting world criteria and standards in terms of sustainable development of tourism.[10]

Overall tourist offer as well as existing lodging offer, distinguish themselves by structural defects which relate to modest investment of other basic types (11197 beds) in relationship to hotel facilities (37104 beds—for detailed information look at table 15), inadequate structure of hotels where dominates category B (69%) and category A (16%)as well as old age of hotel and other facilities (82% of hotels have been built twenty years ago or are older). Furthermore, the equipment of the hotel is inadequate with low percentage of utilization of capacity in the conditions of inadequate demand and market disturbances.

Territorial disposition also shows aspects of unilateralism. The main portion of basic lodging offer is located in Beograd, Nis, Subotica and other major cities in Serbia (54%) which means that about 87% of total lodging offer is located in central Serbia. On the other hand, 25,884 lodgings are located in private rooms, which lead in complementary lodging, while 95% are located in spa tourist locations.

In the following years the main influence on removing numerous, structural defects of lodging offer, would have to concentrate on the tourist market as well as determination to accept foreign and domestic demand in line with the goals of long-term development of tourism of Serbia.

Build up of tourist offer can be viewed from the aspects of human resources and their training for executing dealings and working operations (in various economic and no economic fields) which secure offers of services to domestic and foreign visitors. One should keep in mind that Serbia has relatively built up system of education for tourist needs, in which are educated and trained personal of various profiles and different types of qualifications. Serbia has at its disposal three faculties at which are educated and trained personal for work in tourism (Beograd, Novi Sad, Kragujevac), three junior colleges (two in Beograd, one in Nis) and four vocational schools. However, curriculums are rarely innovated so there is no contemporary knowledge from the aspect of strategic management of tourism in adequate form. Also the structure

Table 3: Employed According to Qualifications in %

	total	*college*	*PhD*	*ma*	*other*	*Junior college*	*High school*	*elementary*	*Highly Qualify*	*Qualifie.*	*Semi quaify*	*Non Qua.*
total	100											
Buss.	100	5,8	0,02	0,2	5,7	4,7	23,1	5,08	9,7	32,3	9,7	9,5
Tour.	2,26	2,7	0,006	0.02	2,7	4,9	21,6	6,6	6,8	35,57	10,7	11,0

Izvor: Statistical Office of Serbia for 2005. and personnel evaluation.

of personal employed in tourist economy of Serbia is very interesting (see Table 3).

In the tourist and catering industry of Serbia in 2005, according to the official figures, there were employed (excluding Kosovo and Metohija) 35.891 employees which makes up 2,8% of the total number of employed in Serbia. Also, from the following it could be stated that in tourist economy of Serbia the presence of personal with college degree is far more below average of Serbia and that dominate under qualified (66%) while personal with college degree make up 2,7% of the number of employed.

Particular problem is not following of innovations, knowledge and technological advances as well as market advances in tourist business dealings (through adequate forms of advanced training) in domestic tourist companies. Because of all of that it is essential to adapt tourist economy of Serbia strategically to market changes, as well as elevating the quality of tourist offer, securing qualitative personal structure for offering tourist services, which need to be basis for development of tourist offer.

On the other hand, harmonized development of tourism (on strategic and program basis) in mountainous, as well as in other areas, makes foundation not only for its safety but for increase in employment and countering migration towards regional and local urban centers. Through production of organic food as well as presentation of anthropogenic colorants to domestic and foreign tourist segments as well as advancement of tourist village offer, significant economic and social effects can be expected in regional development of Serbia.

In the building up of tourist economy of Serbia, as well as total tourist offer, what is significant is the qualitative factor and that is market oriented behavior of offer and demand, and its reaction to adequate impulses in economic and total social environment.[11]

b) Traffic conditions

While in Europe traffic development is carefully monitored and directed, in Serbia and FR of Yugoslavia due to adverse economic conditions as well as conflict destruction, has brought about falling behind of traffic development.

In connection with road transport, it is necessary to upgrade the quality of traffic services, and here it is inevitable to modernize transport capacity (obtaining vehicles which satisfy EU standards, in terms of security, protection of environment, economic utilization). Transit traffic along our motorways does not answer to possibilities of geostrategic position of Serbia (one of the problems is toll payments which need to be addressed according to EU regulations which means that it have to be the same for domestic and foreign vehicles).

Priorities in building up of motorways need to have those ones that have secured foreign resources. In that should be included main motorways which encompasses Hungarian-Serbian border with the corridors leading to Greece, Bulgaria and Romania, and over long-term Western Morava corridor.

Railway traffic has over a long time been the most significant branch of transport, and as a consequence of rapid development of road and air transport, was significantly neglected. This is proven by a fact that the scope of transport of passengers in railway traffic has been ten times less, then in road traffic. Priority in modernization, build up and securing higher speeds, have those routes which can enable better connections between Balkan and European states. However, long-term problems of limited scope of transport of passengers and bad quality of services are influenced by lack of financial resources, general technical lagging behind and other factors.

In air traffic, during last years were absent significant revues (due to air traffic ban) so it also needs modernization (although in terms of foreign currency revenue it mainly comes from over flights).

c) Tourist Destinations

Complementary development of all this elements of tourist economy, and in that sense tourist offer, imposes as a necessity. The most important questions from the aspect of tourist offer can be systematized in the following way:

(1) Realizing selection of priority tourist places and centers;

(2) Stimulating development of complementary industrial branches;

(3) Securing import of products which are not produced domestically;

(4) Increase of cooperation with food industry;

(5) Long term development and modernization of transport;

(6) Creative role in development of tourism of travel agencies.

For the development of tourism, and keeping in mind its adaptability and competition, it is necessary to differentiate tourist offer of Serbia in the following way:

1) Business approach
- transit tourism
- business
- health
- sport-recreational
- culture and historic
- manifestations
- hunting and fishing
- tourism for special professions/photographs, explorations, rafting, mountain hiking/

2) According to holders tourist product
- mountain tourism
- urban tourism
- lake and river tourism
- spa tourism
- Village tourism
- hunting grounds
- protected areas

3) Other
- summer and winter
- excursions
- picnics

From the strategic point, build up of tourist offer could be realized by formation of selective products at the level of particular destinations in Serbia. In that context, it is necessary to define following tourist entireties, and according to our estimates they are the following:

(1) Tourist zones—widest possible functional scope of complete and integral thematic offer of one region or part of Serbia with characteristic of existent and potential tourist activities and contents;

(2) Tourist region—basic tourist territory encompassing existing and potential activities and contents of offer of major trends of tourism in tourist zone;

(3) Transit tourist routes—separate, specific areas of tourist offer along main corridors of international and national road highways and waterways, both inside tourist regions and zones, as well as separate offer;

(4) Urban tourist centers—cities with particular tourist offer or offer inside tourist zone, regions or along tourist corridors;

(5) Spa-health and recreational tourist centers, with characteristic offer inside tourist zones, regions and along tourist corridors.

Serbia, as tourist destination, may encompass six tourist zones[12]

(1) Eastern zone (with two regions: Stara planina, Krajiste sa Vlasinom)

—skiing and other winter sports, summer recreation, ecology, hunting and village tourism

(2) Main zone (two regions mountains Kopaonik and Golija)

—winter skiing, summer recreation, hunting tourism, spa tourism, village tourism;

(3) South zone (two regions: mountains Sara and Prokletija)

—winter sports, summer recreation, hunting and village tourism, cultural heritage;

(4) West zone (regions: Tara-Zlatibor and Zlatar) —summer recreation, sport, transit and lake tourism, village tourism, other;

(5) Central zone (five regions: Valjevo mountains, mountains of Sumadija, mountains of Kucevo, Djerdap, sandy terrain-Deliblatska:

(6) North zone (four regions: Fruska gora, upper Podunavlje, upper and lower Tisa) —excursion and nautical tourism, ecology, monuments, picnics, weekend tourism

Inside tourist centers, Beograd has a central place and is internationally significant. Tourist product is differentiated as congress, business and transit destination, with numerous supplementary content- shopping tourism, excursion tourism, and tourism of organized groups and other. Beside this, there are also other cities such as Subotica (Palic), Novi Sad, Kragujevac, Nis and other cities which might differentiate due to their tourist product.

In case of spa, grading should be done according to their attractiveness (for example in the first group are Vrnjacka banja, Soko Banja) and beside thermo mineral, other out of lodging contents (culture, recreation, entertainment) which need to be activated in order to classify into modern centers of active and dynamic recreation.

Also, transit tourism need to be develop along major highways and waterways.

4.4.1.3. Realized Results in Tourist Traffic and Revenue

In the last decade of the XX century dramatic changes took place in political and economical sphere. Process of globalization of world economy is more and more accelerated. Known events in Europe, especially in the Balkans, as well as in Yugoslavia and in its surroundings had enormous consequences on overall economic situation, and as well as on tourist economy.

However, habitual factor and so called structural accommodation enabled that even in adverse conditions; some kind of domestic tourist traffic is maintained[13]. In terms of quality and quantity in the period 1989-2005 many things have changed in tourism of Serbia, which is witnessed by the following facts.

Table 4: Tourist Traffic in Serbia (in thousands)

	1989	*1999*	*2000*	*2005.*
Tourist arrivals	4.158	1.443	2.166	1.988.
Overnight visits	11.899	5.467	7.668	6.499
No.of foreign tourists	941	463	165	452
Overnight visits by foreign tourists	1.515	174	174	991

Source: Federal Statistical Office, Statistical yearbooks for corresponding years, Tourism Organization of Serbia and personnel evaluation.

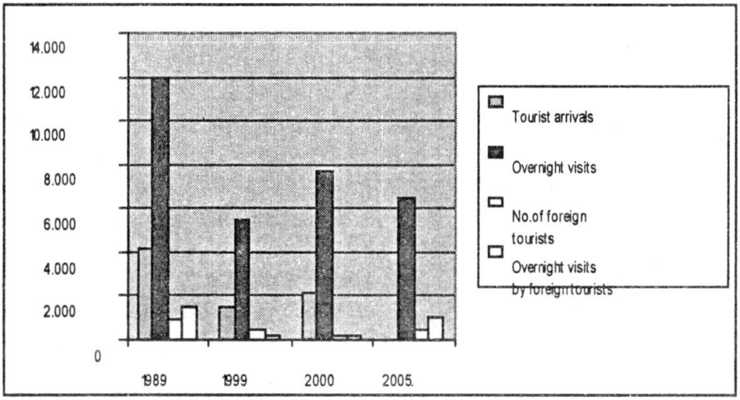

Tourist economy of Serbia has during the last decade of XX century seen lowering of overall tourist traffic for two to three times (depending on year) and lowering of tourist traffic for over ten times. Of course, that resulted in lowering of foreign currency inflow (in 1989 Serbia it amounted 550 million US dollars while in 2000 it was 26, 5 million US dollars, which is 25 less amount).

In general, in the period 1989-2000 achieved was a drastic fall of tourist traffic and revenue, and tourist economy of Serbia survived because of domestic tourist.

Table 5: Tourist Places According to Number of Overnight Stays-2005

Tourist place	*Total number of overnight stays*	*In terms of %*
Belgrade	1,183	18,2
Novi Sad	0,126	1,9
Spa places	2,012	30,9
Mountain places	1,765	27,3
Other tourist places	1,413	21,7
Total	6,499	100,0

Source: Facts of Tourist Organization of Serbia.

For example Serbia has in the years before the crisis (1985-1990) realized annual income from tourism around 500 million US dollars, while in 1999 17, 9 million US dollars. In 2005 Serbia realized a total foreign currency inflow of 304, 1 million US dollars. At the same time average occupancy of hotels in Beograd[14] (as biggest and most important tourist destination in Serbia) in 1989 was 51,2%, in 1990 47,1%, while in 1998 it was in 1985) and it fell to 89.000 in 1997 (or in 1993 when it was 41.000), with ten time less number of foreign transit visitors (due to the unfavorable political and security situation in Serbia: conflicts in former Yugoslav republics; UN sanctions; NATO campaign of 1999).

4.4.2. Tourism in Total Economic and Regional Development of Serbia

Development of tourism so far in Serbia confirms that its effects are complex and in a significant degree integrated into the overall economic and tourist development of Serbia. However,during the 1990s Serbian tourism was exposed to numerous, exceptionally unfavourable,factors of economic and political nature,which essentially influenced conditions of development of Serbia. Interruption of long-term development was particularly reflected in foreign tourism.It is in the export sector where development possibilities of tourism are best expressed.

With development of tourism, Serbia could increase foreign and domestic tourist traffic, foreign receipts and consumption using existing capacities and available products.[15] Increased share of exports in gross domestic product predetermines tourism to achieve high foreign currency revenues with total development effects on tourism.[16] Taking into account expected effects on tourism over the longer term,one should proceed with dynamic growth which could enable its greater share of GDP as well as an increase in employment rate of around 6-8% (up to 255,000 employed in tourism).To this,one should add an increase in basic and additional employment in other support activities,especially in trade.If other business activities are included,it becomes clear that increased employment could bear on the future development of tourism in Serbia.

The generator role of tourism in the economic development of Serbia as well as the multiplying effects that are brought about by tourism will contribute to an increase in basic and additional employment.This is true especially in underdeveloped regions of Serbia when speaking about tourist and complementary activities and an expanding market (including multiple effects of overflying-related consumption from abroad) for the supply of domestic products and services in all sectors. For that reason it is necessary to determine priorities in the development of Serbia as a whole, which in our opinion are tourism, agriculture and communications. Therefore it can be ascertained that "the main task is to determine which sector(or group of sectors)of the economy will,according to the present structure of the balance of power,in that moment,express its driving force and capabilities and be a degree of growth".[17]

4.4.3 Strategy of Development of Tourism in Serbia

4.4.3.1. Goals and Direction of Strategic Development of Tourism in Serbia

Goals and direction of strategic development of tourism in Serbia could be defined taking into account that Serbia has quality resources for tourism development. By inclusion of numerous activities which have their own interest in the aggregate development of tourism or its sub-sectors individually, tourism could become one of the generators of the development of the entire economic sector of Serbia and its integration into European and world processes.In the long run, tourism could become a factor of stability and thus contribute to the growth of economic activities in Serbia. Mainly, the following basic goals and directions of tourism of Serbia could be defined:[18]

1. Stepping up of overall development through full use of existing capacities.
2. Speedy and significant presence of Serbia on foreign markets;
3. Creation of conditions for the further development of domestic tourism;
4. Improved organization as part of efficient managing of development of tourism;
5. Building up of such economic environment in tourism as would stimulate investment in dealings in this field (privatization and entrepreneurship).

In order to achieve these goals and tendencies related to the strategic development of tourism of Serbia,it is necessary to fulfill a number of assumptions and conditions, among which there are three sets of questions:

1. Conditions for dealings in tourism (stability of economic sector, investment, fiscal policy, credit policy, internationalization);
2. Advancement of tourist product and other instruments of market performance on selective basis (assortment, quality, standards, technological changes, selective development, marketing instruments)
3. Protection of the environment (coordinated development and environment)

Development of tourist economy of Serbia, in terms of defined goals of development, demand determination of priority types of tourism. In order to achieve that it is necessary to keep in mind the following:

- Basic trends of development of international tourism;
- Long-term goals of tourist development of Serbia (especially those which are linked to the accession

to international market);

- Achieved degree of development and quality of service;
- Basic resources and other factors.

Taking this into account it is possible to select following, most important, types of tourism:[19]

(1) Big city tourism

- In international scope (especially in Europe) visits to big cities are much faster then visits to the seaside and this because of the rise of short travels, taking into account vacations based on cultural and other content, as well as rise of all kinds of business travel and attendance of various manifestations.
- Big city centers (Beograd, Novi Sad, Subotica, Nis, Kragujevac) need to develop business, congress, manifestation, youth, vocational and other types of tourism;[20]

(2) Mountain tourism

- One of main trends of future international tourist demand;
- This type of tourism includes not only vacation, but various sport and recreational activities, hunting and other throughout the year, especially during winter and summer season;
- Tourist product should not be linked to ski sports (relatively massive segment) but needs to be adjusted to various other segments, with a possibility of stay during summer season (for example sport tourism);

(3) Transit tourism

- This type of tourism needs to be developed along main highways;
- It means creation of adequate content alongside highways (using corridor Vienna-Budapest-Beograd-Nis);

(4) Spa tourism

- Encompasses various tourist segments, and not only health and recreational;

- Adjusting offer with development of adequate contents (sport, vocational, cultural)
- Increase in quality of services for foreign and domestic tourists with adequate price;

(5) Tourism along river Danube
- It is complementary part of tourism on rivers and lakes of Serbia;
- Needs to utilize natural beauties, cultural-historic and total anthropogenic values;
- Development of nautical tourism (with other types of water sports);
- Development of international cruising along river Danube (ships-hotels on water);
- Significant regional aspect of development of areas along river Danube, with development of port, commodity and passenger traffic;

(6) Tourism based on special interests
- hunting and fishing
- culture
- religious tourism
- village tourism
- photo

When developing priority types of tourism in Serbia one has to take into account the following characteristics:

- In between all types of tourism there exists a high degree of correlation on a given area (it is not rare to find destinations in Serbia which do not encompass a great number or all types of tourism),
- Necessity of integral development of tourism in concrete areas;
- Ambient plan encompasses (in line with long-term development of tourism) following ambient and functional segments: tourist zone, tourist region, transit tourist highways, city tourist centers and spas.

Beside this, it is necessary to know that Serbia is not a suitable destination for development of massive tourism, especially not on an international market. However, her tourist values bring her into high correlation with growing trend of individualization and international sophistication, as well as domestic tourist demand. From that stems certain demands when formulating acceptable tourist product and her advancement, and those may include following positions:

- It is necessary to precisely define target markets and target segments;
- Faster positioning (and repositioning) of a known tourist product of Serbia;
- Within market (domestic and foreign) it is necessary to define target segments (for example congress participants, business travelers, transit passengers, nautical personal, hunters and others);
- Large number of smaller segments and individualization which influences faster adjustment to turbulent tourist demands (as in room and board facilities so in outside facilities);
- Sale and promotion must be made more directly with constant monitoring of market happenings.

Strategic basis for development of Serbia as tourist destination must be based on selective determination of target markets and target segments in tourism of Serbia. They can be disaggregated on three types of markets:

(1) Markets which can be rapidly entered by tourist product of Serbia, and from which it is possible to secure initial foreign currency inflow (former Yugoslav republics, Russian federation, Greece, Ukraine, Czech, Slovakia, Israel, Bosnia and Herzegovina, FYROM)

(2) Perspective markets which, in short time, could generate significant foreign currency income (with a major effort in positioning and repositioning, with adequate adjustment). These are: Germany, France, UK, Italy, Netherlands, Sweden, Norway, Austria and other)

(3) Potential markets, over a long period of time, which require adjustment (for example USA, Canada, Japan, China and other).

On the other hand, on all of these markets, it is necessary to determine small homogenous groups of consumers from which could, as target groups, Serbia expect success. These priority market segments could be: participants to various congresses, sport, cultural and other manifestations; those that prefer utilization of mountain centers (in winter and summer season); those that prefer spa centers; hunters, fishermen, transit passengers, youth segment, retirees and others. Also, for some of this segment part time travel could be developed i.e. package arrangements for organized groups of consumers.[21]

Table 6: Targeting Markets and Segments

TARGETING MARKETS		
PRIMARY	*SECONDARY*	*TERTIARY*
Germania	Austria	Bulgaria
Great Britain	Slovenia	Rumunia
Italy	Hungary	BiH
Spain	Czech	Croatia
France	Slovakia	Macedonia
SEGMENTS		
➢ Younger persons		
➢ Younger childless couples		
➢ Older couple with grown-up children		
➢ Groups of friends		
➢ Business people		

4.4.3.2. Intensified development of existing offer

With full use of existing capacity in tourist trade, the development of Serbian tourism could be intensified. That is possible on the basis of better quality of tourist services and advancement of the tourist product of Serbia, combining this with other basic instruments of market performance.

Changes in everyday life, living standards, techniques and technology have all influenced modification of the tourist demand. Tourists, especially foreign, more and more take a vacation in two parts. On the increase is their demand of beds in detached hotel buildings (tourist vacation establishments), outer activities with adaptable services, modern communications which will contribute to an exemplary tourist offer.

Intensification of development of tourist offer should be focused in these directions:

- greater orientation to development of tourist apartments, vacation homes and recreational contents;
- more wholesale and retail stores, special catering buildings and handicraft shops;
- innovation as to techniques and technologies of preparing and expanding tourist offer;
- standardized and computerized services on offer in tourist establishments;
- organization and business connections of tourism, catering, trade in agricultural products, communications, fisheries and other activities which form part of the tourist offer.

4.4.3.3. Development of tourist trade and offer in the function of economic revival of Serbia

Creation of conditions for further development of domestic tourism is in the function of its positive influence on the totality of economic and social life in Serbia. Developing Serbia as a tourist destination could make room for all aspects of domestic tourist demand. Ultimate aim is to secure economic and for certain segments of the population (young and retired people) special conditions for their participation in tourist changes. Beside positive economic influence on the balance of payments, development of domestic tourism is always strategically important for the tourist offer of a country and for its business results.[22]

Primary task for further development of tourist trade of Serbia is adaptation of its tourist offer to international demand. It is necessary to create conditions for intensified development, which means creation of qualitative integral tourist product (suitable development of all components of the "total" product),together with the continuous (extensive) development of lodging capacities and exemplary tourist offer. Necessary for the development of tourist trade, as a contribution to the economic revival of Serbia, is creation of conditions for efficient dealings in tourism in order to have a positive influence on the entire economic sector of Serbia.

For tourism, three areas of development of economic policy are essential: fiscal system, system of international economic affairs and credit policy (in terms of securing investment and conditions for current dealings). The main preconditions for the development of tourism are as follows:

> a) consistent tax policy b) tourism needs status for exporters and suitable incentives c) financial loans to stimulate exports d) shareholder capital e) foreign capital f) internationalization of dealings in tourism and commerce

Thus, any further loss of speed in the development of the services sector(as well as development of new services)may disrupt further economic development and perpetuate the existing gulf with the developed countries. Strategic adaptation of the tourist sector of Serbia to market changes as defined in development goals requires identification of priority areas of tourism.

The following among them are considered to be the most important:[23]

(1) big city tourism
(2) mountain tourism
(3) transit tourism
(4) spa tourism
(5) tourism on the Danube river
(6) tourism connected to special interests:

> a) hunting and fishing, b) culture tourism, c) religious tourism, d) village tourism, e) photo tourism

4.4.3.4. Transformation of companies as a transition process

The current dealings,whose characteristics are globalization of markets and technologies, have helped promote new forms and ways of competition. This has reflected itself on the internal configuration and content of strategic management of companies. Dynamism of market, technology, business and other factors have diminished the relevance of the current company standing (creating new challenges, obstacles and pitfalls) so that devising a business strategy always means smaller or greater changes which lead to transformation of companies.

In tourist-catering sector of Serbia commercial activities are performed by 4,179 companies out of which 60% are in catering and 40% in tourism consultancy with around 100,000 employees (accurate data on total employed does not exist). Out of these, on 31 December 2000, there were 536 insolvent companies, which reported a loss of 3.4 billion dinars.Besides this,it should be noted that 24 companies have initiated bankruptcy proceedings.[24] On average,on each 100 dinars expended, there were 8.5 dinars in earnings. Just a few of these facts indicate the necessity for radical changes in the transformation of companies.Capital restructuring in our companies has not been followed up by organizational restructuring, so that the positive effects that may have originated from the restructuring process have not materialized yet.This shows that in companies (private, mixed and stockholder) in the last thirteen years no structural and strategic changes have been made, which means that nothing has been done to adapt to market demand and tendencies.

Table 7: Tourist Companies by Property Type (Status as at 30.09.2003)

TOTAL	*socially-owned*	*private*	*collective*	*mixed*	*state-owned*	*Other*
3760	250	3293	9	186	18	4
100%	6.62%	87.6%	0.22%	4.98%	0.48%	0.1%

Source: Statistical Office of Serbia and personnel evaluation.

From Table 7 it is clear that the dominant role in the tourist-catering sector is played by private companies. However, this gives a false picture about their influence in the entire tourist sector, since most employees in this sector are employed by the public or state-owned sector (although there is no official data). GDP share of Serbia's tourist-catering trade has varied over the years, though not significantly (in the period 1996-2002 this scale varied between 1.93-2.27%).

In the process of modern strategic management of tourist business, market adaptation has played a central role. Also, in the selection and implementation of successful business strategies, companies have to maximize competitive advantages and minimize weaknesses. Strategy presents a wide-ranging company action plan for its interaction with the surroundings in order to achieve long-term development goals.[25] It is a way in which companies meet their long-term objectives.[26] Defined through strategy are resources and works to be mobilized in order to achieve growth and development of companies[27] in the conditions of change of all surrounding factors. Restructuring of tourist trade companies begins with a comparative analysis of strategic management.

Known as SWOT analysis, which means analytical method of examination and facing of organizational strengths(S), weaknesses(W), organizational opportunities (O) and threats (T). In other words, it means that the main conditions for development of tourism are:

1. Political stability
2. Tourist infrastructure(especially road network)
3. Selectivity of markets
4. Consistent fiscal policy
5. Stimulation of investment

4.4.3.5. Property transformation in the tourist sector

Property transformation in tourist trade, in our conditions and in order to achieve greater business efficiency,is essential. However,the speed and types of privatization of companies in the tourist business (which includes transformation of the whole economic system) depends on the scope of joint ventures and attraction of foreign investors.

Process of company restructuring from the aspect of implications for its volume, property and financial structure has three directions:

(1) expansion (through merger, acquisition and diversification);

(2) shrinking of certain activities/parts and contraction of business

(3) maneuvering as to ownership structure and system of management

This maneuvering regarding ownership structure may have several options:

- purchase of shares by management or employees;
- purchase of shares by certain groups(and through that their withdrawal from the market);
- repeated purchase of company through exchange of shares.

According to the work schedule in the period 2000-2003 there were ownership transformations[28] in 48 companies which became private or stockholder companies with 4177 employees. Also, according to the Ministry of Privatization there are plans to change ownership in around 50 tourist-catering companies. However,the underlying problem of this transformation is that it is not accompanied by company restructuring in the field of business policy and management that would allow modern management and marketing policies to be pursued.In that way,it is apparent that there is no qualitative advancement of dealings of these companies and that there are even examples of manipulation on the part of some new owners.

However, notwithstanding the course of restructuring, companies need environment in which they would not do any kind of business dealings, and especially not those which they cannot do solidly. Instead, companies could be enabled to contractually, with partner firms, do relocation i.e. division of labor and thus maximize effects under the terms of specialization.

In contemporary form of transformation of property of tourist companies, a total of 130 auction sale of tourist-catering companies was completed.[29] Two companies were sold on tender. These are companies ATP 'Puntnik' and 'Srbija turist Nis'. A total of 86 tourist companies were sold for 3 790 209 000 dinars or 4 407 219,67 EUR (1 EUR=86 dinars). Contracts for two tourist catering companies, sold on auction, were severed. These companies are socially owned tourist catering company "RESAVA' and socially owned company for tourism and catering 'SRBIJA". In the meantime, also sold on auction were hotels Jugoslavija (31 000 000 EUR), Hotel Metropol-Belgrade (27 400 000 EUR) and Hotel Junior Brzece and Hotel Breza Brus.

4.4.3.6. Adjustment of Economic and Other Policy

The main areas of adjustment of economic and other policy, within the context of activity for the realization of long term goals of development of tourism are:

(1) Improvement of legal regulations,
(2) Induction of investment (foreign and domestic),
(3) Creation of integral programs of development of tourism,
(4) Joint foreign investment.

Thus, it is necessary to form a complete, consistent and selective system of measures which would, on long term basis, stabilize and induce development of tourism. These measures cannot be partial and must be changed often, but must be directed in the direction of continental tourism in all its aspects.

However, for the realization of given growth rate in tourism, beside long-term measures and changes of systematic laws, also are needed short-term measures of economic policy:

- Efficient functioning of legal state, with changed legislations and its adjustment to EU regulations (with independent judiciary and efficient police),
- State financing from real sources, with a possibility of financing of deficit up to 5%, but only through valuable papers, sold on financial markets;
- Lowering of taxes and contributions, so that they can be stimulative to gradual scaling down of gray economy and its transformation into legal one,
- Strengthening of financial discipline, at the same time honoring all instruments of payments and implementation of fiscal obligations,
- Activation of all inspection services and financial police (with rigorous control of corruption and bribes),

- Persistent implementation of anti-monopoly laws and control of monopoly behavior;
- Creation of social programs as well as conditions for new jobs in economy of small enterprises,
- Creation of market for trade in valuable papers (government bonds, cashier bills, commercial bills, foreign currency bonds and shares stemming from privatization).

In general, economic policy needs to be efficient in the following spheres:

(1) Fiscal policy
(2) Credit-monetary policy,
(3) Foreign trade policy,
(4) Price policy.

All this means that government must enable faster development of tourist economy of Serbia by introducing incentive measures. This can be achieved by lowering the rate or abolishing income tax on all investment for the development of tourism; exemption from taxes and customs on all goods which are necessary to import in order to upgrade the quality of tourist facilities and modernization of its business dealings; exemption from taxes on used good and repro-material; introduction of grace period for new-built objects or new-formed tourist centers; favorable credits for preparation of tourist season; giving status of exporter and other. All this would enable formation of free financial resources for investment or reinvestment into tourist economy.

4.4.4 Election of Strategy in Future Development of Tourism of Serbia

Analysis of potential marketing strategy of tourism of Serbia can be realized through Ansooff matrix which takes into account two key elements: product (what is being sold) and market (to whom it is sold). Basically, it brings into vision tourism of Serbia with generic strategy (positioning, specialization and differentiation).

Ansooff matrix points out to strategic possibilities which Serbia has. These are:

Rewiew 2: Ansoff-a Mmatrica[30]

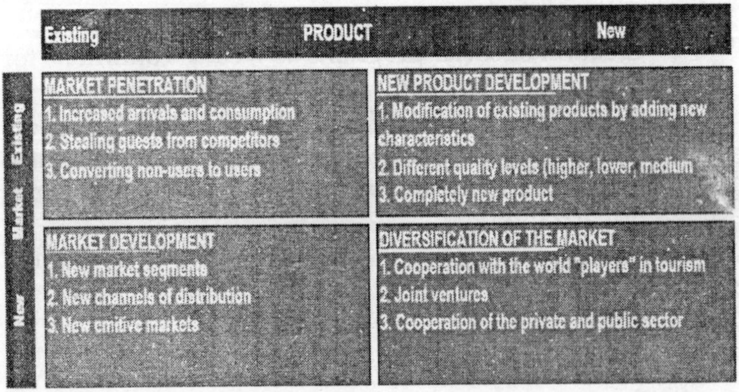

Matrix gives four strategic possibilities with detailed options within each possibility. If one takes into account portfolio of future tourist products of Serbia, as well as markets which are being counted in, we come to a focused Asnooff matrix which is adjusted to the tourist needs of Serbia. Here is where different directions of development of future tourist products are determined.

Rewiew 2: Development of Tourist Product of Serbia

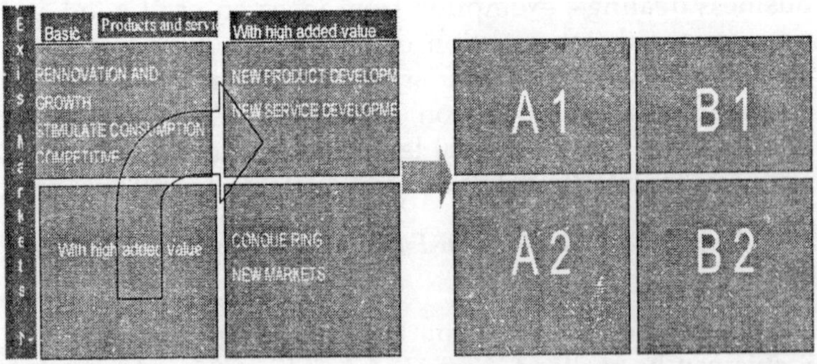

The main directions of tourism development in Serbia will start at the initial quadrant A1 (renovation, growth,consumption, competitiveness) and will continue in the direction of quadrant A2 (selective investments) and B1 (new products and services). So, it is of key importance to begin with the renovation of tourism in Serbia (by means of the said options) and then, depending on the product in question, take a direction toward the selected quadrants. Once development directions have been placed in the context of selected products, we arrive at the following table:

Rewiew 4: Development Phases of Tourist Product

	Product development stages			
	Stage 1	Stage 2	Stage 3	Stage 4
City stopovers	A1	B1	A2	B2
Business tourism + MICE	A1	B1	A2	B2
Mountains and lakes	A1	A2	B1	B2
Rural tourism	A1	A2	B1	B2
Health tourism	A1	A2	B1	B2
Special interests	A1	B1	A2	B2
Events	A1	B1	A2	B2
Nautical tourism	A1	A2	B1	B2
Touring	A1	B1	A2	B2

**MICE- Meetings, Incentives, Conferences and Exhibitions*

Each product shall have four development stages:

- Stage 1 shall be identical for all the products.
- Stage 2 shall be different depending on the product in question. Quick win products might start in B1 stage, that is, they can create new products and services. Products demanding great investments must start in A2 nad proceed with selective investments, that is, where the creation of the products starts from zero (bottom-up approach).
- Stage 3, for all the products, is the opposite of Stage 2. Here, the products proceeding from the development of the new product segments, start from selective investments (the creation of landmark product characteristics), while products starting from selective investments develop new product segments in the next stage.
- Stage 4 which concerns new markets relies, logically, on all the products, but this does not mean one cannot approach new markets during the preceding stages.

After determining competition guidelines for the development of tourist product with phase processing, it is necessary to have this "timeless" model put into relationship with real market changes. Degree of market growth has influence on potential managing of financial and strategic direction, while relative market participation has direct connection with profitability. Structural approach of this model gives:

- insight into different option of business portfolio
- gives introspection into market success
- implements allocation of financial resources within portfolio
- tests credibility of foresight in the success of the model

The business portfolio of tourist product of Serbia given in model BCG matrix is shown in review 2. Here the main job of the marketing system is to secure balance between products and services. That is enabled in that way that balance is found between product which generates revenue but have no future in terms of market growth (milk cows) and those which generate revenue with bright future (stars), as well as those which now spend financial resources. and have brilliant future. (Question marks).

Rewiew 5: Attractiveness of Tourist Product of Serbia[31]

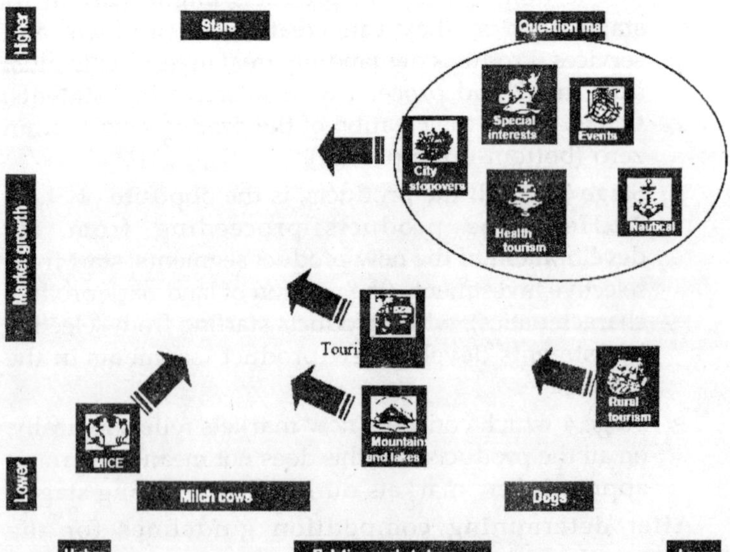

By implementation of these basic market tools one can gain basic insight into processes and strategic aims and main direction of future marketing system of Serbia.

On the basis of the SWOT analysis made as well through the implementation of the cluster model of strategy of the tourist sector of Serbia it is necessary[32]

- *to make a strategy planning* in which it is necessary to analyze beforehand: 1. market conditions; 2. segments; 3. competitive strengths and weaknesses; 4. economic and legal conditions; 5. technological development and availability of resources.
- *to map out the desired strategy*. At present, our opinion is that external method of growth is conducive to present conditions and available resources.

Taking into account market changes, as well as the potential and development of tourist trade of Serbia, from the point of view of scope of generic strategy, an acceptable strategy is that of determination and that of differentiation and lower costs.

In choosing a growth and development strategy, priority should be given to penetration strategy and product development. Also, strategy of vertical integration is suitable for conditions in which tourist trade of Serbia operates. Externally based methods of growth, under examination, show that for tourist trade of Serbia, when taken into account necessities of greater integration into international tourist exchange and faster access to world tourist market, the optimum strategy is that of interconnection and merger. In implementing this strategy it is possible to accept all options(horizontal, concentric, vertical and conglomerate).In that sense, contractual and other arrangements are especially attractive as ways and means of external growth in the forms of: franchise, management contracts, strategic alliance and joint ventures.

- structure, as a component of strategic capability, needs to complement a strategy, even for tourist trade of Serbia. We consider that the optimal solution is a functional structure or for complex forms of organization diversified companies or a divisional structure.

- when speaking about managing of companies of tourist trade in Serbia, we are of the opinion that strategic style of management and control needs to be implemented. For the control of execution of all operations and activities, strategic control is recommended.

Likewise, in the process of strategic adaptation of companies to market changes and tendencies, it is necessary to pass through the process of change of strategic management of companies. For that a process can be used which is represented in the review no 1.

Rewiew 6: Strategic Menagement of Tourist Companies[33]

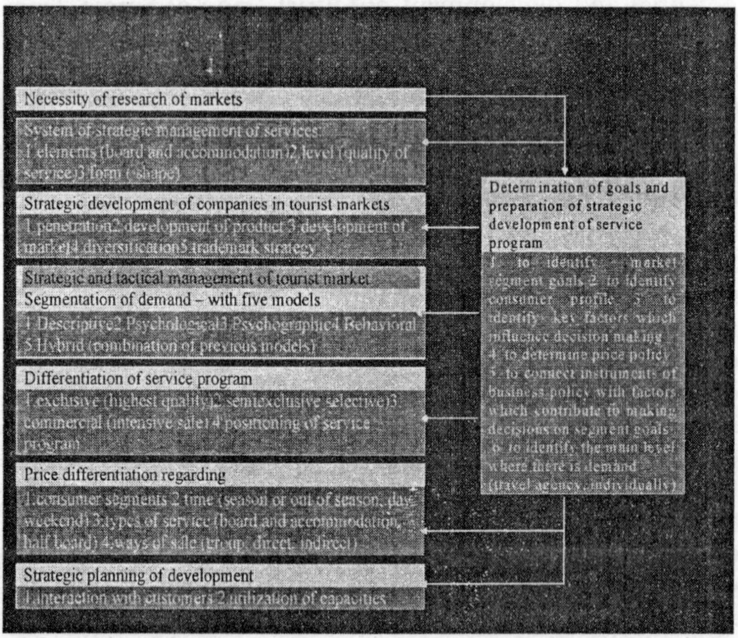

4.5. Conclusion

Taking into consideration that Serbian tourism is striving to be predominantly export oriented and in view of strategic adaptation and orientation towards doing business based on market conditions, it would give scope for successful overcoming of barriers in international markets. By being exposed to competition in international tourist market, conditions would be created for its efficient inclusion into integration processes in Europe. It is well known that this is an activity, which speedily adapts and demands very few conditions for normal functioning and activation of a huge potential in order to achieve wide and significant economic effects. At the same time, we have in mind that tourist products of Serbia, always to a larger or lesser extent, are present on the advertising markets of Europe. Today, there is a need to have these products viewed in their proper perspective and improved as well as to incorporate them into new and contemporary market trends and tendencies, taking into account wide ranging changes in its surroundings (demographic, economic, geographic, natural, technological, political, legal, socio-cultural, etc).

Tourist trade, more exactly tourist trends and consumption which stems from it, in contemporary conditions are exclusive components of international business and overall world business relationships. For many of these areas, and even for a relatively large number of countries, tourism is the principal or one of the main driving forces behind business and general social development.

Globalization, as a process, enables strengthening of international economic integration. It clearly defines efficient market dealings of modern companies, as a principal motor of business transactions, efficient development and functioning market forces as a whole. Incorporation of tourist trade of Serbia into processes of integration and globalization is best realized by incorporation into strategic alliances, joint ventures with foreign partners, franchise contracts, conclusion of contracts with management companies, horizontal and vertical interconnection with domestic and foreign companies.

Also, this process demands fast and efficient adaptation of legal regulations as well as further harmonization regarding specialization and management of quality on aggregate.

Literature Review

1. Ansoff, I & McDonnell, E., *Implanting Strategic Management*, Prentice Hall, 1990.
2. Bentley, B.R. Information Technology and Tourism: An Update, Tourism Management, N 2/1996.
3. Burns, T. & Stalker, G.M., The Management of Innovation, London, Tavistock, 1961.
4. Čačić, K., Tendencies and General Characteristics of Development of International Tourism, Ekonomski anali no. 133, University School of Economics, Beograd, 1995.
5. Čerović, S., Management and Tourism, Čigoja štampa, Novi Sad, 2003.
6. Čerović, S., Strategic Management of Tourist Trade of Serbia, Želind, Beograd, 2002.
7. Chamber of Commerce of Serbia, Notice No. 209, 2001, p. 2.
8. Cowell, D., *The Marketing of Services,* Heinemann Ltd., London, 1987.
9. Drucker P., Management, Pan Books Ltd., London 1997.
10. Gaibrath, J.R & Kazanjan, R.K., Structure, Systems and Process, sec. ed., West Publishing Company, 1986.
11. Harvard Business School Press, 1993.
12. Katzenbach, J. and Douglas, S., *The Wisdom of Teams: Creating the High-Performance Organization,* Boston.
13. Kotler, P., *Marketing Management, Analysis, Planning, Implementation, and Control,* Ninth Edition, Mate d.o.o., Zagreb, 2001.
14. Krippendorf, J., *Travelling Mankind,* Institute for Research of Tourism, Zagreb, 1986.
15. Milisavljevic, M., Todorović, J., *Planning of Development Policies of Companies,* Savremena administracija, Beograd, 1994.
16. Ministry of Privatization of the Government of the Republic of Serbia.
17. Mintzberg, H., The Strategy Concept: Five PS for Strategy, *California Management Review,* Fall 1987.
18. Nickels, W., *Marketing Principles,* Englewood Cliffs, Prentice Hall, New Jersey, 1978 of *International Marketing*, Vol. I, No. 1, 1998., pp. 16-28, MBC Publications.
19. Petrović, P., *Marketing Strategy of Companies,* Institute of Foreign Trade, Beograd, 1995.

20. Porter, M., *Comptetive Strategy*, Free Press, New York, 1990.
21. Raičević, B., *Economic Rewiew*, No. 4/1968, Beograd, Shuptrine, F.K., and Toyne, B., *International Marketing Planning: A Standardized Process*, Journal.
22. Slobodan Unković, *Economics of Tourism*, Savremena administracija, Beograd, 2001.
23. Steiner, G.A.; Miner, J.B.; Gray. E.R., *Management, Policy and Strategy*, Macmillan Inc., New York, 1996.
24. Štetić, S., Attraction of resources, motiv for election of tourist destination, Collection of Works: 'Tourist Potentials of Yugoslavia', Novi Sad, november 1996.
25. *Strategic Development of Tourism in Serbia*, Beograd, 2000 in 2006.
26. Thompson, A. JRANDA., Strickland J., Strategic Management: Concepts and Cases, 6th. Ed BP/IRWIN, Homewood, Illinois, 1992.
27. Todosijević, R., and Others, *Changes and Contemporary Company*, Prometej, Novi Sad, 1995.
28. Vukonić B., *Tourisma and Development*, Školska knjiga, Zagreb, 1987.
29. WTO, *Compendium of Tourism Statistics*, Twentieth Edition, Madrid 2000.
30. WTO, *World Tourism Barometer*, No. 3, October 2004.
31. Zemke, R., *Scandinavian Management—A Look to the Future*, Management Review, 77, No. 7, 1988.
32. Žižić M.,Tourki M., *Sectoral Analysis of Serbian Trade*, Beograd, 1993.

NOTES

1. Under the assumption that for example new lodging capacities and especially non-room and breakfast contents are sold, Serbia could in a certain period of time attain foreign tourism consumption level that existed in 1989, when it acquired US 550 million income from tourism, although overall tourist consumption was much more. It is estimated to have been around US 1 billion.
2. Popesku J., *Marketing in Tourism*, Cigoja stampa, Beograd, 2002.
3. *Strategic Development of Tourism in Serbia*, Belgrade, Horwath Cosulting Zagreb i Ekonomski Fakultet Beograd, 12.04.2006., str. 2-3st.

4. In that respect, Serbia has numerous resources such as Belgrade area, Kopaonik, V. Banja, Zlatibor, Fruska Gora, Tara etc.
5. This resource in particular is the important basis for development of tourism in Serbia. Some of the jewels of the cultural and historic heritage of Serbia (Studenica, Sopocani, Stari Ras) were included among specially important monuments in the world and put under protection of heritage of UNESCO.
6. For e.g. one of those processes represents the erosion of the ground, pollution of water and air of natural or anthropogenic origin
7. Travel agencies would have a significant role to play taking into account their activities and transport capacities, especially in land transport. About 400 member of Yugoslav association of tourist agencies (YUTA) use 600 buses for realizing travel in domestic and international tourism. Severe conditions in international land transport and EU standards especially would demand modernization of bus capacities and achievement of adequate standard of transport.
8. Within basic capacities, major shares goes to hotel capacities 74,2%, and tourist settlements 17,1% while in complementary capacities private rooms are in the majority (35,4%), rest houses (worker, children and youth) participate with 27,2% and camps with 22.94% (see Table 15, capacity for lodging of tourists in the FRY in 1999).
9. For example, Serbia and Portugal have the same population and approximately have the same territory, but Portugal has four times more basic lodging capacities. In case of Austria it is smaller and has less population but that country has 13 time larger scope of basic lodging capacity, while Greece has 10 times more.
10. Space exists, but it is reliable question of its further utilization, i.e. striving of Serbia to secure reconciled development of tourism and strengthen it as its tourist advantage.
11. Tourist demand makes travel during summer holidays, school vacations, lengthened state and religious holidays and on other occasions.
12. This example is made up according to Spatial plan of Serbia, strategy of development of tourism (1999) and domestic expert analysis (Bakic, O., Cacic, K., Maric, R., and other).

13. Structural accommodation of offer means shortening of time spent during holidays, lowering of number of members of family which travel (in majority cases it is youth member who utilize it), selection of cheap transport, lodging, food and other. Thus, even in adverse social and economic circumstances and with lowed ring of standard of living, there is no abandoning of tourist travel.
14. In 1990 hotels in Beograd had at their disposal 7.749 beds, while in 1997 7.474 beds.
15. Assuming that new beds are provided and sold and that there are other contents outside board and accommodation, Serbia could over a certain period of time get back to the 1989 level of foreign tourist consumption when its earnings from foreign visitors were US$ 550 million,although it was estimated that tourist consumption was much higher, around US$ 1 billion.
16. In the strategy of overall development of Serbia (up to 2010 and beyond up until 2020) it is estimated that tourism, through foreign visitors' consumption, could achieve 6-8% of the GDP with justifiable tendencies of increasing that potential (Strategy of Development of Tourism of Serbia, Beograd, March 1999, p. 60).
17. Raičević, B., Ekonomska misao No. 4/1968, Belgrade, p. 735.
18. Adapted according to the Strategy on the Development of Tourism in Serbia, Beograd, 1999. and 2006.
19. Strategy of development of tourism in the Republic of Serbia, Beograd, 2000, p. 40.
20. Business reasons and other types of visits to Beograd, Novi Sad, Nis and other major cities in Serbia participated with over 70% in the total number of foreign tourist visits. Beograd, and other major cities, in reality could and need to reactivate status of an important European congress center.
21. At the same time, into account could be taken smaller segments, such as bird watchers, incentive travelers or segments which have special interest.
22. This is confirmed by the data provided by major tourist nations, for example France, Italy, Switzerland, Mexico, Spain and other where development of tourism is based on domestic tourism.
23. Strategic development of tourism in the Republic of Serbia, Beograd, 2000, p. 40.

24. Source: Chamber of Commerce of Serbia, Notice No. 209, 2001, p. 2.
25. Thompson, A. JRANDA., Strickland, J., Strategic Management: Concepts and Casses, 6th ed, BP/IRWIN, Homewood, Illinois, 1992.
26. Mintzberg, H., The Strategy Concept: Five PS for Strategy, *California Management Review,* Fall 1987.
27. Milisavljević, M., Todorović, J., Planning and development policy of companies, Savremena administracija, Beograd, 1990, p. 81.
28. Ministry of Privatization of the Government of the Republic of Serbia.
29. Agency for privatization-auction center.
30. Taken over from Strategy of development of tourism of Serbia-Horwath Consulting Zagreb and Economy faculty, Beograd, p. 7.
31. Taken over from Strategy of development of tourism-Horwath Consulting Zagreb and Economic faculty Beograd, p. 9.
32. Čerović. S, *Strategic Management of Tourist Trade in Serbia,* Zelnid, Beograd, 2002, pp. 152 and 203.
33. Čerović, S., *Management and Tourism,* Čigoja štampa, Novi Sad, 2003., p. 80.

5

Application of Marketing Concept within the Airline Industry: The Case of Albania

*Areti Stringa**

The objectives of the research were defined through the following tasks:

1. To synthesise the features of daily marketing activities of the airlines operating on the Albanian market and establish their strengths and weaknesses.
2. To analyse and establish if there are marked differences in marketing activities of the airlines operating on the Albanian market.

Different sources of primary and secondary data were used in analysis of marketing of services of airlines operating on the Albanian market. The nature of the research was exploratory. Primary data were mostly gathered from expert opinion by means of personal interviews. The depth interviews took place in offices of the respondents.

Introduction

National economies of developed countries are dominated

* PhD, is an Associate Professor in Faculty of Economics of the University of Tirana, Albania.

by the service sector. In their efforts to differentiate and diversify from competition, the companies in the service sector are developing yet unknown marketing and management models. Their competitive edge is that they provide services but in relation to achieved satisfaction and loyalty of the customer as well. The features of the service sector in the Republic of Albania are still very different from characteristic features of such sectors in the developed market economies. Nevertheless, and as a reflection of many different changes that have occurred in the past twelve years in political, business, cultural and legislative environment, service companies on the Albanian market are constantly faced with business regulations and attitudes characteristics for companies from developed service sectors. The gap is narrowing and the importance of the service sector is increasing. Gathering of the statistical data for the service sector is made on the basis of the data from "Statistical Yearbook 2004" where the service sector in 2004 contributed to 64,4% of employment and 65% of gross domestic product.

Methodology of Research

The airline companies are markedly exposed to challenges and needs for permanent differentiation from their competition—the services of many airlines offer similar concept of benefits as they are provided on the same type of aircraft and destinations. In comparison to the competition—the services of many airlines offer similar concept of benefits as they are provided on the same type of aircraft and destinations. In comparison to the competition, how the services are provided and their quality still remain the main source of differentiation. That is why the airlines are among the leading service companies. The objectives of the research were defined through the following tasks:

- To synthesise the features of daily marketing activities of the airlines operating on the Albanian market and establish their strengths and weaknesses.
- To analyse and establish if there are marked differences in marketing activities of the airlines operating on the Albanian market.

- Different sources of primary and secondary data were used in analysis of marketing of services of airlines operating on the Albanian market. Statistical publications, international magazines, books and internal sources of some of the airlines were the most frequent sources of secondary data. Time series models were used for data analysis.

The nature of the research was exploratory. Primary data were mostly gathered from expert opinion by means of personal interviews. The depth interviews took place in offices of the respondents. The unstructured—undisguised questionnaire was used. Interviews were carried out with the managers of airlines' representative offices or members of their management and the purpose was to obtain, on the basis of their company business activities and their experiences, opinions, views and answers to the questions determined by the objectives of the research.

Quota sample was intentional and it comprised twelve world renowned airline companies: Albanian Airlines, Alitalia, Malev, Ada Air, Austria Eirlines, Olympic Airlines, Turkish Airlines, Adria Airlines, Swiss, Jat, Hemus Air and Club Air.

Figure 1: The List of Airlines According to their Number of Passsengers

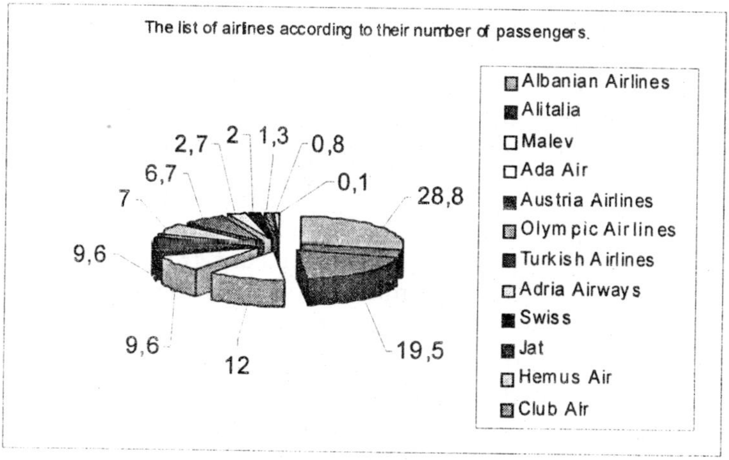

Figure 2: Airlines According to their Number of Flights

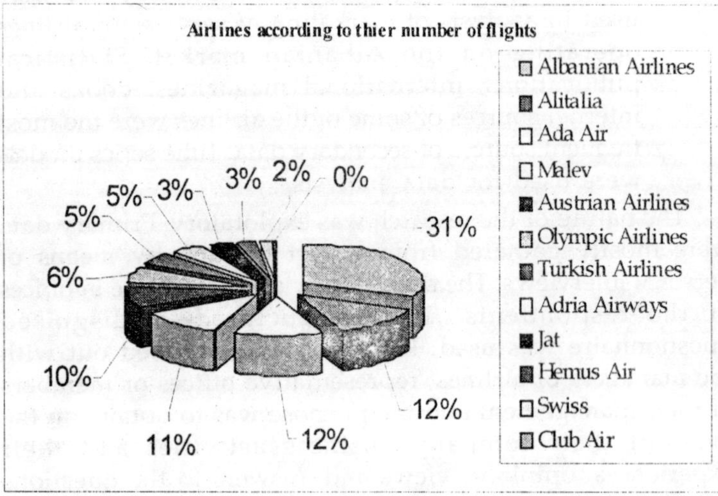

Analyzis of the Air Travelling Market

Recent profitability of airline companies has not been too high. The business has been limited to bare survival. Here, the airlines tend to explain the causes of their problems through structural difficulties that the industry is faced with and through their insufficient size due to which they are not fully able to enjoy the benefits of economies of scale. Demand for air traffic services and its permanent growth were not matched by respective financial results hence simultaneous coexistence of high demand growth rate and decline in profitability became one of the most important features of modern air traffic. Physical and financial indicators in the air traffic in period 1991–2003 show the following:

- Demand for air traffic services expressed through passenger numbers shows constant growth. Only in two years an insignificant drop in the number of carried passengers was recorded.
- Total operating revenues show constant growth, but their growth is not matched by adequate profit.
- Despite constant growth in demand and in total operating revenues airlines recorded significant losses,

both operating and net, on two occasions. Loss intervals were simultaneous to periods of great economic crisis.

- Strong demand, deregulation and free market entry of new airlines led to the fair that the existing capacities would be inadequate. As a consequence, orders for new aircraft rose hugely. The number of aircraft on the market grew two times faster than the demand for air traffic services. The consequence of this was many more seats than passengers. Overcapacity led to lower prices and decline in average yield per passenger or per flight.

Observing business activities of the leading airline companies it is possible to single out some of the factors that might have a significant influence on the successful financial results of an airline company:

- Basic features of airline's route network
- Basic features of flight economics derived from passenger load factor, duration of flights and frequencies.
- The role of computer reservation systems, FFP and concentration of flights through hubs.
- University educated company management with good experience in economy.
- Corporate costs
- The influence of deregulation and liberalisation of air traffic.
- Disloyal competition from airlines

The majority of above mentioned factors bear no direct relation to the size of company, except maybe ownership of computer reservation system. Namely, every company can try to fly at low costs, build an efficient route network and employ experienced management. Equally, institutional problems such as regulation, that is deregulation of air traffic, allowing of airline companies to come under protection of "Chapter 11", which entire industry faced, could not bear all the blame for bad financial results. Primary causes must be sought in bad planning within companies themselves, inefficient adjustment to changes that economic crisis brought about, Gulf War, Afganistan and Iraq War and the increase in fuel cost, that is factors that were beyond control and could not be anticipated.

The Basic Findings of Research

What follows is the presentation of the findings of the research on the marketing of services by the airlines operating on the Albanian market according to individual areas of the marketing of services.

Specifics of Operating on the Albanian Market

Despite the differences in the time length and continuity of their operations on the Albanian market, and also in the importance that the Albanian market has for each respective company, it could be concluded that they share common assessment about the specifics of operating on the Albanian market. Generally they feel that it is expensive market. Their arguments for such assessment are landing, cargo and passengers handling fees, prices for aircraft cleaning and maintenance, catering prices, leases for business premises, accommodation prices for crew which are too high and not competitive. They also underline the payment problem. Late payments or difficulty to collect payment for provided services is characteristic for entire Albania and is a result of lack of financial discipline. Most airlines also point to low prices and payment benefits as dominant demand features of air traffic services on the Albanian market.

Customer's Features on the Albanian Market

The research findings reveal that significant changes have occurred in the area of market segments. Genuine tourist passenger segment has almost vanished while ethnic travelling (visits to relatives and friends in Canada, USA, Australia, and Western Europe especially Italy, Greece and Germany) have gained prominence. Unfortunately strong business passengers segment does not exist (e.g. business people fly in economy class or even worse, buy complete package as the cost is lower than price of business class ticket). In recent years, refugees, displaced persons and members of international forces formed a specific segment. The main reason behind the changes in the market segmentation lies, and this view is shared by most airlines, in the price which is the key element in the selection of an airline company. Some companies stated that the demands of Albanian passengers in terms of the services standards were not much different from other markets—passengers are increasingly aware of what they can demand and that is how they behave. Some companies stated that it was easier to satisfy Albanian passengers as they still did not demand details (as oppose to passengers from developed Western countries). Evident is also the view that Albanian passengers select airline company out of "habit", that is they are not fully informed about full range of services offered on the Albanian market.

Internal Marketing

The findings of the research show that each airline has defined staff policy, but they significantly differ in concrete actions that are created and implemented in order to educate, motivate, award and build staff loyalty. In certain number of companies the governing form of education is self-education through manuals prepared by companies or courses (formally not a condition for promotion, but in reality yes). Education (basic and advanced) is organised in company's headquarters or through chain process where the knowledge is passed from headquarters to regional centres, and finally to staff in the local representative offices. Alternatively, representative office in Tirana has the status of profit centre and that determines the nature of bonus for achieved results. It is not unusual to observe declining staff loyalty in such companies—there is no enthusiasm, and no extra efforts are put to keep the staff. Finally there are companies that stand out for their exceptional care for internal marketing and human resources management. Loyalty of staff and keeping of the best can be achieved through combination of methods and techniques and the most important ones are: team work and aspiration towards company's common goals, continuous investment in staff education and training, active involvement of staff in decision making in all levels, stimulation of self-initiative, remuneration by achieved results, profit sharing. Among such companies it is not rare to find those that are characterised by informal structure—personalization of relations is present, staff, irrespective of their position in the company, is on the first name terms.

Conduct Towards Customers

All airlines underlined that the market research was one of the fundamental functions of marketing and it its importance for business was indisputable. However majority do not carry out local market surveys and their main arguments are lack of staff and time for such tasks. Some airlines included the Albanian market in customer satisfaction survey that was carried out on flights where Tirana was either arrival or departure airport. Passenger complaints were mostly about lost luggage, check—in (here airlines have very little say as service is provided by airport), aircraft delays, unsatisfactory in—flight service—e.g. food in the economy class. In Albania lost luggage complaints are predominant and are solved locally. Most companies have general guidelines and flexibility up to a certain level is tolerated; however certain issues such as the refund level are strictly regulated. The companies also tend to satisfy the customer as much as possible. If a passenger is not happy with offered solution, he or she is referred to claims department which is either located in the regional office or in headquarters. Some companies have very elaborate complaints systems (as a part of company's general standards manual); if complaint type and how—to—handle—it guidelines are not covered by the system, managers in the regional centre or company headquarters are contacted. The loyalty of Albanian passengers is not on the level that the companies would wish. Loyal passengers do exist but most of them will explore competition's offer and will purchase the ticket from those that offer better payment conditions. Economy class passengers are underlined as the most interested in the programme. Most of these programmes are characterised by collection of air miles (including hotels, car hire) and large and versatile selection of awards (free flight tickets, free package tours).

The Quality of Service

All companies deem the quality of services as the main tool in gaining and maintaining competitive edge position on the market. Passengers compare the benefits of services provided by respective companies but are not interested in how much has been invested in development of services. The quality of service is very important area of investment and the following investment areas should be emphasised:

- New aircraft:
- Improvements in aircraft comfort
- Changes in the services offer—passenger classes are becoming increasingly frequent: economy and enhanced business class
- Enhancement of in-flight and ground services
- New corporate identify
- Strategic alliances due to changes in demand (declining) and other trends on the global air traffic market.

(Above statements are not in the order of importance)

Consistent quality of service is necessary for all markets, and there are no reasons why company standards should not also be applied on the Albanian market.

Strengths and Weaknesses of the Airline Companies

All companies are in agreement that in the creation of services to be offered to potential passengers, irrespective of their origins, particular attention is given to spotting and emphasising of competitive advantages and constant efforts to overcome their weakness. Globally, airline companies underline the following features as their strengths:

- Numerous destinations and quality time table.
- Punctually, reliability and safety (particular characteristic of top ranking airlines in terms of service quality).
- Strategic alliances that result in greater market coverage and synergy effects by joint use of company's individual strengths.

- Professional conduct towards passengers (e.g. relaxed or even friendly conduct towards passengers, prompt reaction in the case of customer's complaint).
- Professional conduct of staff.
- Air craft comfort (on long haul flights in particular).
- In-flight service (catering, entertainment).
- Good airport service.
- New and modern aircraft.
- Corporate image and identify.
- Attractive prices.
- Attractive loyalty programme.

In fierce and uncompromising competition, the strengths of one company often become the weakness of its competition. As stating of individual strengths and weaknesses would be beyond the objective of this research, these issues have not received detailed consideration. Among particularly conspicuous strengths for the Albanian market the companies indicate; good timetable that offers daily connections even with the most distant destinations, attractive prices, good relations with agents—which serve as distribution channels, professional conduct of staff in the representative office, interesting offer of "stopover programme" with possibility to stay in one of the destinations that is neither passenger's departure point nor final destination. The companies recognise certain weaknesses present on the Albanian market and not elsewhere; price policy on the market that demands attractive prices and payment conditions is not competitive; potential customers are not informed about company's offer (they a priori consider company as expensive or attribute the image of company exclusively catering for business class passengers).

Conclusions and Recomandations

Considering that internalisation of Albanian economy is necessity, and that Albania intends to export through tourism, the air traffic services become key element in developing and maintaining of Albania's competitive edge in a service sector but of Albanian economy in general. All airlines that took part in the research are characterised by their very high level of international business. Because knowledge about their marketing practices and performance in Albania was not extensive, the exploratory research was carried out. As stated earlier in the paper, the general objective of the research was to gain insights and ideas about similarities and/or differences among marketing practises and performance of surveyed airline companies regarding Albania and other markets of their operations.

The research results reveal that day to day marketing activities on the Albanian market are clearly not different from standards and practices used on other, domestic and international markets. Albanian market has its specifics but required adjustments by airlines operating on the Albanian market should not demand drastic divergence from company's global marketing strategy.

In conclusion, the major task for the management of airlines operating on the Albanian market should be to learn lessons from hitherto crisis and to respond with adequate business strategy. It is necessary to find means for more efficient control of operating costs and to improve load factors. Profit should not be increased through price increases at the expense of passengers. On the contrary, through restructuring of existing flight network and increased productivity significant cost reduction could be achieved and that could lead to lower prices for customers. Better forecasting of economic trends, planning and more cautions and prudent decisions in the development of the company exposure to destabilising effects of economic crisis.

REFERENCES

Bateson, John E.G. (1989). *Managing Services Marketing: Text and Reading*, Dryden Press.

Christian Gronroos, (May, 1983): *Strategic Management and Marketing in the Sector*, Cambridge, MA, Marketing Institute.

Coivell, Donald. (1984). *The Marketing of Services*, London: Heinemann.

Heskett, J.; Sasser W.E. (1990): *Service Breakthroughs—Changing the Rules of the Game*, New York, NY, The Free Press.

Wells, A.T. (1989). Air Transportation: A Management Perspective, Wadsworth Publishing Company, Belmont CA. *Statistical Yearbook 2002, 2003*.

6

On-line Advertising and Distribution of Touristic Services

*Tatjana Petkovska Mirchevska**
*Nada Sekulovska***

Introduction

The Internet approach has a unique placement technology of the economic propaganda message and has an innovative campaign for development and maximization of the marketing message effectiveness, as well as information distribution and a feedback for its valorization.

This medium arrays over 70 million unique visitors per month. More than 7 billion web site marketing messages are delivered monthly on over 1900 web sites. According to demographic and geographic characteristics, there are specific channels which help companies to locate their desired audience. The Internet approach is exposed to innovations which are developing continuously in order bigger creative role to be accomplished. Those (Such) innovative elements of the Internet approach can be media signs, floating messages, sound- audio effects, streaming, video etc.

* Ph.D., University "St. Cyril and Methodius", Macedonia.

** Ph.D., University "St. Cyril and Methodius", Skopje, Macedonia.

The Internet as a Media

The Internet as a marketing and promotional media has appeared in 1994. First, it can serve not only as a communicational channel but also as transaction and distribution channel. Customers can gain information and can perform the buying and paying process over the Internet. No other medium can reach these marketing functions at once without looking for other meanings. Second, the Internet is interactive. Users can initiate the buying process by visiting a website and clicking on a hyperlink text for better information. This is a two-direction communication, the Internet as a provider with customized content which meets the customers' needs. Third, the Internet has a multimedia content capacity. It can transmit not only text and graphics but audio and video contents as well. Multimedia characteristic of the Internet give a high shut to the promotion. The Internet has become an integral part of multimedia mixed with lot of promoters and new promotional forms have filled the WWW landscape including animated messages with signs, sponsors' logos and 3-D visualizations.

Measuring the Audience

Measuring the audience size is the currency of the promotional media. Internet audience is usually measured by research and follow-up activities. There are two basic, often used methods for audience following: web centric and user centric. Web centric method is using coded files on a web server in order to measure the number of people who has visited the website. This method has a tendency to assess the actual number of visitors, which is called "catching" in the network practice, by which the internet service is providing copies of the shops on popular websites for fast access.

The user centric method requires an appropriate software installation on the computers in households and offices. The software automatically locates the websites which are continuously visited. The information is combined with demographic data on users in order different website profiles to be created. Telephone calls analyze are also used in order the number of internet users to be calculated. For example, a research conducted in 2001 by UCLA centre for communication has find out that 73% of the Americans have an online access which is bigger than 2000 when it was 66, 9%.

Online Promotion and Distribution of a Tourist Service

Today, in business competitive environment every hotel manager wants more distribution on its services, more clients and more profit. Cendant—Travel Distribution Service (TDS) has a solution which can be optimized by a distributional strategy, both, online and offline—through agencies.

Table 1: Cendant Distribution Channel—Total, Summary

Channel	*Online visitors per month*	*On line distribution partners*	*Tourist agencies*
Galileo			44.000
Orbitz.com	15.2 millions		
CheapTickets.com	8.0 millions		
Lodging.com	2.6 millions	8.000	
HotelClub.com	4.0 millions	12.000	12.000
RatesToGo.com	1.6 millions	12.000	12.000
ebookers.com	3.6 millions	7.500	
Travel2Travel4			6.000
THOR			3.400

Source: Cendant, March 2005.

Online visitors
Offline visitors

That is why the worlds leading hotel brand names like Starwood, World hotels, Accor, Four Seasons, Marriot and Mandarin Oriental are using TDS internet service, and worldwide independent hotels are joining Cendant whose online portfolio is growing and it widens its goals and area of performance against competition.

Graphic No. 1: Tourist Arrangements Sales in America

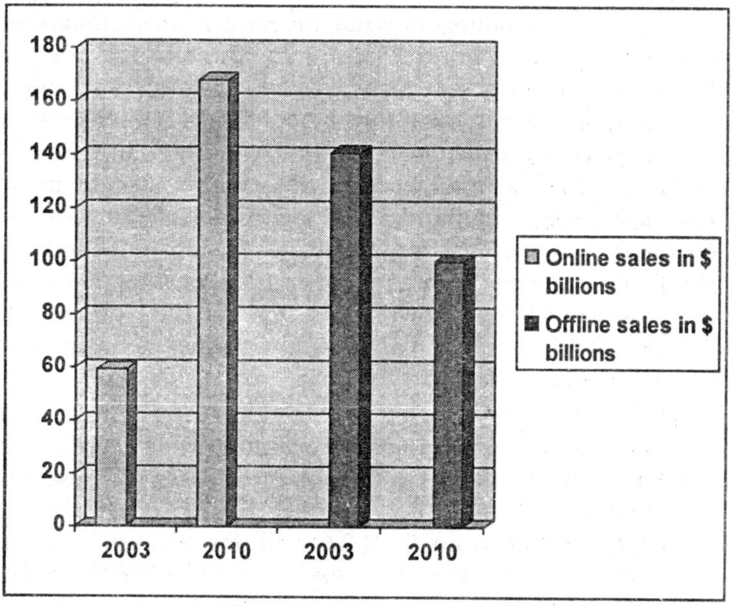

Source: PhoCusWrigt and Cendant estimations

Hotel managers are using Cendant as a distribution channel because of its financial power, controlled price, capital creation potential and amazing ROI. Managers are forming their price, service and their possibilities on the same way they do on their internet pages.

The distribution enables them to completely follow the online strategy. Every month, PDS helps the managers to fill in their hotel rooms, reaching the number of 35 millions visitors on their web sites through their online distribution channel. The loyalty that doesn't ends, combined with the innovation ensures constant growth. Doesn't matter what are the distribution needs, PDS has a product that will be helpful to every business to improve itself. One size doesn't fit all the hotels. Every hotel's manager has its own needs, but every manager wants and asks for results.

With more than 15 millions visits Orbits can be, by size, ranked as third online tourist web site (based on the total number of tourist reservations). The distribution growth of 40% or more on yearly level is a direct result of giving the clients and the managers what they want most: maximum choice, maximum control and maximum usage comfort. Ranked by size as forth and fastest growing web site is CheapTickets.com in USA, it has more than 8 millions visitors per month. The direct contact with the hotel supplier, i.e. with the desired hotel and the reservation system means that the hotels' managers can aggressively do a guests evidence in the last moments. Working with on-line distribution there is not more work with allocation. The issues here are to put the right offer in-front of the right person. The portfolio of online distribution channels is designed to help the managers to do that.

The availability of that what Lodging.com is doing as one of the leading distributors of hotel suppliers? This dynamic distribution channel makes the hotels available by presenting them on the Internet distributing it their product through own web site to more then 2.6 millions visitors and plus 8.000 associated Internet partners. Around 14.000 businesses have chosen Lodging.com because of its large presence on the international as well on the USA market.

Graphic No. 2: Hotel Arrangements in America in the Period of 2002-2006

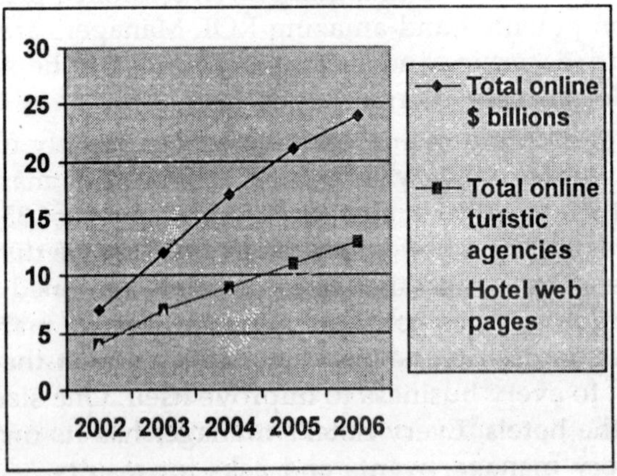

Source: PhoCusWright Inc.

Table No. 2: Cendant Channels—World Markets

Channel	*North America*	*South America*	*Middle East*	*Australia*	*China*	*India*	*Japan*	*New Zealand*	*South Korea*
Galileo *	X	•	•	X	•	X	•	X	•
Orbitz.com	X								
CheapTickets.com	X								
Lodging.com	X								
HotelClub.com	X	•	X	X	•	X	•	X	•
RatesToGo.com	X	•	X	X	•	X	•	X	•
THOR	X		X						

Source: Cendant Inc, March 2005.

X - Presented on the English language market

• - Presented on the local language market

* - Galileo available worldwide in 115 countries

Online Sales
Offline Sales

Online expansion in Europe and Asia

ProCusWright plans to have a growth of 46% or more on the European online tourist market. Till the end of 2006 the European online tourist market will be two times bigger than it was in the last year. The Chinese billion populations are starting to make bum on the home market as well on the foreign tourist market. HotelClub.com and RatesTOGO.com provides two different models that make the world their market. HotelClub.com makes the hotels available to potential tourists 365 days in the year, while RatesTOGo.com distributes in the last minute the arrangements. These two distribution channels connect them with more than 5.6 potential clients during one month through all over the world. The managers know the importance of developing their service distribution and they also know that is too expensive to concord the world market alone. Because of that Cendant helps 14.000 hotels by satisfying their needs and odds on the world market or through complete menu of services or through partnership.

Chart No. 3:
Sales of Turistic Packages in Asia

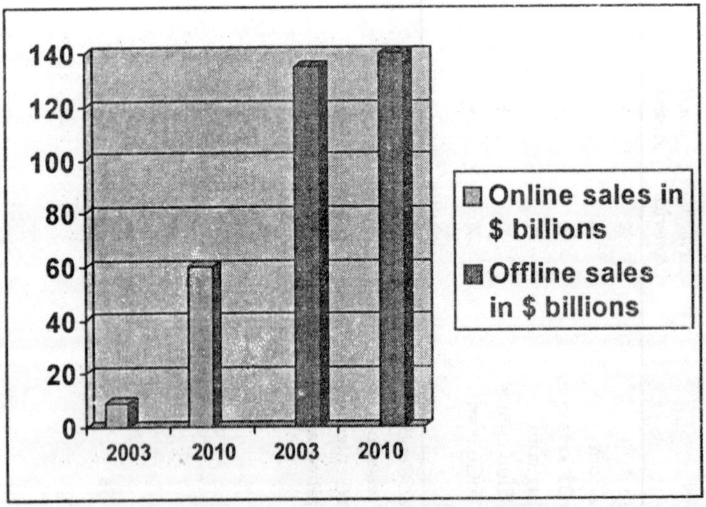

Source: PhoCusWrigt according the estimations of Cendant

With presence in 14 states, ebookers is one of the granules in the pan European online tourist service, according to PhoCusWright, Also it is one of the most effective web pages: for example the group ebookers holds 25% of the market between the clients from Great Britain to Australia. The special way of paying, large dividends for 1500 hotels in form of highly valuable business for which in average every single reservation is in value of 900 dollars compared with the typical reservation of 290 dollars for short distances and in-state traveling reservation through the Internet.

Picture No. 1:
European Online Tourist Market

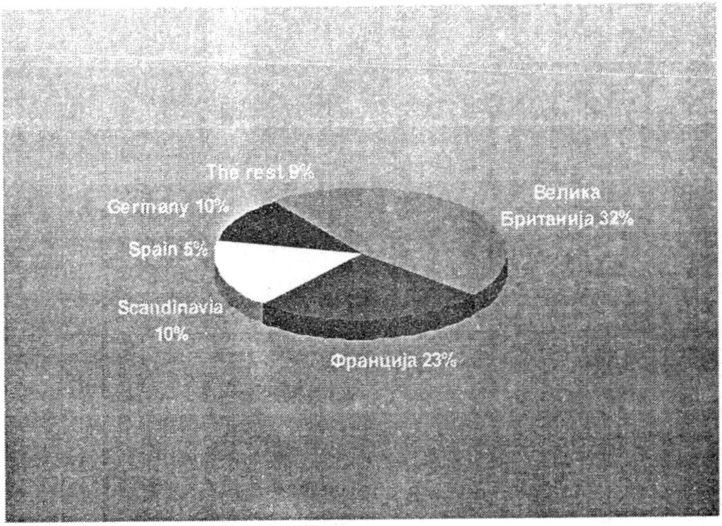

Source: PhoCus Wright Inc.

Global Distribution through Tourist Agencies

While online distribution is moving forward with full speed, the tourist operators make reservations for more hotels and arrangements to cover the losses from airplane tickets. The tourist agencies not only that they have largest number of confirmed reservations, but they, generally looked, bring the largest number of clients. As the hotels' managers enlarge their online presence, they also need to ensure that that for

Table no. 3: Cendant channels – European markets

	Austria	*Belgium*	*Denmark*	*Finland*	*France*	*Germany*	*Ireland*	*Italy*	*Netherlands*	*Ireland*	*Portugal*	*Russia*	*Spain*	*Sweden*	*Switzerland*	*Great Britain*
Galileo	X	•	X	X	•	•	X	•	X	•	•	•	•	X	•	X
CheapTickets.com		X														
HotelClub.com	X	•	X	X	•	•	X	•	X	X	X	X	•	X	X	X
RatesToGo.com	X	•	X	X	•	•	X	•	X	•	•	X	•	X	X	X
ebookers.com	•	•	•	•	•	•	X	•	•	•		X				
Travel2Travel4			X													

Source: Cendant Inc, March 2005

X - Presented on the English language market.

• - Presented on the local language market.

• - Galileo available worldwide in 115 countries.

Online Sales
Offline Sales

them is additional, and not replacement for the tourist agencies, their main tourist channel".

Through Galileo (Galileo is company of Cendant), Cendant has maximized the globalization of the hotels by enabling reservations and marketing opportunities to 195.000 tourist agents in 44.000 tourist agencies located all over the world, that brings 254 millions of reservations in one year. By adapting its self to the growth of online traveling, "Galileo" has the leading role in the distribution process of traveling with key innovative things like the systems:

- Galileo agents' network—it enables the tourist agents to sell the dynamically prepared travel arrangements.
- Galileo internet! Hotels (Only USA) and Galileo Hotel Club securing pre-paid model program for the Galileo agents.
- The best possible pricing program—over 100 groups of hotels at this moment provide the best possible guaranteed offer to Galileo agents that their web sites offer to the clients.

THOR is involved in one of the leading companies specialized for providing services to tourist agents. This popular program secures hotels with advertising possibilities for increasing the sales and strong known brand, while the agencies that provide easy access have the possibility for making the reservations in all three systems. THOR is also providing adequate marketing program for large specter of hotel partners. Their program "Best possible prices" provides to the hotels a flexible daily prices, and the program "Bloc Space" to the agencies with assigned values provides it to get hotel room for VIP clients prior to others or in situation when in the hotel there is no place.

Conclusion

In contemporary conditions, with the development of the computer technology, grows and the importance of the Internet as a medium for exchange of information, goods and services. The big destinations are bypassed by using the virtual space, in which the information becomes one of the main tools for success. The promotion and the distribution of those information, in the conditions of the digital economy, basically it is distribution of goods and services. Of course that and from the aspect of the tourism, the development of the Internet communications gets its importance. In more simple way the potential buyers of the tourist service get that information that they need to choose that what is of their interest. In that direction and the marketing opportunities are changing for more efficient and successful marketing tourist services on the global market.

REFERENCES

1. Quick answers to Web Marketing Questions from Alison Asbury and Sean McManus
2. The Internet: Amazon.com; Buy.com; E-bay.com,
3. www.cendant.com
4. www.orbitz.com
5. www.ebookers.com
6. www.travelbag.com
7. www.lodging.com
8. www.hotelclub.com
9. www.trevael2.com
10. www.galileo.com
11. www.travelbag.co.uk
12. www.consumerpsychologist.com/distribution.htm

7

Community Based Tourism: Bringing Marketing Closer to the Society

*Babu P. George**

The present paper attempts to weave together the theory and practice of community based tourism. Though the idea of community based development is age-old, its adoption into tourism is relatively recent. The paper examines how community based tourism can be a panacea for many of the evils of the mainstream industry driven mass-tourism. It exhorts that, while community is at the centre stage, there are important roles for governments and non-governmental organizations in community-based tourism. The role of public-private partnership is also examined.

Introduction: Community Based Development and Community Based Tourism

Community-based development is a strategy used by tourism planners to mobilize communities into action to participate in broadening the scope of offerings in the industry. The goal is socio-economic empowerment and a value-added experience for local and foreign visitors. This process opens new niches for destinations, most notably for the nature,

* University of Southern Mississippi.

culture, and adventure travelers. What this achieves is a policy objective of creating a culture of inclusion in the industry, whereby communities participate and share in the wealth of the industry, dispelling a long held perception of tourism as an exploiter of wealth where only the rich can benefit.

Community-based development empowers people to be more aware of the value of their community assets—their culture, heritage, cuisine and lifestyle. It mobilizes them to convert these into income generating projects while offering a more diverse and worthwhile experience to visitors. Every citizen is a potential business partner to be trained in small business management, environmental awareness, product development and marketing. This type of 'people-centered' tourism promotes a sense of 'ownership' which augurs well for the industry's sustainability.

Continuing with the above line of thinking, community based tourism (CBT) is may be defined as tourism that takes environmental, social and cultural sustainability into account. It is managed and owned by the community, for the community, with the purpose of enabling visitors to increase their awareness and learn about community and local ways of life. Existing terms like heritage tourism, eco-tourism, agri-tourism, cultural tourism, etc can all be forms of the community tourism product, within the constraint that these are to be promoted with the spirit of community centeredness and sustenance.

The key benefits of CBT are seen to be: job creation; poverty reduction; less impact on an area's culture and environment than that exerted by mass tourism; community capacity building and pride; and revenue for maintaining or upgrading the community's cultural assets. The relationship between resources and actions in CBT is illustrated below:

The key rationale underlying the approach and objectives of CBT for conservation and development is that CBT through increased intensities of participation can provide widespread economic and other benefits and decision-making power to communities. These economic benefits act as incentives for participants and the means to conserve the natural and cultural

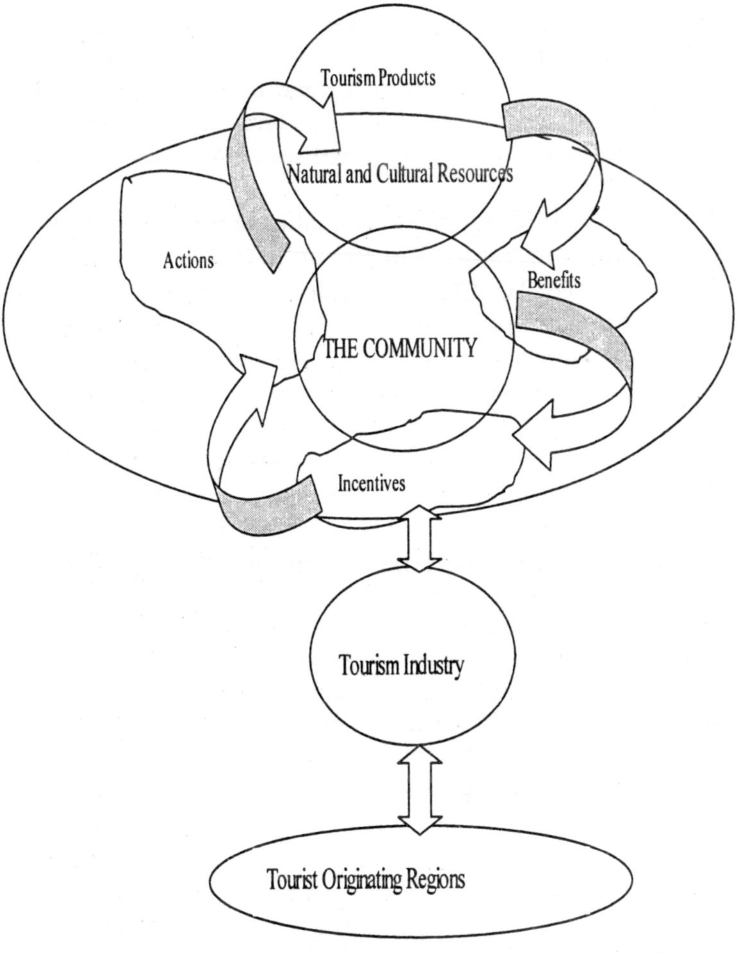

resources on which income generation depends. Note from the diagram that the community is at the centre and is occupying the commanding position with regard to the management of its natural and cultural resources which can be reformulated as tourism products. The relationship of the industry to the tourism products developed out of the natural and cultural resources of the community is not a direct, one-to-one relationship; on the contrary, it is through the intermediation of the community. This is aimed to ensure that the aspirations of the community are never bypassed by the extraneous industry interests. One can see CBT as an interaction among the three major groupings of the community, the tourism industry, and the tourists themselves. In the language of cost-benefit analysis (CBA), community based tourism may be expressed in terms of the following inequalities:

i. CB>IB>IC>CC (The inequality of interaction between the community and the industry)
ii. CB>TB>TC>CC (The inequality of interaction between the community and the tourists)
iii. IB>TB>TC>IC (The inequality of interaction between the industry and the tourists)

(CB=Community Benefits; CC=Community Costs; IB=Industrial Benefits; IC=Industrial Costs; TB=Tourist Benefits; and TC=Tourist Costs)

Note that the maximum benefit with the least cost goes to the community. This is the essential condition for CBT and the other conditions are not as consequential as this. The third condition may even be contested; however, we feel this is desirable since only if the industry benefit is significant than the industry cost shall it survive and not move on to unsustainable practices; tourists shall visit a CBT destination as long as tourist benefit is more than tourist cost.

Defining Characteristics of a Community Based Tourism Project

Community-based Tourism can and should encompass a range of activities that collectively contribute to improved conservation and development. Some of the most noteworthy characteristics of community based tourism projects are listed below (adapted from TPDCO, 2005):

- A community-based tourism project is a profitable and sustainable activity that enhances the environment while adding value to the experience of both locals and visitors.
- It directly involves the community—providing both social and economic benefits.

- Its ultimate goal is to satisfy consumer expectations without harming the community interests.
- It is market driven and has to meet high standards in order to be sustainable.
- Private entrepreneurs, community groups, and or organizations may own it. It should aim to educate, train develop, encourage, and utilize any skills and human potential within the community, towards the delivery of professional service.
- It should be operated within a business structure that adheres to government regulations, financial obligations, good labor relations and sound management systems.
- All Business Plans must be scrutinized to ensure owners/organizations understand the opportunities, pitfalls and risks and to show the long-term viability of the Project.
- Environmental awareness and sustainability should be top priority. It is the responsibility of the community to maintain clean healthy surroundings.
- Members of the community are expected to exhibit friendliness, honesty and professionalism amongst themselves as well as in their dealings with the visitor to ensure the integrity of the project.

Every community based tourism developer must ask the following questions from the very first stage of idea generation for the same:

- Will the project enhance environment while adding value to the visitor's experience?
- Will the project be developed, operated and protected by the community?
- Will the project provide social and economic benefits to the stakeholders/shareholders?
- Will the project be operated with sound ethical business practices including adherence to regulations and standards set by government, agencies, stakeholders, shareholders and consumers?
- Will the project offer professional services and value

to the visitor and be competitive in the global marketplace?

If not properly devised and implemented, CBT is highly likely to fail. The International Centre for Responsible Tourism (ICRT) at the University of Greenwich, UK, is evaluating CBT projects around the world and reviewing literature on CBT. Preliminary findings from this research suggest several reasons why CBT projects fail:

- Few projects understand the need for commercial activities: local people must sell crafts, food, accommodation and wildlife or cultural experiences to tourists. This is the only way to ensure a sustainable supply of local income or conservation funds.
- CBT projects must engage with the private sector, including travel agents, tour operators and hoteliers. The earlier this engagement takes place and the closer the partnership, the more likely it is to succeed.
- Location is critical: for poor people to benefit, tourists must stay in or near to these communities. Very few communities have tourism assets which are sufficiently strong to attract tourists—they rely on selling complementary goods and services. Tourists need to be close by for this to happen.
- CBT projects do not always provide appropriate tourism facilities for generating income. For example, too many CBT initiatives rely on building lodges, which are capital intensive and need considerable maintenance, or walking trails from which it can be difficult to secure revenue.
- Protected areas increasingly rely on money from tourists to pay for conservation initiatives. Local communities often have to compete with conservation projects for revenues.

The ICRT summarizes the recipe for successful CBT as that providing:

- Collective benefits: for example providing funds for community assets such as grinding mills or school books.

- Individual benefits: paid employment (full - or part-time) and opportunities for micro-enterprise earnings (for example craft sales).

The Blueprint for Developing Community Based Tourism in a Destination

In order that CBT be developed in a systematic manner, a methodological framework needs to be adopted. An outline of a suggested framework is provided below (Source: Tuffin, 2005):

1. Choose a destination.
2. Complete a feasibility study with the community.
3. Create an action plan.
4. Set up an administrative system.
5. Prepare for operation.
6. Monitor and evaluate.

Step 1: Choose a Destination

Choosing an appropriate destination requires collecting information that leads to an understanding of the community. A detailed study of the village context includes collecting information about the community from organizations working there, government agencies, other communities in the area, and the community members themselves.

Step 2: Complete a Feasibility Study

The community needs to be fully involved in the process of deciding if they want to be involved in a tourism project. The process for building consensus in the community requires that the information and data be studied with the public and private partners and then an action plan be formulated. It is important to be open and honest about the limitations of the community when deciding whether to continue or not. The decision to develop CBT must be agreed upon by all parties. During this process the community will be stimulated to think about the reasons and motivations for developing CBT. They should be able to discuss the issues and visit communities which are already involved in CBT. The community members need to answer questions like:

Do you want CBT to raise income?

Do you want CBT to preserve culture?

Do you want CBT to conserve natural resources?

Do you want CBT to bring more knowledge and skills into the community?

Step 3: Create an Action Plan

If all parties reach a consensus, the planning process can begin. In this stage the community creates an action plan and enters into agreement with external agencies like tour operators. Some of the key issues that need to be considered include: Programs for the tourists; Services that will need to be provided; Development of facilities and infrastructure; Training that will need to be provided; Carrying capacity; and, Tour program and price.

The public partner (association of the community members) will need to formulate a monitoring and evaluation plan that includes the associated indicators and the private partner can begin to draft a marketing plan and strategy.

Step 4: Set up an Administrative System

Without transparent organization, confusion, suspicion, and conflict can arise in the community. It is crucial that the community sets up a clear administrative system to effectively manage CBT.

The administrative organization will focus on the following: Participation level of community members; Division of roles in operation; Division of benefits; Transparency of management; Measures to control economic and social impacts; Measures to control natural and cultural impacts; and, Cooperation and communication with public and private partners.

Step 5: Preparation of Operation

Before full operation of the tour program can start the community and its partners need to acquire skills and experience in operating CBT. The infrastructure must all be designed and built and the equipment acquired and put in place. At this stage emphasis will be placed on:

Training: including guiding skills, language learning, food preparation, housekeeping and simple accounting systems

Preparation of information: involving the educational content of the tour program; the things about themselves that the community members will share with tourists

Infrastructure design and construction: community lodges, trails, water systems, power systems, toilets, etc.

The community members will need to gain experience in guiding and operating the tour program and distributing benefits. It will be necessary to bring pilot groups of tourists into the community so that the community members can see what works and what does not and so that they can practice their skills and test the administrative systems.

Step 6: Monitoring and Evaluation

Monitoring and evaluation starts once the program is in full operation. It helps to identify problems, impacts and benefits, as well as to ensure the sustainability of the operation. It examines the extent to which the project is meeting its objectives. It should also result in plans and efforts to compensate for weaknesses, correct problems, adjust systems and improve the program. Monitoring and evaluation is a participatory process. All stakeholders should play a role in gathering the monitoring data, assisting in the analysis, and in actions taken as a result of the final assessment and evaluation.

The aspects monitored include: Environmental impacts; Economic impacts; Cultural impacts; Social impacts; Efficacy of CBT as a development tool; etc.

Information can be gathered from the tourists, the community members and from physical inspections of infrastructure and the environment. Tools used for monitoring can include questionnaires, interviews, focus groups, guest books, photographs, checklists, trend lines, seasonal calendars, and so on.

Often in CBT the locations are remote and subject to national policies regulating access by foreigners as well as domestic visitors. Thus while initial assessments show considerable potential as tourism destinations, there may be regulations that restrict access by numbers and by seasons. International policies and actions have complex linkages with the visitor to a protected area and the local entrepreneur. Political instability can also affect the volume of visitors.

The Koroyanito CBT Development in Fiji: A Case Study

(Summarized and published by The Mountain Institute, 2000, from the Proceedings of the Ecotourism for Forest Conservation and Community Development Conference, 1997).

This example from Fiji has been chosen to highlight the linkages between conservation, economic development and participation in Community-based Tourism products. A key feature in this case was the nature of participation where there appeared to be considerable power held by local communities in the development and management of the tourism product.

As part of the management strategy for Koroyanitu National Park in Fiji the following activities and organizations were established.

Village Ecotourism Co-op Society Limited: Each village with an ecotourism facility established their own Ecotourism Cooperative Society Limited, with the main objective to "establish and manage projects in such a manner, which maximizes benefits to the community and ensures equal opportunities for all". Membership is restricted to landowning units on the basis of the amount of their land included in the project area and villagers who earn their share through direct involvement and/or capital contribution. The first criterion provides an incentive for landowning units to dedicate as much of their land as possible and discourage poor practices, which may disqualify a parcel of land. The second provides for allocation of equity, distribution of benefits, commensurate with one's contribution to the project. The feature to note here is who owns the land that is to be conserved and serves as an attraction. With local ownership, the economic incentives to conserve are much stronger since local people who derive economic benefits also make the decisions on land management.

Koroyanito Development Trust (KDP): All landowning villages agreed to establish the KDP and the objectives were to:

- o ensure the protection and integrity of the natural and cultural heritage within the national park
- o facilitate efficient and controlled flow of visitors to facilities
- o award contracts and approve participation
- o and, hold shares in Fijian Vanua Tours Inc.

An institutional arrangement was established to manage conservation and development activities associated with the site.

Fijian Vanua Tours Inc. (FVTI): The objectives of this entity are to:

- o promote participation in the protection of their natural and cultural heritage
- o secure funding for the establishment of ecotourism facilities and other activities which lend to sustainable development
- o conduct relevant training and development programs for owners
- o provide management and technical assistance to Village Tourism Cooperatives
- o and, hold shares in Fijian Vanua Tours Limited on behalf of accredited facility owners Fijian Vanua Tours Limited

This entity is a limited liability company designed to:

- o promote Koroyanitu as a desirable ecotourism destination
- o facilitate efficient and controlled flow of visitors to FTVI facilities
- o set and enforce standards
- o approve accreditation
- o generate income

Participation is restricted to two parties - 50% for FVTI and 50% for a private investor who can inject expertise and capital to ensure survival in the tourism industry. Both of the above entities serve to increase participation in tourism and related activities from deriving economic returns to quality control to market and product development.

Noted achievements of the scheme are:

Education: participation in business management and tour guiding courses

Women's participation: active club that makes and sells handicrafts

Environmental protection: logging has not been reintroduced; area set aside for tree nursery; enrichment planting in previously logged areas; etc.

Income: project earned in 1994 the equivalent of the entire communities yearly income before the project, two thirds was retained in the village

Capital additions and improvements: in 1994 another accommodation facility designed especially for school groups who want to camp in the park during field trips. Education groups have regularly used this facility.

The Role of Non-Governmental Organizations in Community Based Tourism

Nongovernmental organizations, or NGOs, are generally accepted to be organizations which have not been established by governments or agreements among governments. In the early 1990s there began to be recognition of the importance of NGOs. They are found to have closer ties to on-the-ground realities in developing countries and, perhaps more important, to be able to deliver development aid considerably more cheaply than states or intergovernmental organizations.

Aided by advances in information and communications technology, NGOs have helped to focus attention on the social and environmental externalities of business activity. Multinational brands have been acutely susceptible to pressure from activists and from NGOs eager to challenge a company's labor, environmental or human rights record. Even those businesses that do not specialize in highly visible branded goods are feeling the pressure, as campaigners develop techniques to target downstream customers and shareholders.

In response to such pressures, many businesses are abandoning their narrow shareholder theory of value in favor of a broader, stakeholder approach which not only seeks increased share value, but cares about how this increased value is to be attained. Such a stakeholder approach takes into account the effects of business activity—not just on shareholders, but on customers, employees, communities and other interested groups.

There are many visible manifestations of this shift. One has been the devotion of energy and resources by companies to environmental and social affairs. Companies are taking responsibility for their externalities and reporting on the impact of their activities on a range of stakeholders. Nor are companies merely reporting; many are striving to design new management structures which integrate sustainable development concerns into the decision-making process.

NGOs have been involved with tourism related issues for a long time. Current international activities in community tourism planning and development reflect a strong interest and involvement by NGOs, particularly those focused on resource conservation. Traditionally, they have been critical. They have campaigned against contentious issues, such as tourism links to child prostitution and the forced relocation of peoples for new developments. NGOs have frequently been concerned with tourism related environmental issues, opposing, for example, the establishment of golf courses in developing world locations that have exploited land and water previously available to local communities. NGOs have also focused their attention on the flow of income from tourism, particularly in the developing world, examining how this has been generated and how equitable its distribution is. Most NGOs commenting on tourism have had their major interests elsewhere.

However, NGOs can play an important constructive role in the development of management strategies and in the planning process of tourism development for various reasons. Tourism is becoming far too commoditized, and NGO involvement offers alternative ways of viewing the tourism experience. NGOs have prioritized development approaches that include host community perspectives, emphasized host–

visitor interaction and stressed nature and cultural conservation. A number of NGOs have been actively involved in tourism related projects. The motives of NGOs in these circumstances appear to have been to boldly go where government or private commercial organizations would find political or economic resistance. Being nongovernmental institutions they can establish and facilitate the participation of local stakeholders. Being non-profit organizations, they can promote the sustainable use of biodiversity and cultural resources and point out the economic benefits of the integration of tourism development and nature/culture conservation. Being experts in ecological sciences, social development and project management, and having a deep insight into the regional political and economic structures, NGOs can contribute significantly to the sustainability of community based tourism development. NGOs can sensitize the public and even organize mass movements if avaricious industrial interests placate the wider goals of community centered tourism development. Thus, they can act as brokers between conflicting groups and some of them have the potential to act in a conflict management capacity.

Another role that NGOs can take over is that of a co-operative agency that manages a community's initiatives towards CBT. Where international tour operators are unable to contract ground services to in-country operations or do not employ residents of that country, the amount retained in the destination is obviously lower than if this was not the case. Some NGOs appear to have special skills in collaborative partnerships based upon shared aims with local communities, the private sector and other NGOs. The NGO can become a unified marketing front for the small and medium scale tourism enterprises run by the community members. With the help of e-commerce technologies, such a body can bypass the middlemen like travel agents and tour operators and reach the tourist originating markets directly. With tour operators invariably demanding payment in the visitor's country of origin, the benefits to national economies can vary considerably. This has the potential to make the community's tourism offerings more cost-competitive, too. In these situations the development work of NGOs can be directly supported by tourism income flows, active tourist participation in projects, or through direct and indirect donations to their work.

Thus, NGOs are shown often to be both campaigning and proactive bodies, capable of operating in a wide variety of natural, economic and political environments. In sum, NGOs in community based tourism does one or more of the following things:

1. Contribute to the development of policies and plans for the CBT industry
2. Assist the government in developing a standard for responsible community based tourism
3. Assist the government, private sector and communities in implementing, monitoring and evaluating CBT
4. Attract funding from donor agencies to develop specific CBT projects
5. Assist communities and community groups in organizing themselves, preparing themselves for CBT and implementing CBT projects
6. Assist the government in conducting tourism and environmental awareness programs among communities and the tourism industry at large
7. Liaise between the private sector and communities to generate more community involvement in the tourism sector and stronger private sector commitment
8. Deliver education, training, bridging courses, and other capacity building exercises to local communities
9. Resist against inequitable tourism development by campaigning and mobilizing community support
10. Manage and market the community tourism product for the community, at least until the community gains experience to manage on its own.

Some of NGOs that do outstanding work in the area of tourism are:

- Tourism Concern (www.tourismconcern.org.uk)
- Equations in India (www.equitabletourism.org)
- Ecumenical Coalition on Third World Tourism (www.ecotonline.org)

- World Wide Fund for Nature (www.wwf.org)
- Conservation International (www.conservation.org)
- Rainforest Alliance (www.rain-forest-alliance.org)
- Cultural Restoration Tourism Project (http://home.earthlink.net/~crtp)
- International Council on Monuments and Sites (www.icomos.org)
- International Society for Eco-tourism Management (www.ecomanage.com)
- Partners in Responsible Tourism (www2.pirt.org)
- Retour Foundation (www.retour.net)

Governments and Community Based Tourism

Community Based Tourism can not be implemented successfully without the constant and coordinated facilitation by the various governmental bodies. Governments play a critical role through their institutional leadership, guaranteeing stakeholders' participation. The Governments' role is also essential in the establishment of regulatory and policy frameworks, ensuring their enforcement, the application of appropriate economic instruments (including the removal of environmentally perverse subsidies), and monitoring environmental quality. What communities do in tourism depends on the opportunities and power they have, the incentives and prices they face, and their access to skills, training, capital and markets. All of these are shaped by government policies, regulation and taxes. Only governments can provide the strategic planning base for CBT which is so clearly needed. Only they can ensure that valuable and fragile habitats are identified, that baseline studies and monitoring are carried out, and that overall infrastructure needs and implications are assessed. And only they can establish emissions standards and citing and design requirements, and ensure that they are enforced.

Governments need to make resources such as national tourist boards accessible to CBT operations, while ensuring that systems of licensing or tourism standards do not act as barriers. Government, especially, the local government, provides the core utilities and infrastructure on which the tourism industry is based. This includes district and city roads, lighting, water and sewerage, public transport systems, signs, airports, and ports. If local government operates attractions such as museums, art galleries, sports stadiums, convention centers, parks, gardens, events, tours, and other amenities, the same become additional motivators for tourists to visit a CBT destination. The government can integrate travel information about the CBT destinations in the country into its Visitor Information Network, too.

Private companies can't be expected to share profits and power with rural communities simply because it's a kind thing to do. But governments can create the conditions under which it is in their interests to work with communities by giving communities market power and giving the private sector more security of investment and incentives for partnership. This can be by means of:

- asking private sector bidders to develop proposals for community partnership, and making this a key criteria in allocating tourism rights. This small change to the planning process can force every new investment to address community tourism issues.
- devolving tenure to communities, to give them market power in forming agreements
- giving communities an equity share in government-private agreements
- helping local residents to start private enterprises.

Policies vary from country to country and over time. It is often the overall approach that is most important in helping community tourism to flourish. Some tips that are suggested from governments in CBT by Africa Resources Trust (ART, 2005) are:

- Create supportive attitudes in government
- Let communities develop tourism over time
- Create opportunities and remove constraints, rather than plan community tourism for them
- Recognize that local people will have multiple livelihood objectives, not just maximizing cash income. Concerns about how land or natural resources are

used, or access to training, can be equally important to livelihoods

- Enhance their power in the tourism market
- Ensure tourism sector regulations encourage rather than exclude the informal sector
- Welcome NGO facilitation—it's usually needed.

There are two extremes to be avoided: one is to ignore community tourism or pretend it will happen with no support from Government and the industry. The other is for government and the industry to try to do everything and do it now, without allowing time for local people to develop their ideas and skills.

Harnessing Public-Private Partnership for Community Based Tourism

Public-private partnership (PPP or P3) is a variation of privatization in which elements of a service previously run solely by the public sector are provided through a partnership between the government and one or more private sector companies. Unlike a full privatization scheme, in which the new venture is expected to function like any other private business, the government continues to participate in some way.

Important variants of public-private partnerships are (*Source:* National Council for Public Private Partnerships, USA): Build/Operate/Transfer (BOT) or Build/Transfer/Operate (BTO); Build-Own-Operate (BOO); Buy-Build-Operate (BBO); Service Contracts (SC); Design-Build (DB); Design-Build-Maintain (DBM); Design-Build-Operate (DBO); Developer Finance: Enhanced Use Leasing (EUL); Lease/Develop/Operate (LDO) or Build/Develop/Operate (BDO); Lease/Purchase; Sale/Leaseback; Tax-Exempt Lease; and Turnkey Arrangement.

Build/Operate/Transfer (BOT) or Build/Transfer/Operate (BTO): The private partner builds a facility to the specifications agreed to by the public agency, operates the facility for a specified time period under a contract or franchise agreement with the agency, and then transfers the facility to the agency at the end of the specified period of time. In most cases, the private partner will also provide some, or all, of the financing for the facility, so the length of the contract or franchise must be sufficient to enable the private partner to realize a reasonable return on its investment through user charges.

At the end of the franchise period, the public partner can assume operating responsibility for the facility, contract the operations to the original franchise holder, or award a new contract or franchise to a new private partner. The BTO model is similar to the BOT model except that the transfer to the public owner takes place at the time that construction is completed, rather than at the end of the franchise period.

Build-Own-Operate (BOO): The contractor constructs and operates a facility without transferring ownership to the public sector. Legal title to the facility remains in the private sector, and there is no obligation for the public sector to purchase the facility or take title. A BOO transaction may qualify for tax-exempt status as a service contract if all Internal Revenue Code requirements are satisfied.

Buy-Build-Operate (BBO): A BBO is a form of asset sale that includes a rehabilitation or expansion of an existing facility. The government sells the asset to the private sector entity, which then makes the improvements necessary to operate the facility in a profitable manner.

Service Contracts: A public partner (federal, state, or local government agency or authority) contracts with a private partner to provide and/or maintain a specific service. Under the private operation and maintenance option, the public partner retains ownership and overall management of the public facility or system. Another way is public partner (federal, state, or local government agency or authority) contracts with a private partner to operate, maintain, and manage a facility or system proving a service. Under this contract option, the public partner retains ownership of the public facility or system, but the private party may invest its own capital in the facility or system. Any private investment is carefully calculated in relation to its contributions to operational efficiencies and savings over the term of the contract. Generally, the longer the contract term, the greater the opportunity for increased private investment because there is more time available in which to recoup any investment and earn a reasonable return. Many local governments use this contractual partnership to provide wastewater treatment services.

Design-Build (DB): A DB is when the private partner provides both design and construction of a project to the public agency. This type of partnership can reduce time, save money, provide stronger guarantees and allocate additional project risk to the private sector. It also reduces conflict by having a single entity responsible to the public owner for the design and construction. The public sector partner owns the assets and has the responsibility for the operation and maintenance.

Design-Build-Maintain (DBM): A DBM is similar to a DB except the maintenance of the facility for some period of time becomes the responsibility of the private sector partner. The benefits are similar to the DB with maintenance risk being allocated to the private sector partner and the guarantee expanded to include maintenance. The public sector partner owns and operates the assets.

Design-Build-Operate (DBO): A single contract is awarded for the design, construction, and operation of a capital improvement. Title to the facility remains with the public sector unless the project is a design/build/operate/transfer or design/build/own/operate project. The DBO method of contracting is contrary to the separated and sequential approach ordinarily used in the United States by both the public and private sectors. This method involves one contract for design with an architect or engineer, followed by a different contract with a builder for project construction, followed by the owner's taking over the project and operating it.

A simple design-build approach creates a single point of responsibility for design and construction and can speed project completion by facilitating the overlap of the design and construction phases of the project. On a public project, the operations phase is normally handled by the public sector under a separate operations and maintenance agreement. Combining all three passes into a DBO approach maintains the continuity of private sector involvement and can facilitate private-sector financing of public projects supported by user fees generated during the operations phase.

Developer Finance: The private party finances the construction or expansion of a public facility in exchange for the right to build residential housing, commercial stores, and/or industrial facilities at the site. The private developer contributes capital and may operate the facility under the oversight of the government. The developer gains the right to use the facility and may receive future income from user fees.

While developers may in rare cases build a facility, more typically they are charged a fee or required to purchase capacity in an existing facility. This payment is used to expand or upgrade the facility. Developer financing arrangements are often called capacity credits, impact fees, or extractions. Developer financing may be voluntary or involuntary depending on the specific local circumstances.

Enhanced Use Leasing (EUL): An EUL is an asset management program in the Department of Veterans Affairs (VA) that can include a variety of different leasing arrangements (e.g. lease/develop/operate, build/develop/operate). EULs enable the VA to long-term lease VA-controlled property to the private sector or other public entities for non-VA uses in return for receiving fair consideration (monetary or in-kind) that enhances VA's mission or programs

Lease/Develop/Operate (LDO) or Build/Develop/Operate (BDO): Under these partnerships arrangements, the private party leases or buys an existing facility from a public agency; invests its own capital to renovate, modernize, and/or expand the facility; and then operates it under a contract with the public agency. A number of different types of municipal transit facilities have been leased and developed under LDO and BDO arrangements.

Lease/Purchase: A lease/purchase is an installment-purchase contract. Under this model, the private sector finances and builds a new facility, which it then leases to a public agency. The public agency makes scheduled lease payments to the private party. The public agency accrues equity in the facility with each payment. At the end of the lease term, the public agency owns the facility or purchases it at the cost of any remaining unpaid balance in the lease.

Under this arrangement, the facility may be operated by either the public agency or the private developer during the term of the lease. Lease/purchase arrangements have been used by the General Services Administration for building federal office buildings and by a number of states to build prisons and other correctional facilities.

Sale/Leaseback: This is a financial arrangement in which the owner of a facility sells it to another entity, and subsequently leases it back from the new owner. Both public and private entities may enter into a sale/leaseback arrangement for a variety of reasons. An innovative application of the sale/leaseback technique is the sale of a public facility to a public or private holding company for the purposes of limiting governmental liability under certain statues. Under this arrangement, the government that sold the facility leases it back and continues to operate it.

Tax-Exempt Lease: A public partner finances capital assets or facilities by borrowing funds from a private investor or financial institution. The private partner generally acquires title to the asset, but then transfers it to the public partner either at the beginning or end of the lease term. The portion of the lease payment used to pay interest on the capital investment is tax exempt under state and federal laws. Tax-exempt leases have been used to finance a wide variety of capital assets, ranging from computers to telecommunication systems and municipal vehicle fleets.

Turnkey Arrangement: A public agency contracts with a private investor/vendor to design and build a complete facility in accordance with specified performance standards and criteria agreed to between the agency and the vendor. The private developer commits to build the facility for a fixed price and absorbs the construction risk of meeting that price commitment. Generally, in a turnkey transaction, the private partners use fast-track construction techniques (such as design-build) and are not bound by traditional public sector procurement regulations. This combination often enables the private partner to complete the facility in significantly less time and for less cost than could be accomplished under traditional construction techniques.

In a turnkey transaction, financing and ownership of the facility can rest with either the public or private partner. For example, the public agency might provide the financing, with the attendant costs and risks. Alternatively, the private party might provide the financing capital, generally in exchange for a long-term contract to operate the facility.

Further details about these variants are beyond the scope of this module. However, learners desirous of knowing the same are advised to consult the website of the National Council for Public Private Partnerships, USA (http://ncppp.org).

There are several basic characteristics of community-based tourism development that make public-private partnerships a possibility (UNESCAP, 2001). First, communities may not have the skills and experience in tourism management. Second, community tourism ventures take time to set up and require a process of intensive capacity building. Third, community tourism ventures may not be profitable when they are initiated.

Partnership is becoming a powerful tool for implementing CBT policies more effectively. PPPs enable the public sector to benefit from commercial dynamism, the ability to raise finances in an environment of budgetary restrictions, innovation and efficiencies, harnessed through the introduction of private sector investors who contribute their own capital, skills and experience. The positive characteristics of PPP arrangements for infrastructure development appear particularly attractive to developing countries like India given the enormous financing requirements, the equally large funding shortfall, the need for efficient public services, availability of a pool of private finance, growing market stability and privatization trends creating a favorable environment for private sector participation (Subramaniam, 2005).

Despite numerous advantages, certain negative aspects—a too large role for governments, partnerships lacking attention to market needs, disproportional investments, inefficiency of public administration, institutionalization of projects and lack of creativity—have to be taken into consideration before going in for any PPP based tourism development since these are antithetical to the spirit of CBT.

According to OECD (1997), good partnership involves a clear definition of roles, competencies, responsibilities and advantages both in public administrations and private enterprises. In particular, the public sector, as an agent of development, may help achieve optimal exploitation of public resources and services, safeguard the environment, and develop human resources. Partnerships must be based on agreements which show the economic benefits for the public/private sector and/or centre/periphery. More and more forms of partnerships are developed in almost all areas of tourism policy. Governments have to play an important role in new ways of organizing this co-operation, notably by defining a clear national strategy for tourism policy which will stimulate and guide innovative partnerships and give incentives to all individual partners to participate in the development.

The Akha Lodge: A Case Study of PPP in CBT

Akha (in Northern Laos) villagers—with their exotic outfits, ancient traditions and traditional way of life—don't usually sit down with urban businesspeople and hammer out business deals. But, that is the scenario set up by GTZ, a German development agency (www.gtz.de) and Exotissimo Travel (www.exotissimo.com). GTZ is working with Akha villagers to set up their own trekking tours in order to offer them an alternative means of income generation. And, Exotissimo has built a reputation as a leader in the travel service industry in South-East Asia. Dedicated offices are situated in Vietnam, Cambodia, Laos, Myanmar and Thailand. In total, we have 14 offices and more than 320 full-time staff.

This Public-Private Partnership coupled with Community-based Tourism (CBT) offers the opportunity for rural communities to access the potential of a global market while helping to minimize any negative impacts tourism development may bring. The model offers an opportunity for the tour company to invest in an authentic village based tour program without having to develop all the skills in community development approaches. The partnership between communities and tour operator is formalized through a contract, in which rights and responsibilities of both business partners are stated. The approach creates local ownership, jobs and sources of income, trains local personnel, and transfers business know-how and technology in a sustainable and participatory manner while at the same time adding an authentic experience to the tour operator's program.

Concluding Remarks

Raising awareness of all stakeholders involved in community-based tourism is essential for promoting an understanding of the beneficial link between conservation and community development. Awareness raising and information dissemination to the community allows for greater self-determination and informed decision-making. Awareness campaign is equally important to other stakeholders involved, as it leads to greater understanding and sensitivity toward the variables involved in implementing community-based tourism.

Conservationists and development professionals have tried to promote community-based tourism since the 1970s. The CBT was a popular intervention during the ecotourism boom of the 1990s. It is now being suggested as a form of pro-poor tourism. However, only a few projects have generated sufficient benefits to either provide incentives for conservation—the objective of ecotourism—or contribute to local poverty reduction.

Community-based tourism is a complex and nascent field of study, and much remains to be learned. Continued information sharing and dissemination of research results are needed to identify better solutions for linking sustainability to the tourism enterprise. Ongoing research is integral to understanding the means by which CBT can be made more economically, environmentally and culturally sustainable. Policy and action should promote continuing research through the provision of financial, academic, technical, and dissemination support.

REFERENCES

Africa Resources Trust (2005). Community Tourism in Southern Africa. Last accessed from www.resourceafrica.org on 26th August 2005.

Brandon, K. (1996). Ecotourism and Conservation: A Review of Key Issues. World Bank Environment Department. Paper No. 033. Washington. DC: World Bank.

Cooperrider. D.L. (1990). Positive Image. Positive Action: The Affirmative Basis for Organizing, in Srivastava. S., Cooperrider. D.L., and Associates, (eds) *Appreciative Management and Leadership*, San Francisco: Jossey-Bass.

Liburd, J.J. (2004). NGOs in Tourism and Preservation – Democratic accountability and Sustainability in question. *Tourism Recreation Research*, 29(2), 105-110.

OECD (1997). *OECD Conference on Partnerships in Tourism*. Conference organized by the OECD, the Italian Department of Tourism and the City of Rome on 27-Oct-1997.

Pretty, J. N., Gujit, I., Scoones, I., Thompson, J., (1995). A Trainer's Guide for Participatory Learning and Action. Sustainable Agriculture Programme. International Institute for Environment and Development, 3 Endsleigh Street. London WCIH ODD, UK.

Responsible Ecological Social Tours (2005). Last accessed from www.rest.org.th on 28th August 2006.

Subramaniam, P. (2005). Partnership in tourism. In India Revisited: A symposium on reorienting our policy on tourism. *Seminar*, October, 19-24.

The Mountain Institute (2000). *Community-Based Tourism for Conservation and Development: A Resource Kit*. Washington: The Mountain Institute.

TPDCO (2005). Tourism Product Development Company. What is a Community-Based Tourism Project? Last accessed from www.tpdco.org on 25th August 2006.

Tuffin, B. (2005). Community-Based Tourism in the Lao PDR: An Overview. Last accessed from www.nafri.org.la on 25th August 2006.

UNESCAP (2001). *ESCAP Tourism Review* No. 22: Managing Sustainable Tourism Development. Last accessed from www.unescap.org on 26th August 2006.

Whelan. T., (ed) (1991). *Nature Tourism: Managing for the Environment.* Washington, D.C.: Island Press.

Wells. M., Brandon. K., Hannah, L. (1992). *People and Parks: Linking Protected Area.*

Management with Local Communities. World Bank. WWF. USA1D. Washington D.C.

Worah, S., Svendsen, D., Ongleo, C. (1999). *Integrated Conservation and Development:*

A Trainer's Manual. WWF-UK, Godalming.

8

Comparative Tourism Marketing Case Studies

*Liljana Elmazi**

*Alexandru Nedelea**

CASE	*THEME*
1. The sleep Well Motel	Marketing for tourism and hospitality
2. The Excelsior Hotel	The role of marketing in strategic planning
3. The Australian Tourist Commission	Marketing information Systems and marketing research.Marketing destination
4. Gomez Executive Bus Service	Consumer markets and consumer buying behavior
5. Hawaiian Sights	Consumer markets and consumer buying behavior
6. New Zealand Heritage Park	Building customer loyalty and consumer satisfaction
7. World View Travel Agency, Inc.	Distribution channels
8. Burger King: Searching for the Right Message	Promoting products
9. McDonalds:	Advertising

* PhD, Tirana University, Albania.

** Stefan cel Mare University Suceava, Romania.

10. The Ritz-Carlton, Millenia Singapore	
11. International Travel Agency	Professional sales
12. USAIRways	Pricing
13. Superior hotel	Marketing plan

CASE: The Sleep Well Motel

In April 1980, Will Shelton was evaluating information received from the owner of a motel that was for sale in Fort Morgan, Colorado. Will had answered an ad in the Whit Street Journal under the heading "Business for Sale". To Will's surprise, he received a call directly from Hank Bennington, the owner of the Sleep Well Motel of Fort Morgan, Colorado.

During the conversation, Mr. Bennington described his motel and his reason for wanting to sell. He also described the many advantages of living in Colorado and promised to send Will more information on his company. The next day an overnight package of information arrived at Will's home from Mr. Bennington.

Background on Will Shelton

At 44 years of age, Will felt that he had climbed the corporate ladder about as high as he was likely to go. He also had doubts about remaining in a large corporation the rest of his working life. The present position held by Will was director of marketing research for a large electronics corporation located in Houston, Texas. Despite the title, Will felt his position was not satisfying.. "Marketing research in an industrial company just isn't very exciting or personally rewarding in fact, it's down right dull. This statement pretty well summarized Will's feelings toward his position.

Although Will had been trained as an engineer, he discovered that engineering, wasn't his primary interest and began to move into marketing. When the position of marketing research director opened in his company. Will applied and was elated when he learned he had received the position. In reviewing this move, Will stated that he believed the fact he had recently completed an MBA during part-time studies had helped him to obtain the position.

Will had recently gone through a divorce and his former wife had been awarded :a of the two boys Since the laws in Texas called for a division of hared property and child support, Will had suffered a financial setback hit was not faced with large ongoing payments to his former wife other than for child support. Despite his recent financial problems, Will felt he could raise sufficient money to purchase the motel with a bank mortgage.

In earlier years, Will had studied and worked in New Mexico. He had learned to ski and also enjoyed hunting and fishing in that state. Will felt the people n that part of the United States were somehow more genuine and that life 'a better in many ways than his present life in Houston, As a result, when be read about a motel for sale in Colorado, Will had an automatic interest.

Background on the Sleep Well Motel

A Will began to pull his thoughts together. he reviewed what he had already learned about the Sleep Well Motel. This information had been gained though telephone conversation with Mr. Bennington plus sales literature a brief historical sketch that had been included with data sent by Mr. Bennington.

The motel had 80 rooms and had been affiliated with a chain several years ago but was no longer associated with this company. The property was located off U.S. Highway 76, which carried traffic between Denver and Nebraska. He didn't have data concerning the profile characteristics of his customers but told Will that his customers were commercial travelers such as repair crews, independent sales reps, middle-aged retired couples, and young budget-minded travelers. The motel did not have an attached restaurant hut there was a cafe about two blocks away. There was also a Laundromat nearby that was frequently used by his guests. The property was IT years old and was described as clean and comfortable but in need of cosmetics and new carpeting. Mr. Bennington said he had a dependable night clerk hut served as the manager front-desk clerk himself during the day. I- said that dependable maid service was a problem for all the motels in the area and his was no exception.

Reason for Selling

In the telephone conversation, Mr. Bennington stated he had recently lost his wife in a tragic car accident. Since at time lie bad been unable to concentrate on the business and now w noted to return to his borne state of Illinois to be near his son's family. In addition, Mr. Bennington said he wanted to he perfectly candid, He said that after the car accident he failed to keep as close a watch on the business as he should have. Mr. Bennington admitted that he felt ill at ease in the field of marketing and felt the company would need strong direction in that area. He went on to say that Will should be a 'natural" to manage this type of business.

After skimming the material, Will became increasingly enthused about the possibility of owning and managing this motel. He knew there were many additional questions he would need to ask in his next phone conversation. At the moment, the most exciting part was the possibility of living in Colorado and being his own boss. Will knew he would have to develop a list of penetrating questions to ask Mr. Bennington and also knew he needed to study the financial sheets in detail. That could come later. For the moment, Will was picturing himself on the slopes of Colorado's beautiful mountains gracefully skimming down tile snow.

Discussion Questions

1. Discuss the pros and cons of Will Shelton owning and operating the Sleep Well Motel.
2. Do you believe that Will's marketing/marketing research backgrounds will he of great assistance to him in running this motel?
3. Why do you suppose Mr. Bennington said that Will s marketing background would be a real benefit?
4. What kinds of marketing sales tactics are best suited for a motel such as the Sleep Well Motel?

CASE: The Excelsior Hotel

A most significant competitive threat was about to affect the four-star Excelsior Hotel A new luxury hotel was under construction directly across the street The staff as concerned that there might not be enough business to support two upscale hotels in the same market.

Hotel history

The 30 Excelsior had operated in the cm for 10 years. During these years it had served as the only upscale hotel in the city. It had an excellent location downtown between a 600-space parking deck and the Convention Center. The hotel featured an indoor swimming pool, a Jacuzzi, two restaurants, a cocktail lounge, and several unique amenities. Many of the rooms had balconies o the garden level dining area and Greenhouse Café. Each floor was accessed by three glass-enclosed elevators. Other major attributes of the hotel were the ice skating rink located under the hotel and tunnel connecting the hotel with the Convention Center.

The Excelsior was managed by a management group hut was owned by the Concept Corp., a real estate and investment company. An interview with the general manager of the Excelsior revealed the following:

What are your goals for the hotel?

Locally, for the next year, we would just like to he competitive productwise. Our long-term goal is to he one of the leading hotels in our state."

How do you perceive the increasing competitive pressure?

It has been tremendous. The increase in hotel rooms over the last file years within our competitive market has been unbelievable. The Stouffer will open up on July 1, and a new Sheraton will open up later this year. Radissons are going up left and right. A lot of smaller hotel chains are putting up budget hotels. Right now I would say we are overbuilt until the city gets its convention center expanded so that we can attract larger groups. There is not enough corporate business to go around to supply all of us with a decent occupancy.

What actions does the Excelsior plan to take within the increasingly competitive environment?

To be competitive, you have to have the product. Once again that's our first step. We want to bring our over all product of service hack up to a competitive level, meaning that we have to renovate and make some other adjustments decor-wise- new rooms, new furniture, and some other things. Those are tangible things.

Describe the relationship between the management and the hotel owners?

We are a management company. We don't own a nickel here. Our ownership is another company. They ha e a little different philosophy on how to make money and to provide quality service to the guests. They don't have the same idea regarding bottom-line profits and quality rendered to the guests. Obviously, you have to realize the relation between profit and quality service to the guest. If you put in "turn-down" service, it is costing you money. If you give your employees benefits, it costs you money. Anything you do other than supplying them with one towel and a clean room costs you money. It means that the profit level between what we feel is obtainable provided that e give the guests great service and what a ownership thinks we should make as a hotel is different. They feel we should make a lot more money.'

The general manager was perplexed as to what direction the hotel should take. The building is in need of renovation to maintain its attractive ness and "image." There is pressure from the owners to offer less and make more, which is inconsistent with long-standing image. The biggest threat, though, is coming from the increased competition for the lucrative group business from newer hotels and convention centers. However, the cit was beginning to enter a "renaissance" period with the planned expansion of the Convention Center, the completion of the Super Block area, and a push for retail stores and businesses to relocate downtown.

Discussion Questions

1. Why should a conflict exist between the philosophies of the hotel Excelsior's management group and its owner, The Concept Corp?
2. What steps in addition to renovation should the Excelsior he taking to prepare for increased competition?

CASE: The Australian Tourist Commission

The Australian Tourist Commission (ATC) was planning a marketing research study within the United States. The plan had originated in the home office in Melbourne and was sent to regional offices for comment before soliciting bids. These regional offices were located in London, Frankfurt, New York, Los Angeles. Tokyo, and Auckland. Visitor traffic to Australia from the United States had grown at a slower rate than other major market areas. It was apparent that marketing strategies were needed to increase the number of American visitors to Australia. Before developing a new marketing plan, it was felt that a study should be conducted within the United States to identify target markets.

Research Objectives

Objectives had been identified for the study:

1. To identify and quantify groups in the U.S. population with the highest potential for holidaying in Australia.
2. To investigate in detail the factors that determine holiday destination choice among the high-potential groups.
3. To provide information indicating the types of holiday products taking into account time and cost factors, which would satisfy the holiday needs of the high-potential groups.
4. To investigate the awareness of and preferences for alternative destinations.

5. To provide information to guide publicity agencies as to the type of creative approaches that will appeal to and motivate the high-potential groups.
6. To provide a guide to media patterns that will enable efficient communication to the high-potential groups.
7. To identify the best distribution modes for holiday products aimed at the high-potential groups (e.g.. airlines, travel agents, bank travel departments).
8. To in the role of the travel trade and its importance in determining holiday destination choice.
9. To determine past and intended future holiday behavior among the high-potential groups and to describe them in socioeconomic terms. Detailed information must he collected on the destinations visited on past trips and the sequence of these visits.

In addition to the objectives, the ATC felt that the study should be de signed with the following purposes in mind:

- To enable the development of a comprehensive understanding of the destination selection process-essential if Australia is to he marketed more successfully in the United States.
- To enable the design of products of greatest appeal to the high- potential groups, in terms of cost, length of holiday, preferred standard of accommodation, and domestic transportation.
- To enable Australia to be promoted in a way that will capitalize on its perceived strengths. overcome its perceived weaknesses, and com Pete more effectively with the strengths and weaknesses of competing long-haul destinations.
- To provide an adequate measurement of the extent of awareness of and interest in various Australian features e.g. the Barrier Reef, the outback, Sydney Harbor).
- To provide a detailed knowledge of the holiday planning process, including the time involved and the sources of information used.
- To enable more efficient communication and

distribution of available products to the high-potential groups.

Proposed Methodology

It was the opinion of the ATC that the study should he divided into two stages. The first would he of a qualitative" nature for the purpose of developing personality and attitudinal questions which would then he used in the second quantitative phase. The general opinion was that face-to-face interviews of 30 to 35 minutes each would he needed for both parts of the study. The use of telephone interviews was considered but rejected since it was feared that they could not provide the depth of answers needed, particularly since "trade-off' questions were being asked.

Due to the high cost of field research in the United States, it seemed imperative to minimize the sample size. Consequently, a total of 1000 face-to-face interview s during the primary research were considered to he sufficient to provide good precision for estimates from the total sample and from the various subgroups.

The ATC felt that respondents should be selected on the basis of four criteria:

1. past travel experience,
2. future travel intentions,
3. travel desire, and
4. interest in Australia.

Those who should be interviewed would include people who had never traveled and had no intention or desire to travel. The term *travel* was defined as long-haul international travel for pleasure purposes, excluding Mexico, Canada, and the Caribbean. In addition, people with immediate family living in Australia were to he excluded.

In the interests of efficiency it was felt that the sample should overrepresent key markets. Hence a screening process was to he used in the interviews. The screening questions were to he administered in sequential fashion, with the first criterion being "past travel experience". The sample structure emphasized those with extensive travel experience, as research indicated that this was a prime market for Australia. The recommended structure was:

• *Past travelers:* traveled in the last five years to a lung-haul destination for pleasure, with or without a stated intention to travel.

N= 600 broken down as:

(a) At least 200 "experienced travelers"

(h) At least 200 with "stated travel intention"

(c) At least 200 with "interest in Australia"

• *Potential travelers:* stated intention to travel in the next three years, to a long-haul destination for pleasure. without past travel experience, *N* =300 broken down as:

a) At least 100 whose primary intended destination is not U.K/Europe

(h) At least 200 with "interest in Australia"

• *Non latent travelers:*

N = 100 comprising persons with no past travel experience and no stated intention to travel, but who:

(a) Have an expressed desire to travel (to a long-haul destination for pleasure purposes)

(b) Express an interest in visiting Australia.

Although a random sampling technique was desired, the sample was to heavily biased toward upper-income groups and not representative of the general mix of the U. S. population. Further sampling restrictions that: felt to he necessary included the following:

1. No interviews from persons who lived in rural areas or small centers.
2. Undersampling from the east coast, with the exception of New York.
3. Undersampling from the southern states, with the exception—Florida.
4. Oversampling from California, Hawaii, New York, Texas, and Florida. The reason for this was an observation of incidence based on data generated from past international visitor un the ATC.
5. Use of a form of multistage sampling in which Cities

would to be the primary unit. For reasons of cost, no more than 20 Cities should be selected. This selection of cities should not be "purposive it should be a random selection of cities within the constraints specified below.

Responses	*Cities*
100	New York
50	Florida
50	Texas
150	California
100	Hawaii
50	New England
150	Eastern North Central
50	Western North Central
100	Other South Atlantic
50	Other Western South Central and Eastern South Central
100	Mountain
50	Pacific
1000	

One of the reasons for the suggested sampling procedure was that the ATC had data on a large sample from the United States known as *Travel Pulse* plus data from an earlier ATC study known as the *International Visitors Survey*. It was felt that the new study should provide data that would be cross- comparable with the results from the previous studies.

Table. U.S. Arrivals in Australia by Purpose of Visit (%)

Purpose of Visit	%
Holiday	43
Visiting Relatives	15
Business	23
Other	19
Total	100

Table. Age of International Visitors to Australia

Age of International Visitors	%
0-4	8.3
15-24	14.5
25-34	20.4
35-49	23.5
50-64	22.3
65 +	11.0

Table. Occupation of International Visitors to Australia (%)

Occupation	%
Professional (excluding teachers)	13.1
Teachers	3.5
Administrative workers	15.9
Clerical and sales workers	9.8
Service workers (including armed services)	3.9
Other	11.1
Inadequately described	5.8
Total (working persons)	63.1
Children (0-14 years)	8.3
Students (15 years and over)	4.8
Home duties	14.8
Independent means, pensioners, etc.	9.0
Total (nonworking persons)	36.9
Total	100

Table. Seasonality of Foreign Arrivals to Australia Ranked By number of Monthly Arrivals

Months	*OCEANIA*	*AFRICA*	*AMERICAS*	*ASIA*	*EUROPE*
January	7	6	5	5	3
February	6	4	3	4	12
March	4	2	4	3	10
April	3	8	7	8	4
May	9	9	11	11	5
June	11	12	12	12	9
July	2	7	10	7	6

August	12	11	8	10	2
September	5	10	9	9	8
October	10	5	6	6	7
November	8	1	1	1	11
December	1	3	2	2	1

Table. Top Ten Origin Countries of Visitors to Australia (%)

Country	%
New Zealand	28.9
UK and Ireland	14.6
USA	13.5
Japan	5.5
Papua New Guinea	4.4
Canada	3.2
Germany	2.7
Netherlands	1.9
Malaysia	1.8
Hong Kong	1.8

East South Central	3.77	*Mid Atlantic*	1.56
• Kentucky	3.9	• New York	13.3
• Tennessee	4.6	• New Jersey	10.5
• Alabama	3.6	• Pennsylvania	6.4
• Mississippi	2.4	East North Central	10.57
West South Central	9.06	• Ohio	10.7
• Arkansas	7.4	• Indiana	8.6
• Louisiana	3.4	• Illinois	13.3
• Oklahoma	12.6	• Michigan	9.7
• Texas	10.4	• Wisconsin	7.3
• Mountain	29.13	West North Central	14.67
• Montana	28.4	• Minnesota	18.3
• Idaho	25.1	• Iowa	14.6
• Wyoming	10.8	• Missouri	14.5
• Colorado	28.1	• North Dakota	8.7
• New Mexico	22.8	• South Dakota	13.4
• Arizona	22.8	• Nebraska	10.9
• Utah	26.2	• Kansas	13.5
• Nevada	18.6	South Atlantic	11.12
Pacific	43.91	• Delaware	6.6
• Washington	33.0	• Maryland	52.0

- Oregon 29.9
- California 42.5
- Alaska 88.7
- Hawaii 148.5
- New England 9.06
- Marine 5.4
- New Hampshire 2.4
- Vermont 8.1
- Massachusetts 9.7
- Rhode Island 5.7
- Connecticut 11.8
- District of Columbia 7.3
- West Virginia 3.1
- North Carolina 4.2
- South Carolina 4.8
- Georgia 5.5
- Florida 23.7

Discussion Questions

1. What is our opinion of the research objectives and purposes for the study?
2. What is your opinion of the proposed methodology?
3. Why do you suppose that travel to Australia from the United States was than desired? In answering this question, consider the cost of travel, time required, and other factors.
4. In your opinion, will information from the survey permit the ATC to address the issues raised in Question 3?

CASE: Gomez Executive Bus Service

After three months of operation. it was apparent that something needed to be done to increase the use of Gomez Executive Bus Service. The bus service was established to provide a new type of service between the two principal cities of Honduras. This service consisted of two nonstop trips each way. The trip was completed in 31 2 hours. Buses left from the Hotel Maya in Tegucigalpa and the Hotel Sula in San Pedro Sula. Trips began at 6 A.M. and 6 P.M from both cities and arrived in the other at 9:30 .AM. and 9:30 P.M.

The Notch Maya and Solo were considered to be the best hotels in each of the respective cities. They catered to business travelers, foreign tourists. and convention trade. Many of the guests lived in the United States, Europe, and Japan.

The buses were made by Mercedes-Benz and were considered to be the most comfortable and luxurious available anywhere with room for 36 passengers and a bar in the rear. A pair of uniformed and attractive e young hostesses accompanied the passengers. During the trip, passengers their choice of free alcoholic beverages, soft drinks, coffee, tea. and sandwiches. Since the bus left from the best hotels in town, there was no reason for passengers to he exposed to long waiting period iv crowded bus terminals or to wait in long lines to purchase tickets. The could instead purchase tickets at a counter in the hotel lobby Tickets sold on a commission basis by a company that also sold sightseeing excursion trips.

In the Hotel Maya, the service u as advertised by the use of a hand drawn sign about the size of ordinary notebook paper. The sign read:

BUS

EJECUTIVO

GOMEZ

SALE A SAN PEDRO SULA

6:00 A.M

6:00 PM.

Despite the fact that each bus had a capacity for 36 passengers, an average of onl seven or eight were taking each trip. This was less than the number required for break which had been estimated at 12.

Tegucigalpa, the capital of Honduras, had a population of approximately 300,000. San Pedro Sub. with 160,000 people was known as the industrial center of Honduras, The highway between the two cities was in good condition. The countryside consisted of beautiful mountains and a few valleys.

Advertising

Prior to the beginning of the set-vice and shortly thereafter, a series of news paper advertisements were used in the two cities. These were later discontinued and television advertisements were used hut were not scheduled for any particular program. The theme of the ads v directed to people ho drove their cars between the two cities.

Although a grand opening was never held, a total of 50 free tickets were sent to members of the press. It was not known if any of these tickets had been used, but as far as an one could see, there had been no free publicity in any of the media, A free ticket was also sent to the Minister of Tourism, hut no reply was received. A total of 400 letters were also sent to companies within San Pedro hula and Tegucigalpa.

The typical customer who had been using the executive bus service came from the Honduran upper classes. There seemed to have been quite a hit of repeat business. The primary problem according to Sr. Gomez, owner and manager, was a lack of advertising and publicity.

None of the passengers were tourists. It was felt that very few tourists, to Honduras simply to wander about as they do in Mexico and Europe. Most seemed to have a planned itinerary and pre-purchased tickets for airline travel. The aid of an ad agency in helping to plan strategy had been dismissed since it was felt that no agency existed in Honduras that s as sufficiently knowledgeable about marketing to assist in this project.

Pricing and Competition

To obtain permission for a new bus service from the Honduran government, Gomez was required to charge twice the regular fare charged by existing bus lines on this route. Four companies offered regular bus service between the two cities. These were San Juan, El Sol. Colombo, and Gomez, Each had n bus terminal and ticket office,

El Sol. The company El Sol offered bus ser ice every two hours between the two cities. This Service was generally considered good but not luxury class. Buses sere not air conditioned nor was there ser vice on hoard, There were also stops at small towns along the way. This company owned a small hotel in Tegucigalpa and would deliver and pick up customers directly from this hotel.

- *Colombo.* The service on this bus was nonstop and was considered to be very good. hut buses were not air conditioned nor was there on-board service.

Colombo owned a middle-class hotel in Tegucigalpa and picked up and delivered customers from this hotel.

- *San Juan*. This company offered service with stops between the two cities and ran every two hours. Service was generally considered average.

Airline Service

Commercial airline travel between the two cities was provided by SAHSA air lines, This airline was 40% owned the ex-president of Honduras. The cost of single-class round-trip travel on SAHSA was five times the price of travel by the Gomez Executive Bus Service. The flight normally took 25 minutes. hut Sr. Gomez felt that it was really a t\\ o-hour trip counting waiting time and trips to and from the airport. Flights were sometimes overbooked and canceled due to mechanical or weather problems.

It was also believed that a certain number of people were afraid to fly due to the difficult airport at Tegucigalpa. This airport had a short runway which literally ended on the edge of a mountain. There was no train service between the two cities, so the only other competitive means of travel was private auto. The distance between the two cities was 265 kilometers.

Although statistics were not available, it appeared that most of the customers of the Gomez Executive Bus Service paid for the ticket with their own funds. By contrast, it was felt that a great number of those who flew SAHSA did so with tickets purchased by their employers. It appeared as though SAHSA had chosen to ignore them, as the new bus service was not considered a threat by the management of SAHSA. Sr. Gomez believed that SAHSA v as wrong and that he just needed time and the right marketing formula to experience success.

Discussion Questions

1. Why do you believe the Gomez Executive Bus Service has not yet reached the break-even point?

2. Why do you believe that two competitive bus companies were vertically integrated with hotels?
3. What marketing strategies and tactics should Sr. Gomez use at this point?

CASE: Hawaiian Sights

After nine months in operation. Hawaiian Sights was struggling to solicit support from tour operators. Despite earlier comments from many that this type of tour was needed and should sell without any problems, sales success had been elusive.

As a walking tour, Hawaiian Sights covered the least explored areas of *"Old Honolulu"* ordinarily bypassed by tour buses:

(1) the Civic and Historical Center.
(2) downtown Honolulu, and
(3) Chinatown.

The tour allowed tourists to mingle and make friends with Hawaii's "real" people—away from Waikiki was viewed as an oral, historical excursion.

Tours began with an escort guide meeting clients at a predetermined location in Waikiki. The group would board the city bus and disembark (20 minutes later) in front of the state capital building. The narration continued for the next four hours. The group spent one hour for lunch and shopping on Fort Street Mall and returned to Waikiki on the city bus.

The idea for Hawaiian Sights occurred to Evelyn Wako when she noticed that conventional city tours ignored the most important part of Hawaii, its people. The majority of tourists rode through Honolulu viewing the city through bus windows. Evelyn felt that if tourists really wanted to learn about Hawaii. they had to get off those buses, E knew that walking tours were successful in Europe, so why not Hawaii?

The concept of a tour that forced customers to take the city bus and to walk was so different that operators of travel desks and travel agencies gave Hawaiian Sights little encouragement or cooperation. They also said that the original commission structure of 20°o on a 20 (retail price) item did not pro duce enough revenue to interest them.

Lunch was not included hut clients could eat at any of the restaurants or food concessions around the Fort Street Mall area. Tourists were encouraged to eat with the "natives" on benches in the tree-shaded mall. They could get to meet Hawaiians, observe life in Hawaii, feed the birds, or just he alone to shop in stores which were less expensive than those in Waikiki.

During each tour the escorts would hoard city buses with their groups at the Historical Center. Prior to hoarding, the group was given a short briefing as to what would transpire. They were informed that more than 0[illegible]o of Hawaii's population was "non-Caucasian." The tourists observed how the bus would change from a touristy one into a local bus the farther it moved away from Waikiki.

The unusual nature of Hawaiian Sights enabled it to he included in the tour brochures of several tour operators and two airlines. With sales lower than expected, Evelyn was searching for ways to advertise her tours. She felt that one way might be to distribute brochures to tourists on the street. She a thinking of hiring girls dressed in grass skirts to act as salesgirls. This was are to bring some negative reaction from certain segments of the Hawaiian population. Evelyn knew' that the hotel travel desks remained a key sales.

Operators of one desk were negative from the beginning. They felt that their clientele were too upscale to ride the city bus.

Tourists who had taken the Hawaiian Sights walking tour rated it far superior to conventional bus tours, Hawaiian Sights offered a "satisfaction guar or money back" guarantee, and so far no customer had expressed dissatisfaction. Despite this, Evelyn had not yet found a way to attract sufficient numbers of tourists to make the new business profitable.

Discussion Questions

1. Do you believe that Hawaiian Sights would appeal to most tourists who visit Hawaii? If not, why not?

2. What is the probable profile of the market segment for Hawaiian Sights?
3. What promotional techniques could Evelyn use to sell this tour to tourists? To the tour tourists? To the clerks at the travel desks?
4. Why do you think the travel desks and travel operators have been unenthusiastic concerning Hawaiian Sights?
5. What do you think of Evelyn's idea to hire girls and dress them in hula skirts to distribute brochures on the sidewalks of Waikiki to passing tourists?

CASE: New Zealand Heritage Park

Heritage Park in Auckland, New Zealand, was designed as New Zealand's first and only tourist theme park. It was modeled to international standards but not intended to become another Disneyland-style operation. The purpose a to present a 100% New Zealand content in as lively and dynamic a v as possible and to encourage visitors to participate, not merely observe. The operation hoped to establish itself quickly as a major tourist attraction and also to plan an important role in encouraging visitors to venture out and see the real New Zealand for themselves.

Conceptualization

New Zealand Heritage Park (NZHP) was the idea of Terry Beckett, who formulated the concept with the realization of New Zealand's tourist potential and the lack of entertainment facilities to accommodate them, The planning phase for the NZHP involved input from t groups of internationally renowned theme park consultants. The first, Economic Research Association (ERA). v based in San Francisco and had performed over 130 studies for Disneyland and worked on projects for Universal Studios and Knotts Berry Farm.

The Product

The attractions within the park represented the three main themes around which the park revolved:

1. Natureworld. This included displays of native plants and animals. Native birds were housed in a large free-flight aviary which allowed visitors to walk through. There were trout pools that could be viewed from above and below the surface, swamplands, and two is lands in the man-made lake, which included a children's play ground.
2. Agriworld. This featured various aspects of New Zealand's farming, horticulture, and forestry and included deer and a number of farm animals, some of which formed part of the park's farm show. There was also a period sawmill, a giant kauri log, and gum digging and goldpanning displays.
3. Cultureworld. This was designed to display aspects of the nation's Maori culture, including their heritage, history, and legends. Included in this area were carving and weaving displays and an audio visual show. There as also a professional Maori concert party per forming songs and dances.

The park also offered a restaurant, serving New Zealand food and wines, various snack bars, a souvenir shop selling native products such as Maori carvings, and a miniature golf course. The participatory nature of the park was emphasized in such activities as gold panning, wood caning. and weaving, which visitors encouraged to try.

Pricing

The park opened initially with admission prices of $ per adult and $3.50 per child, with those under 5 years old free. There as also a fee for admission to the Maori concert party, set at $3 and $1.50 for adults and children. respectively. Research revealed that this price was perceived as being too high (mainly by residents of Auckland, who were the major patrons of the park at the time). There was a downward revision to $6 for adults with all children free, The admission fee to the concert was dropped. However, the admission price was still perceived as being too expensive, and a further adjustment resulted in a $5 adult and a $2.50 child's admission. Beckett felt the price was extremely reasonable considering the fact that the park was a four-hour experience and many other tourist attractions in the Auckland area enjoying patronage for only one-fourth of that time were charging comparable rates,

Promotion

Promotion of NZHP was aimed at two major groups: New Zealanders. either out-of-towners or residents within the Auckland area, and overseas tourists. Advertising to the former group was a relatively simple matter with a number of newspaper advertisements. One series was designed to increase aware ness of the park and the other to advertise special features and events. This group was not intended to he the park's major market segment.

Promotion to overseas tourists was different, NZHP prepared a trade pack. including a personalized letter of introduction from Beckett, a selection of' brochures and pamphlets providing information on park features, the summer and winter program of activities, restaurant menus, and park charges. There was also a schedule of commission arrangements for travel agents. This pack was distributed to selected travel agents in the defined overseas target markets of the United States, Japan, and Australia.

Overseas missions were organized to the various New Zealand tourist and publicity departments in conjunction with the Inbound Tour Operators' Council. Beckett saw these missions as fulfilling three objectives: the promotion of New Zealand as a tourist destination, the promotion of Auckland as a tourist stopover, and the promotion of NZHP as a tourist attraction. One such venture was the inclusion of six Cultureworld employees in an August tourist and publicity department Asian mission to Kuala Lumpur, Singapore, Bangkok, and Jakarta. Other promotions for NZHP included the production of a video about the park for distribution to all New Zealand overseas tourist offices and for show on inbound cruise ships before docking in Auckland, There was additional advertising in the Air New Zealand and JAL in-flight magazines,

Promotion was also aimed at tourists in Auckland. Beckett scored what he considered to he a major coup in being allowed to deposit pamphlets in the guest rooms of Auckland's premier hotel, the Regent. A joint promotional campaign was launched in conjunction with three other tourist attractions:

Victoria Park Market, Kelly Tarleton' s Walk-Through Sea Aquarium, and Harbour Cruises on Board the Pride of Auckland. Each attraction actively promoted the others, and a concession ticket to all four was introduced with a free bus link. The latter project provided immediate success in boosting attendance. The relative efforts of other promotional efforts had yet be felt since there was up to 12 months' lead time before material had fully filtered through the overseas distribution.

Markets

In the first eight of operation, the largest market was New Zealanders. However, Beckett expected this situation to alter with the dissemination of promotional material overseas. He believed that Australians would become the largest per capita market, followed by Americans and then the Japanese, although he stated that US market would provide the greatest returns in terms of per capita expenditure.

Research for the months of July and August revealed the following approximate visitor percentages:

Auckland residents	50
Other New Zealand residents	5
Schools and special- interest group	10
Overseas tourists	35

Of the overseas tourists, Australians represented approximately 51%, Americans 19%, and Japanese 10% of the total. The remaining 20% were from other countries.

Discussion Questions

1. In your opinion, has New Zealand Heritage Park selected the right market targets?
2. Why do you suppose attendance has been slow from overseas visitors?

3. What additional promotional strategies/tactics should the park use to attract overseas visitors?
4. What is your opinion of the pricing employed by the park?

CASE: World View Travel Agency, Inc.

The president and the general manager of World View Travel were discussing the possible need for new strategies to meet increased competition and to take advantage of a market they both regarded as unsaturated.

History of the Company

World View Travel was located in a southwestern U.S. city of 150,000 population and was owned by Rene Townsend and her husband, Bob. Although Bob was a full partner, he continued to work full time in his career as a pathologist and did not participate in active management of the company. Rene served as president and shared management responsibilities with Sylvia Franklin, the general manager.

After 10 years of operation, World View had become the largest travel agency in town, Prior to establishing World View, Rene had v two years for a competitive travel agency. At that time only two travel agencies existed in town, with eight or nine employees each. The growth of World View had been fairly constant and some in the industry regarded it as extra ordinary. In the first sear of operation, World View recorded over $1 million in billings. Growth occurred each subsequent year, despite the existence of two recessions in the 10 years.

City Location

The southwestern city in which World View was located consisted of approximately 150,000 residents with approximately 30% classified as minority. The largest part of the minority population were Mexican Americans. Blacks represented approximately one-fourth of the minority group.

The city was heavily represented by a middle class, and although there were lower-income areas, there were surprisingly few areas that could be regarded as slums. This was due to a combination of a good industrial base, good public administration, and a civic pride among the residents. There were four major employers in the area and mans smaller ones. The city was corporate headquarters for a company listed on the New York Stock Exchange and one listed on the American Exchange. These were involved in electronics and pharmaceuticals.

The predominant industries in the city were banking-finance, insurance, pharmaceuticals, and electronics. The city also boasted a large medical complex which attracted many patients from outside the area and two universities. The city was located on a major interstate highway and was served by three major airlines and two commuter airlines. Two national hotel chains operated downtown properties, and these chains operated motels along the interstate highway.

Competition

Eleven travel agencies existed in the city. One of these was an in-house agency for the largest employer in town. Consequently, very little direct business generated by this company for any of the 10 independent agency. All agencies offered a mixture of services and were not particularly distinguishable in terms of product offering or market segments served. The largest increase in numbers of travel agencies three or four years earlier and there currently seemed to be relative stability in the industry. There were no rumors of non-firms opening in or major expansion by competitors.

Description of World View Travel

After establishing World View Travel, Rene personally called on companies in the area and asked for their travel business. This approach proved to be so successful that after only three years of operation, her agency was as large as that of an competitor. Most of the calls were made to people n ho Rene or her husband knew through prior business or social settings. Rene admitted to having a distaste for 'cold calls" to organizations and firms unknown to her and preferred to call persons with whom a prior contact of some kind had been established. In several cases these were referrals by friends or satisfied clients, Time after time she was told by the prospect that this was the first time the on nor or manager of a travel agency had ever asked for their business.

Location

The location of World View was not conductive to walk-in. World View leased space in a new office building located on a side street in a light industrial park. The street was not a thoroughfare and dead ended in a cul-de-sac. A sign in front identified World View Travel but was not large or particularly distinct from the signs of neighboring businesses.

Client Mix

The mix of billings for World View was approximately 56% commercial and 44% group and individual. Of the commercial accounts, six clients had billings of 500000 or more. These were the larger companies in town. World View did most of the travel business for the second-largest employer in town. However, Rene said that this business was not evenly distributed among all departments within the company. She was certain there were two or three major departments within the client company that did not deal with World View.

The rest of the commercial business came from a mixture of small and medium-sized companies. Rene emphasized that she had purposely tried to have a large mix of commercial clients. She stated that it was likely that on a time-per-client basis, the sales productivity and earnings were less for small clients than for large ones and felt that from a standpoint of the bottom line, her agency would probably be better off with fewer of the smaller commercial clients and more of the larger ones. For instance: 'We probably could get every bit of the business of the second-largest employer in town. However, that frightens us since we would then have too many of our eggs in one basket. At this point, no feel we're better off with a larger number of corporate clients, even if some are relatively unproductive."

Revenue comparisons between international and domestic billings revealed that revenue from all international billings contributed 15% while domestic contributed 85%. Nearly all the services performed by World View could be considered as outbound. A small percentage consisted of making local reservations for corporate client and helping with inbound groups such as sales meetings and seminars in which corporate clients brought visitors to the local area.

In reviewing, in current customer and product mix. Rene commented that she felt commercial business would be significantly more important in the future. The failure of other agencies to gain reputations as strong corporate sees ice firms meant that World view could strengthen its relationship with the area's major employers, resulting in more travel billings. Rene also expressed interest in moving toward the meeting and convention planning business on both an inbound and an outbound basis. She believed that corporate clients were receptive to professional outside assistance in this area and that in the future professional fees could be charged for this service. If a decision was made to expand in this area. changes or additions to the number of sales personnel would be needed.

Advertising and Promotion

Advertising was not regarded as an activity that deserved a heavy budget appropriation. Rene confined advertising to the Yellow Pages. Advertisements ore purchased in high school annuals and theater programs, but these regarded as contributions in terms of their effect on sales. A limited number of baggage tags and flight bags were purchased which had the name World View. but these were limited in quantity and given only to selected clients. Rene felt that the best advertising was word-of-mouth referrals based on professional service for clients.

A special corporate relations program existed which seemed to has e been very successful. This consisted of the following factors:

1. A free 5100,000 automatic free flight insurance policy for corporate clients who flew on tickets issued by World View.
2. A corporate-rate hotel program. A handbook of nearly 350 pages was given to all corporate clients. This contained names of hotels and the best corporate rates available to them.

3. An emergency 800 number that could be used in case of a travel problem anywhere in the United States.
4. A special training program for executive secretaries to acquaint them with the basics of business travel. This seminar was conducted at the offices of World View and had been popular with executive secretaries.
5. A regular newsletter that was sent to clients.
6. The addition of a special staff person to recheck all fares to ensure the lowest cost to the client.
7. A computer-generated statistical capability to assist major client in analyzing their travel expenditures and trends.

The Future

The past 10 years had been rewarding ones for World View. Rene and Bob were confident that their travel agency was as well equipped to meet future opportunities and challenges as any in town. Rene spoke very encouragingly of the future. She felt that the most difficult years were behind and that the future offered excellent opportunities for growth. Rene summarized her feelings by saying, "World View Travel may look quite different 10 or more five years from now, but we intend to remain the leading travel agency in this area, In fact, there is no reason we have to confine our plans to this area. We proved we were capable of success in this market and there is no reason we can't think in broader terms. We have the organization, the know-how, and the desire to grow; its just a matter of setting our objectives, deciding on a strategy and getting on with the task."

Discussion Questions

1. How would you describe World View Travel? What kind of agency is it?
2. What kind of an image do you feel this agency has?
3. What do you consider to be the primary strengths and weaknesses of this agency?

4. What are the primary target markets for World View in the next year? the next five years?
5. Which of the four marketing P's' (product package, price, place, promotion) ha contributed directly to the success of World View?
6. Which of the following general strategies should World View employ: sell out, retrench, do nothing status quo. or planned growth?
7. If you believe World View Travel should adopt a marketing plan for continued growth. Which strategy or strategies should the agency employ?

Use the chart below to answer question 7.

	YES	NO
A. *Product*		
1. Product line extension (use same product mix but go after new market segments) Why?		
2. Product offering expansion?		
Examples:		
New product		
Examples:		
Will we need to find new market segments?		
If so, what are they?		
B. *Place*		
1. A centralized strategy? Why?		
2. A decentralized strategy? why		
C. *Promotion*		
Paid advertising:		
• To reinforce corporate image?		
• To sell products?		
• If yes, what kinds?		

CASE: Burger Kings Searching For The Right

Advertising's Ups and Downs

Burger King has shown how powerful and yet ineffective advertising can he. In 19 with its market share hovering about 4%, Burger King introduced the *"Have It Your Way"* advertising campaign. The ad focused on Burger King's strategy of making burgers according to customer requests instead of serving already prepared, standardized burgers. Many people still consider this campaign to be Burger King's best ever.

In the early 1980s, however, Burger King began to flip from one advertising campaign to another, trying to keep its sales growing. In 1982, it introduced "Battle of the Burgers" campaign, featuring the slogan *"Aren't you Hungry for Burger King Now?"* The "Broiling s-s. Frying" campaign followed in 1983, driving home the point that Burger King flame broiled its burgers rather than frying them. "The Big Switch" theme guided advertising until 1985. All of these centered on Burger King's advantages over McDonald's, and they helped increase market share from 7.6% in 1983 to 8.3% in 1985.

Then disaster struck. With its market share peaking at 8.7%, burger King unveiled its now infamous "search for Herb" ad campaign. The campaign centered on Herb, an eccentric nerd who was supposedly the only person never to have tasted a Burger King Whopper. Consumers were supposed to search for Herb and earn a change to win valuable prizes. The campaign flopped. Sales inched up only 1%, far short of executives' 10% projections. The campaign led consumers to focus on Herb rather than the Whopper, and Burger king found itself in the uncomfortable position of associating its image with a "nerdy personality".

Following Herb, Burger King's market share began a steady decline. Burger King tried to reverse its slide with its *"This is a Burger King Town"* theme in 1986-1987, and followed it with a *"Best Food for Fast Times"* message. In 1988, the chain tried the *"We Do It Like You'd Do It"* campaign, which again focused on flame broiling. However, because of confusing situations, bad humor, and bad acting, the campaign never succeeded in increasing sales. In 1989, Burger King launched its "Sometimes You Gotta Break the Rules" campaign. Burger King wanted this slogan to convey the idea that it was "breaking the rules" of the burger industry by flame broiling, not frying its burgers, and by making the burgers to meet individual customer requests.

The most recent and most disappointing campaign, "BK Tee Vee", featured MTV personality Dan Cortese, rapid editing, and voice-over that shrieked, "I love this place." Ads targeted teenage males, but the majority of Burger King's customers—parents and people on the go—found the commercials to be loud and irritating.

Thus, since the mid-1980, Burger King has had trouble persuading consumers that they should prefer its restaurants to those of McDonald's and other competitors. With its long string of lackluster, quick-changing advertising campaigns, Burger King has failed to establish a solid image that would differentiate it from competitors. If anything, the ads only confused consumers as to what advantages Burger King offered.

By 1993, Burger King held a 6.1% market share, barely ahead of Hardee's 4.4% and Wendy's 4.1%. It lagged far behind McDonald's, which dominates the industry with a 15.6% market share. Moreover, Burger King's sales were growing more slowly than those of its rivals. So far the fourth time in five years. Burger King's managers decided to put its advertising account up for review, seeking a new agency and a new ad campaign.

Not the only Problems

Failed advertising campaign are only the most visible of Burger King's problems. Its marketing stumbles involve other, deeper issues. Since the 1980s, Burger King has wrestled with internal problems. Management has lacked focus and direction and has struggled with marketing mix decisions. Franchisees, who often felt that headquarters had no well-thought-out strategy, became confused and angered. To make matters worse, in store operations were less than spectacular—service in many Burger King restaurants was slow, and food preparation was inconsistent. Many stores needed remodeling.

Burger King lost its focus on its core product- flame-broiled burgers made the way the customer wanted them. It introduced a variety of unrelated products, ranging from pizza and tacos to ice-cream bars. A failure to concentrate on its leading products, the Whopper, confused customers. Many customers also believed that Burger King served lower-quality food.

In the age of the price-conscious consumer, McDonald's and Wendy's listed and responded with lower- priced combo meals. Burger King's higher prices and its refusal to provide discounts contributed to its below-average sales growth.

Burger King's promotion problems also involved more than just its television commercials. Many in – store promotions failed. And the dinner- basket program- combo meals along with table service – showed that Burger King was not listening to its customers. Fast –food patrons really wanted low prices and quick but high- quality food, not a higher – priced, sit – down meal. In addition to chewing up a number of advertising, the company also tossed out some marketing managers.

Back to the Basics

With the help of CEO Jim Adamson, a former marketer from Revco Drug Stores who came to Burger King in July 1991, Burger king has begun a turn-around. Adamson came to Burger King as president of company-owned out-lets. In 1993, he moved up to become the eighth Burger King CEO since 1980. Adamson took a hands—on approach that pleased franchisees. He listened and responded to franchisees. For example, Burger King initiated Operation Phoenix, a program to improve sales, service, and quality by offering franchisees help with menus, pricing, and local advertising.

Management finally locked into a strategy of concentrating on Burger King's core product—flame—broiled, bigger burgers. Since last year, the company had pruned 30 items from the menu. It also launched a new pricing structure featuring $0.99, $1.99 and $2.99 value meals that allow it to compete on price with McDonald's.

In addition to resolving its internal problems, Burger King is also attending to its major external problem- lack of effective advertising. It has hired a new advertising agency, Ammirati and Puris/Lintas, to communicate a new "Back to Basics" positing. Ammirati's Helayne Spivak describes Burger King's image as "The Voice of the People," as opposed to McDonald's image as the "Voice of a Corporation," and Wendy's image as the "Voice of Dave." Burger King is a company that listens to its customers. To communicate this message, the advertising agency will use about $180 million of Burger King's total $250 million promotion budget.

Burger King has been spending $180 million on television and radio, with about 40% going for national advertising and 60% to local. Ammirati and Puris/Lintas must now create an advertising campaign that will successfully communicate Burger King's competitive advantages and pull more customers into its 5700 restaurants.

Discussion Questions

1. What are the objectives of Burger King's advertising?
2. Why did Burger King's corporate strategy and past advertising fail to achieve these objectives?
3. What suggestions do you have for Burger King's new advertising campaign?
4. What recommendations would you make regarding future sales promotions for Burger King's?

CASE: McDonald's: Where To Go From Here

Who does' not remember "You deserve a break today" or "Two all beef patties, special source, lettuce, cheese...."? Although we haven't heard these slogans in a long while, they nudge our memories and cause a lost of thoughts and feeling to flood our consciousness. They might evoke memories of scenes from specific ads"shots of juicy burgers and crispy french fries, or of McDonald's birthday parties when we were young, or of dinner out with our folks. These our attention, caused us to think positively about the product, and left us with warm, fuzzy feelings about the brand. In doing so, they may have caused us to think, "We haven' been to McDonalds for a while let's go there for lunch."

But can you recall any recent McDonald's ad campaign or slogans? Probably not, and that's a problem for McDonalds. If you can remember ads, do they give you a warm, fuzzy feeling? Again, probably not. Lately McDonald's advertising has not particularly memorable and sales—particularly breakfast sales—have been in a slump for several years.

To attack this sales slump, in 1997 McDonald's instituted Campaign' 55. In this campaign, some items such as the

Egg McMuffin, the Big Mac, and other sandwiches were put on sale for 55 cents. In order to get the advertised item at 55 cents, however, customers had to buy French fries and a large drink at a regular prices. This confused many consumers who had not realized that they purchase the other items. To many consumers, the special prices were not all that special. To inform consumers about Campaign '55, Leo Burnett created ads using the tag the changing specials—for example, Quarterpounders instead of Big Macs were featured. Originally, the ad agency had planned to use price comparisons. However, comparisons were difficult because consumers could not really get advertised products for 55 cents without spending more money on other items.

Why was the 55 cent price chosen? In a word—nostalgia. McDonald's was founded in 1955. The consumer was supposed to think about the McDonald's that they had known over the years and develop a warm glow that would be reinforced by getting burgers at unbelievably low prices. Unfortunately, because it was confusing to consumers, the campaign didn't work as intended. Instead of feeling good about an inexpensive burger, many consumers felt baited by a "false promise of a 55-cent burger." Once they'd had a negative experience with the 55-cent special, they reacted negatively to future advertising for a "new" 55-cent deal. Instead of increasing as expected, sales initially slumped as a Campaign'55 went into effect. Only, months later did sales increase, and then only by about one percent.

Contrast the Campaign'55 experience with McDonald's Teanie Beanie Babies and Monopoly promotions earlier in the year. Both of these were highly successful—the Beanie Babies. Stores initially had trouble keeping up with the demand for Beanie Babies, and sales soared by 15.4 percent in the first month. By comparison, for the Campaign '55 special, some stores initially experienced sales decreases of as much as 6%.

Why did some promotions work so well the other not at all? One answer can be found in the nature of the promotions. The Beanie Babies and Monopoly promotions were clear-cut 9 if you (already knew how to play Monopoly!); they created little consumer confusion. They involved free merchandise rather than reduced prices, and the Beanie Babies promotion was aimed at children.

Who really likes McDonald's? The fast-food giant's major market is children and young adult. Children can't respond to a nostalgia campaign featuring prices based on McDonald's founding. Most of our warm feelings about McDonald's were created when we were young, not when we were older. Cmpaign'55 was aimed at adults, what some analysts view as a lesser McDonald's market. However, McDonald's seems to have trouble getting that message. In 1996, it introduced the Arch Deluxe was supposed to be a more "Sophisticated" adult sandwich—one that children would not want. Add created by Leo Burnett showed children wrinkling up their nose at the Arch Deluxe. This not- so- subtly communicated the message that the Arch Deluxe was for adults. But if adults got the message, it didn't make them flock to McDonald's.

Changing lifestyles, changing consumer preferences, the absence of distinctive products, and the relatively bland taste of most of its products appear to be bigger problems for McDonald's than the current sales slump. The traditional fast- food market has been young families who want to feed their children inexpensively. But lately, the population has aged and means they have higher earnings and may be less price sensitive. These smart shoppers are looking for more than just a burger at a low price.

Over the years, McDonald's has not changed its image greatly. Although the company has modernized its restaurants, it still uses the same basic design with the golden arches. The many board is now so crowded that customers sometimes find it difficult to locate the items they seek. "McDonald's is not an advertising problem; it's much more a strategy problem," says marketing consultant jack Trout. "You're looking at a decade of floundering and trying to be everything for everybody. There's been no focus". Trout is referring to the company's many changes in advertising themes and shifts in campaigns between adults and children.

In an attempt to refocus, McDonald's recently put its main advertising account up for grabs, and DDB Needham won the account that had formerly belonged to the Leo

Burnett agency. DDB Needham landed the account with the slogan "Did someone say McDonald's"? Switching ad agencies may refocus McDonald's advertising on celebrating the experience of eating there. This is important in the restaurant industry. "There's no question we can move a lot of customers through our doors when lower the price", said Brad Ball, a senior vice president at McDonald's. "But customer after customer says price is not the number 1 driver. McDonald's happens to be in the restaurant business, but the experience you have with the food goes way beyond what it is you're eating."

A copywriter at DDB Needham penned the famous "Two all beef patties..." slogan years ago. So a return to Needham should usher in a new era of advertising for McDonald's. The ad firm has been asked to "reconfirm and redefine the brand positioning of McDonald's, what it is and what it should be" says Mr. Ball. To do this, DDB Needham will have to work with Leo Burnett, which retains control over marketing to children, including the Ronald McDonald ads. Thus, the two firms will have to work together to redefine McDonald's.

Last year, McDonald's gave Fallon McElligott, a Minneapolis advertising agency, the opportunity to update its image. That agency created a series of ads aimed at the adult market. One ad featured Ronald McDonald in a bar chatting up women—with beer visible in the background. For obvious reasons, this ad never is not as simple as pitching McDonald's to adults in "an adult way".

DDB Needham will have a difficult task in redefining McDonald's in the "did someone say McDonald's?" campaign. It will have lots of money to spend—the majority of the $500 million that McDonald's anticipates spending. But to be successful, the agency will have to decide what to say, whom to say it to, and how to say it, questions which have eluded answers for a decade.

Discussion Questions

1. What were the objectives of the various McDonald's campaigns discussed in the case? "You deserve a

break today" "Two all beef patties..." Campaign'55, Beanie Babies and, Monopoly?

2. How could McDonald's have presented the Campaign' 55 advertising?
3. What suggestions do you have for McDonalds new advertising campaign? Try creating some different types of advertisements using the "Did someone say McDonald's" Slogan.
4. What recommendations would you make regarding future sales promotions for McDonald's?

CASE: The Ritz Millennia Singapore

The Walter Junger, the executive assistant manager in charge of food and beverage for the Ritz-Carlton, Millenia Singapore Hotel, envisioned an opportunity to create an exciting event for Singapore, the first annual New World of Food and Wine Festival. As a native of Austria, Walter was familiar with the tradition of food and wine festivals, which is relatively unknown in Singapore.

The management of the Ritz-Canton, Millenia Singapore also believed the idea had merit and hacked the concept with an adequate budget, personnel, and managerial support. The event had multiple purposes:

1. To developing a scholarship fund for promising Singapore students to pursue a food and beverage career.
2. To create favorable publicity for the hotel.
3. To provide a forum for the presentation of the Ritz-Carlton, Millenia Singapore Lifetime Achievement Award for Food and Beverage Ex cellence to a person who had dedicated his or her life to the art of culinary refinement or wine appreciation.
4. To provide an enjoyable evening for invited guests.
5. To advance the knowledge and appreciation of wine and fine food.
6. To enhance relations with selected wineries and distributors.

7. To showcase the cutting-edge developments over the last 10 years, especially in the "new world" (such as "Fusion Cuisine"),

The festival was planned and organized as a four-day epicurean extravaganza featuring chefs and winery representatives form North America, South America, South Africa. Australia, and China. During these four days the festival featured exciting and innovative gastronomic creations and wine tasting of premium wines on a grand scale for the first time in Singapore. This festival was on the cutting edge of food and beverage trends, highlighting the achievements of nontraditional food and beverage sources over the last decade.

Just as Singapore is a multicultural crossroad, this festival served as a meeting point for the best new offerings from the New World of Food and Wine. The opening cocktail reception was a superb culina experience showcasing the talents of the Ritz-Canton, Millenia Singapore culinary team. Against a tropical poolside setting. the team led by executive chef Peter Schoch presented innovative creations from restaurants of the Ritz Canton. Millenia Singapore. The culinary delights that evening included oysters from Australia. the United States, and South Africa, and a selection of caviar, black pepper scallops and Hoisin lobster on hot garlic pesto, bourbon-marinated lamb loin on roasted pablano pepper sauce, and a flambe station accompanied by a homemade ice-cream selection. All these, with Green Point sparkling and still wines from the House of Moet et Chandon, Australia. Live music further enhanced the ambiance.

Guests were able to meet and talk with participating chefs and s representatives. These included ,Jeff Cook of Robert Mondavi Winery; Wayne Donaldson from Green Point Winen; Stefano and Franca Manfredi of Bel Monclo Restaurant, Sydney; chef Ramiro Rodriguez Parcho of Argentina; the Arizu family, owners of Luigi Bosca Vineyards of Mendoza, Argentina; and several others, In addition to the opening cocktail reception. The festival was divided into 13 sections of wine tasting and dining, with prices ranging from 850 (Singapore) to 8180.

Walter Junger served as chairman of the festival and received excellent cooperation for a cross-functional team that included the director of public relations, events/ promotion manager, executive chef, director of banquets. beverage manager, room service manager. Greenhouse Restaurant manager, director of catering, Snappers Restaurant manager, and reservations Supervisor. The level of planning and team work by this group resulted in a highly successful festival. Almost all the events during the festival were sold out, and some even had waiting lists.

The highlight of the festival was the presentation of the Ritz Canton, Millenia Singapore Lifetime Achievement Award for Food and Beverage Excellence, worth $7000. to one of the participating chefs, winemakers, and winery representatives. Judges for this prestigious award were Fred Ferretti of *Gourmet magazine*, United States; C.P. Tiong of Wine Review, Singapore; Andre Blanc of Ecolab, Asia; and Walter Junger, executive assistant manager of the Ritz Carlton, Millenia Singapore. After two grueling days 5 of interviews with each nominee, the decision was unanimous: chef Ramiro Pardo was selected the 'a inner. Chef Pardo had been cooking for people from all over the world for +0 years. His restaurant Catalinas was awarded the top prize as "The Best Latin American Restaurant" by the Association of Latin American Gastronomic Journalists.

During the gala dinner, an auction of rare wines was conducted to raise funds for the Ritz-Canton, Millenia Singapore Food and Beverage Scholarship Fund. The scholarship benefitted a promising Singaporean who excelled in his or her profession. The auction was well supported by guests and es entu ally raised over 818.000. The gala dinner ended on a high note: The Ritz Carlton, Millennia Singapore was presented a Five-Star Diamond Award for Food and Be Excellence by the American Academy of Hospitality Sciences.

Discussion Questions

1. Was the New World of Food and Wine Festival a good public relations events? Explain and support your answer.

2. If you were the public relations director for the Ritz Millenia, in what types of Media would you try to get publicity? Explain how your message
3. How does this event create goodwill with the target market of Ritz-Carlton?

CASE: US Airways: The Airline Price Wars

Suppose you wanted to fly from Seattle to San Jose, California. The fare in June 1995 would have been $22; in 1997, it would have been $59. The fare from Detroit to Minneapolis—which is roughly the same distance—would have been $126. obviously, airlines don't set their fares based on distance. So, why do these fares vary so greatly?

One reason is the contrast between operations of discount airlines such as Southwest (the Seattle to San Jose route) and major airline such as Northwest Airlines, (Detroit to Minneapolis). Southwest Airlines, known as the Love Line because its original home was Love Field in Dallas, Texas, is a no- frills airline. It offers no food services, complimentary drinks, extensive baggage handling, or other amenities. It flies a limited number of direct, usually short, routes, carefully selecting its routes based on the popularity of the flights. If lots of passengers normally take a certain route, then Southwest might choose to operate only on that route. There are many passengers flying from Seattle to the San Francisco Bay area of California. So, Southwest cuts fares on the route to lure passengers, and cuts costs by flying into a nearby alternative airport—in this case, San Jose.

When Southwest began operations at Seattle, competing airlines routinely charged fares to San Francisco ranging from $89-$119. Southwest entered with prices between $39 and $59. One of the local airlines reduced its prices to $25 and Southwest responded with $22. How did this price-war tactic work? Not so well. After instituting the $22 fare, a 137-seat Southwest Boeing pulled away from the gate in Seattle with only 19 passengers on board. The revenue from the flight was $418, compared with a cost of $6567.04 – not exactly a recipe for success. Things were so bad that the flight attendant jokingly asked passengers to shift to one side of the plane so that when they taxied past the competition, it would look like the plane was full. Even if the airplane had been full, revenues would not have covered half the cost of the flight.

If fare wars result in such losses, why do airlines engage in them? The primary cause is relatively flat air traffic growth. Although the number of flyers grew rapidly after Word War II, the rate of growth slowed greatly in the 1980s and 1990s. in 1991, the number of airline seats sold actually declined. Facing lower traffic, airlines cut routes and parked surplus aircraft in the Southwestern deserts. Cut- rate companies them leased these surplus planes at low rates and went into business. So, reductions by the major airlines actually provided the inexpensive planes that fueled, competition. As competition increased in a flat market, fares had to decline, with the result that many major and discount lines were forced into bankruptcy, including Eastern, TWA Braniff, and Mark Air.

This explain the situation in Detroit, where you would probably have been flying Northwest Airlines, not a discount airline. Because Northwest carries 74% of Detroit's outbound passengers, it has a lock on the Detroit's to Minneapolis route. With little competition, it can charge higher prices. In fact, Northwest is the nation's higher-priced airline.

"Any passenger who pays more than 30 cents a mile is probably being overcharged" asserts Tim Hannegan, assistant for aviation competition for the General Accounting office, watchdog for the US Congress on federal programs. Using data from 1996, Consumer reports evaluated mileage and fares. Northwest's average cost for flights up to 300 miles was 68 cents per mile. Examples of other Northwest fares and mileage are: Detroit to Traverse City, $154 or 74 cents a mile; Detroit to Kalamazoo, $218 or 90% a mile, and Detroit to Grand Rapids, $135 or 1.12 cents for mile. According to the Consumer Reports study, USAirways says the second more expensive airline at 17 cents a mile, and Southwest was the least expensive at 17 cents a mile. Northwest called the study's data flawed, saying that the study ignored fixed costs for flights on routes with few passengers, which raises its overall costs. To get the kind of lock on an airport and routes that Northwest has in Detroit requires airlines to service all routes, not just the most popular ones.

Not only is northwest expensive, travelers also give it low ratings on factors such as on-time arrivals, ease of airport check-in, and convenience of scheduling. A survey of business travelers on nine major carriers, conducted by J.D. powers and Associates, found Northwest below average in customer satisfaction for flights under 500 miles and only average for longer flights. The best- rated airlines were Continental, TWA, United, American, and Southwest. All this suggests that competition among airlines results in lower fares and better service.

Airlines don't compete only on price. They also offer special promotions. For example, Southwest has launched a mileage war in which it gives fliers in the Rapid Rewards program double mileage credits on that a flier might quality for a free flight by flying Southwest only four times in one year. Other airlines have used tie- in offers. For example, in a recent promotion, anyone purchasing an Aurora Limited Production Numbered Gold Roller Ball pen in a specified time period received 500 bonus Delta SkyMiles. Purchasers of an Aurora Sole Three-Piece Pen set received 100 bonus miles. Sometimes multiple airlines will participate in a promotion. Customers who purchased a 35 mm Samsung camera received a 32-page Travel Saver booklet offering discounts on travel, including a certificate for $500 in airfare discounts good several airlines.

With all this competition, how can an airline get a "lock" on an airport? Usually, the airline uses the airport as a hub. When it first negotiated with the airport, the airline may have contracted to provide service on a large number of rotes and to use most of the available gates. In return, the airport was assured of a steady stream of revenue from the airline and avoided the need to negotiate with a large number of airlines. Over time, however, passenger traffic grows and many airports expand so that they have more gates than are needed by the main airline. This creates a situation in which discounters and other airlines might has still competitive weapons that it can use to defend its market.

The most obvious weapons are price, size, and lots of cash. Consider the situation that existed in Charlotte, North Carolina. Charlotte, with 1.2 million inhabitants, is the second largest city in the Southwest, but its Douglas International airport had no discount airlines. The Atlanta to Charlotte route was heavily traveled and expensive. Douglas International even had 21 available gates out of the total of 64. this seemed to be a ripe situation for a discount airline such as ValuJet. Yet ValuJet chose at first to ignore the Charlotte market, instead starting service on routes producing much less business than would have been realized between Charlotte and Atlanta.

Why did ValuJet avoid Charlotte? The most formidable obstacle in Charlotte was USAirways group, which had 94% of all flights into and out of Charlotte. If a discounter enters the market, USAirways will cut fares to defend its market. A fare war actually would be more costly to USAirways than to ValuJet, because USAirways has much higher costs than ValuJet. However, USAirways had the cash to survive a long fare war- ValuJet did not.

But fares and costs are not the whole story. USAirways also had connections to many other cities to which passengers wanted to travel. So, although USAirways cost more, it was also more convenient for flyers. Notes Ray Martin, sales manager for Southern Bag Corporation "You can get back home quickly and easily". That is very important to the business travelers, who make up only 48% of air travelers, but who account for 66 % of airline revenues. Without access to connecting flights, a discounter would have trouble cracking the Charlotte market unless it also established flights to Atlanta, Washington, New York, and other popular destinations.

Another factor is the willingness of communities to offer incentives to airlines. "We're starting to see a lot of support from communities that know we have other choices", says David Ulmer, vice president of planning for ValuJet. For example, in Newport News, Virginia, a city-operated economic development group paid ValuJet $1.9 million. In Jackson, Mississippi, the Chamber of Commerce provided free advertising for the airline.

With so many cities anxious for their services, discounters can pick and choose where they want to go. There is no need to enter a sustained battle with a major airline such as USAirways in Charlotte.

Eventually, however, the easy picking ran out, and ValuJet chose to enter the Charlotte market anyway. To do so, it had to offer fares that were 68% below those of USAirways and Delta—its major competitors. Moreover, neither the airport nor the city used financial incentives to lure ValuJet—they didn't want to upset their contracts with USAirways. Of course, USAirways responded with lower prices so that, eventually, lower fares will prevail on the more popular routes, but it may mean higher fares on less popular routes.

Discussion Questions

1. What internal and external factors affect pricing decisions in the airline industry?
2. What marketing objectives have the various airlines selected?
3. Which airline industry costs are fixed and which are variable? What implications does this cost structure hold for airline operations?
4. What is the nature of demand and competition in the airline industry? Does demand differ between the business and leisure segments?
5. What pricing and other recommendations would you make to USAirways to help it protect its markets?

CASE: International Travel Agency

The president of International Travel Agency was concerned about the performance of the sales force. It was felt that members of the sales force did not really utilize their sales opportunities, but instead thought only about selling a ticket to a customer from point A to point B. The sales force did not seem to have an interest in maximizing sales and profits by aggressively selling the entire product mix.

In total, the agency had a sales force of eight. Three members of the sales force were referred to as executive sales consultants. These people called on commercial accounts and were expected to spend more of their time outside the office, The remaining five persons were referred to as travel counselors and worked entirely within the agency.

None of the travel counselors who worked within the agency were as signed a quota. The executive sales consultants, who worked outside the office, were assigned a sales quota. Failure to meet a quota would be discussed with the salesperson. hut no other action was usually taken unless this failure continued for several months, If serious and persistent deficiencies existed, the salesperson could be subject to discharge.

The agency provided nine to 12 familiarization (fam) trips for members of the sales force each year. This meant that each salesperson could experience at least one trip per year, as they were assigned on a rotating basis. These trips did not reduce time from the salespersons guaranteed number of days of annual vacation. The purpose of a fam trip was to acquaint travel agents with destination areas and the services of airlines, hotels, restaurants, and so on.

The president felt that the agency could maximize profits by selling more travel services to clients and that the sales force was concerned only about selling tickets. An analysis of, the product mix of International Travel revealed that approximately 85% was accounted for by airline tickets. The remaining 15% consisted of allied travel services, including hotels, rental cars, and entertainment. Of these, the majority consisted of hotel reservations. Less than 1% was accounted for by the sale of traveler's checks.

One of the members of management offered the analogy of a business man entering a clothing store. If a customer purchases a suit, the salesclerk asks if the customer might need a new shirt or tie to go with the suit. Travel agents are no different. They write a ticket from Chicago to Hong Kong or London for a client and never bother to ask if the client needs hotel accommodations, rental cars, travelers checks, or other services that an agency handles.

The president of International Travel had tried to encourage the force to sell other services but felt that they seemed uninterested in taking the time and effort to sell them. The president believed that maximizing sales f the complete product mix would lead to maximum profits and that some thing must be done to encourage cross-selling.

Discussion Questions

1. What can be done to encouraging the sales force to engage in more cross-selling?
2. Does the current fam trip program serve as a motivational tool for the sales force?
3. Discuss what is needed in terms of sales incentives and sales controls to achieve the objectives of International Travel Agency.

CASE: Superior Hotels

Jan Trible. president of Superior Hotels, was concerned with the future expansion of the company. Superior hotels had built a strong reputation in the management of time share resorts in Florida. The company had recently acquired a consulting contract for a ski resort in the Rocky Mountains, which would mark its entrance into a new area of resort management. Now there was serious discussion concerning the advisability of entering the commercial hotel segment of the hotel industry within cities of 100,000 to 00,000 in population.

Management of Time-Share Resorts

The management style of Superior Hotels was exemplified in the manage ment of tile company's time share resorts. Superior managed five time-share resorts, with a total of 2 units. The company maintained a policy of not accepting management contracts for time-share projects that were in trouble. The company philosophy maintained that most of these had been ill planned and probably had little likelihood of long-range success. Jan personally believed that a major shakeup in the time-share industry was coming and that many existing projects would fail.

The Superior Hotel policy was to begin working with the developers of a time-share resort at the beginning of the project. It was felt that development have a short-run viewpoint hut a management company must think of the long run. The policy was to become involved in the entire planning process of the project, including blueprints and interior decorations. If a developer re fused to cooperate, Superior would remove itself from future management

Management believed that a time-share project differed considerably from conventional hotel or resort development.

1. A time share project has hundreds or thousands of owners. A conventional hotel or resort has one or a few.
2. Time-share projects receive high intensity use, with 95°o occupancy being normal. Furniture, carpeting, and other furnishings can wear out in one-third the time, Therefore, rules of thumb developed for hotels would often not apply in time share.
3. The guest assumes a proprietary interest in time share. Guests are extremely critical since they view the units as theirs and complain about things that a hotel guest would accept.
4. A great deal of hype goes into the sales of a time-share unit and guests arrive with extreme expectations. Superior has to bring reality into the dreams that the sales department create.
5. The long-run success of a time-share unit depends on attracting the same guests each year for as long as 20 years or more. If guests be came dissatisfied and enough guests decided to drop their owner ship, resales can be very difficult and the entire project can he in jeopardy.

Several management practices had been developed by Superior to deal with these complexities.

Owner Feedback

Owner comment sheets were distributed to each owner guest during each visit. Tan took pride in the fact that she read each one personal. These sheets covered a variety of areas, from general appearance of the unit to any evidence of insects and rodents. If the comments were particularly had, a member of management, including Jan, would personally contact the owner and report on the steps that had been taken to correct the problem.

Feedback was also received in 'owner coffees." These weekly meetings with owners included attendance by one or more members of management. These could include the resort owner, the head of housekeeping, the director of internal management, and others A quarterly newsletter was published by Superior and sent to all owners. In addition to information of a general nature such as changes in air fares to the resort, the newsletter was personalized to the extent that it reminded all owners of their vacation week.

Recreation Management

Superior Hotels believed that even the most beautiful and best-maintained resort could eventually become boring. To ensure that guests would find some thing new each year, a recreation program was established with a full-time professional in charge. Programs were designed for all ages. These employed some of the successful concepts of Club Med.

Supervised programs for children allowed parents a freedom the could not enjoy at most resorts, Hot dog parties, beach parties, tennis competition. seashell classes, and many other programs offered a variety of recreational and educational pursuits. Each recreational program was monitored as to attendance and guest satisfaction and weak ones were eliminated. A dominant feature of all the programs was the opportunity for interaction among guests. Jan believed that a guest at the average resort could spend a week and never develop new friendships. Hopefully, the recreation programs encouraged friend to develop.

Housekeeping and Maintenance

The turnover of a majority of the guests one clay and the mass arrival of an equal number the next provided special housekeeping and maintenance problems for time share projects. A full-time maintenance crew was employed and a large inventory of replacement furnishings was carried, If a TV set or electric range had a problem. it w as replaced immediately rather than sending a repairman. with only one vacation week. Jan felt that a guest did not want to ‘hare it with a repairman. Housekeeping was performed for the time-share resorts under contract with an independent housekeeping company. Housekeeping managers were responsible for examining each room personally and ensuring that corrections immediately followed discovery of a problem.

The Superior Hotel Image and Philosophy

"All Superior properties must be first class there is no room in this corporation for mundane or second class properties." This statement by Jan summed up the company's philosophy. The philosophy concerning quality had led management to change its policy concerning the new properties it would manage. The company recently initiated a policy of holding an equity position in all future properties. This decision was made for two reasons. First, an ownership position would allow Superior to have a stronger voice in the development and management of properties and would help to ensure quality. Second, superior Hotels had no interest in "bringing up" properties to a de sired quality and performance level only to find that the managers had decided not to renew the management contract.

Corporate Objectives

The management and ownership of superior 1-lotels desired for the company to be recognized as a strong national resort and commercial hotel management company within 10 years. It was felt that resort properties offered limited growth opportunities since the most desirable locations had been developed by others.

The best strategy for the newt few years seemed to lie in the development of first-class commercial properties within sun belt cities of 100,000 to 200 It was felt that the development of three new properties per year in this market was realistic. Sun belt cities were felt to offer the best potential for growth because of the scarcity of 150 to 200 room high-quality hotels. These second-tier cities remained important industrial and agricultural centers and in many cases did not offer truly first-class hotel accommodations. In many cases a respected medical complex had been developed these cities and it was felt that this factor alone would seem as a magnet for visitors.

Discussion Questions

1. What are the core competences of superior Hotels? Management of resorts? Management of time-resorts? Management of ski resorts? Management of commercial hotels? Other?
2. Do you believe that Superior Hotels should he entering diverse markets such as ski resorts and commercial hotels?
3. Do you believe that Superior Hotels can effectively market and manage a wide diversity of properties?
4. What would you advise Jan Trible to do?

REFERENCES

Berry L., Parrasurman, A., *Marketing Services: Competing Through Time;* Free Press; New York 1996.

Brent J.R., Goeldner, Ch., *Travel Tourism and Hospitality Research,* Wiley, New York, 1994.

Buttle, F., *Hotel and Food Service Marketing,* Casell, London, 1993.

Coltman, M., *Tourism Marketing;* Van Nostrand Reinhold, New York, 1993.

Foster, D., *Travel and Tourism Management,* Macmillan Education, Hampshire, 1996.

Gunn, A.C., *Tourism Planning,* Basics, Concepts, Cases, Taylor and Fransis, Washington, 1994.

Holloway, C., *The Business of Tourism,* Pitman Publishing, London, 1999.

Holloway, C., Plant, R.V., *Marketing For Tourism;* Pitman Publishing, London, 1992.

Holloway, J.C and Robinson, C., *Marketing For Tourism,* Longman, New York, 1995.

Jefferson, A. and Lickorish L., *Marketing Tourism—A Practical Guide,* Longman, London, 1988.

Kotler, Ph. Armstrong, G., *Marketing for Hospitality and Tourism,* Prentice Hall, 1999.

Kozak, M. and Andreu, L., *Progress in Tourism Marketing,* Elsevier, 2006.

Ludberg. D., *Tourism Economics,* Wiley & Sons, New York, 1995.

Medlik, S., *Managing Tourism,* Butterworth Heinemann, London, 1995.

Middleton, V.T.C. and Hawkins, R., *Sustainable Tourism—A Marketing Perspective,* Butterworth-Heinemann, Oxford, 1998.

Middleton, V.T.C., *Marketing in Travel and Tourism,* Butterworth-Heinemann, Oxford, 2001.

Sinclair, T. and Stabler, M., *The Economics of Tourism,* Routledge, London, 1997.

Teare, R. and Mazanec, J., *Marketing in Hospitality and Tourism,* Cassell, London, 1994.

Susanu, I., *Services Marketing,* Denbridge Press, New York, 2008.

Tracey Firth., *Marketing for Sustainable Tourism,* University of Western Sidney, www. besteducationnetwork.org

Wearne, N., Morrison, A.J., *Hospitality Marketing,* Butterworth–Heinemann, Oxford, 1996.

Disney: *http://disney.go.com/*

Emirates: *http://www.emirates.com*

Four Seasons Hotel and Resorts: *http://www.fourseasons.com/*

Hamton Inn: *http://hamptoninn.com*

The Ritz-Carlton Hotel Company: *http://www.ritzcarlton.com*

Singapore Airlines: *http://www.singaporeair.com*

Sowthwest Airlines: *http://www.sowthwest.com*

9

KALYPSO ADVENTURES: A CASE STUDY OF INNOVATION, ENTREPRENEURSHIP, AND NICHE MARKETING

*Manoj Edward**
*Babu P. George***

Abstract

This case study focuses on a niche tourism operator in Kerala, India, offering tour packages mainly in the areas of adventure and ecotourism. Started in 2000, the operation has achieved considerable growth by 2008 mainly due to the owners' steadfast commitment and their passionate approach to the product idea they promoted. Over the years the firm has witnessed many changes in terms of modifying the initial idea of the product to suit the market realities, adding new services and packages, expanding to new markets, and starting of new ventures in related areas. In the process, the owners have faced various challenges and tackled most them as part of pursuing sustained growth. The present case study aims to capture these growth dynamics specific to

* Cochin University of Science and Technology, India.
** University of Southern Mississippi, USA.

entrepreneurship challenges. Specific problems in the growth stage like the issues in designing an innovative niche product and delivering it with superior quality, coordinating with an array of suppliers, and tapping international tourism markets with limited marketing budget are explored in this study. Also this study explores certain unique characteristics of the firm's operation which has a bearing on the niche area it operates. Lastly, some of the critical issues pertaining to entrepreneurship in the light of the firm's future growth plans are also outlined.

APPLICATION OF NICHE STRATEGY IN TOURISM MARKETING: THE CASE STUDY OF KALYPSO ADVENTURES

Abstract: This case study focuses on a niche tourism operator in Kerala, India, offering tour packages mainly in the areas of adventure and ecotourism. Started in 2000, the operation has achieved considerable growth by 2008 mainly due to the owners' steadfast commitment and their passionate approach to the product idea they promoted. Over the years the firm has witnessed many changes in terms of modifying the initial idea of the product to suit the market realities, adding new services and packages, expanding to new markets, and starting of new ventures in related areas. In the process, the owners have faced various challenges and tackled most them as part of pursuing sustained growth. The present case study aims to capture these growth dynamics specific to entrepreneurship challenges. Specific problems in the growth stage like the issues in designing an innovative niche product and delivering it with superior quality, coordinating with an array of suppliers, and tapping international tourism markets with limited marketing budget are explored in this study. Also this study explores certain unique characteristics of the firm's operation which has a bearing on the niche area it operates. Lastly, some of the critical issues pertaining to entrepreneurship in the light of the firm's future growth plans are also outlined.

Introduction

Kalypso Adventures is a package tour company started in

2000 by two Naval Commanders of the Indian Navy, Cdr. Thomas, a nature lover and Cdr. Samuel, an adventure lover. Thomas was an electrical engineer and Samuel was a naval pilot. They both loved adventures and shared a passion for exploring nature. Even as naval commanders, they had agreed between them to retire at the next right opportunity and start a venture related to adventurous activities in the lap of nature. So, in 2000, when Thomas and Samuel left the navy, instead of taking the more promising avenues that were available to them at that time, they started up Kalypso Adventures, perhaps the first adventure tourism enterprise in the state of Kerala.

Tourism industry in Kerala in the year 2000 was just showing signs of promising growth and both the entrepreneurs sensed so much more that could be offered to the discerning traveler besides the passive experience of backwaters and beaches in Kerala. They struck upon the fact that Kerala, within a small geographical area, possess a natural diversity which very few other places in the world can claim. The rich mix of diverse terrains, from the beaches to the plains, from the backwaters to the low-lying grassland forests, from the midlands to the rainforests in the high altitude mountains, makes every bit of the state to claim some potential for tourism.

Keeping in mind the vastness of this untapped natural diversity, they saw a business opportunity in developing a tourism product that combines adventure and ecotourism. The concept of ecotourism tourism was just catching on at that time, but the nature of experience offered was only a passive experience of nature. Thus, considering all the favorable conditions, they started Kalyspso Adventures. It was a great start, a realization of long cherished dreams!

But, the honeymoon did not last too long. It did not take much time for the promoters to realize that passion is not enough: domain expertise in tourism is something conspicuous for its absence. With no experience in tourism business they began to face difficulties in taking the dream venture forward. Neither of them had sufficient quantum of money to invest nor were there investors willing to extend a helping hand. Banks declined requests for a loan since they did not have a track record in tourism business and they lacked hard assets to mortgage for getting loans. Coupled with this, bureaucratic hassles and the cumbersome procedures involved in availing the subsidies and grants promised by the state tourism department can easily put one off from the goal of starting a business in the tourism sector. It also turned out to be extremely difficult for them to reach let alone convince international inbound tour operators. Still they ploughed on, believing in the beauty of the concept they were trying to sell. For almost two seasons they stayed on course with very low business, thanks to the courage and endurance they mastered from their service career in the Indian navy.

The initial product mix included adventurous activities like paragliding, rock climbing, and bungee jumping. These were the most popular forms of adventure tourism seen elsewhere in India. While the products were mostly the same, given the geographical uniqueness of Kerala, the environment in which they were offered was greatly different. From the lukewarm response gotten from the market, their optimism began to wane and they began to wonder whether Kerala was a suitable destination for such activities. Kerala is mostly known for its nature appeal with beaches, backwaters, mountains wildlife and hill stations. Yet, they could not believe that the market existed for such hardcore adventure tourism product was insignificant. In any case, they had already procured costly adventurous sports equipments which subsequently had to be discarded for a huge loss if they wind up the business. Adversities they faced are not atypical of what any genuine entrepreneurs with innovative business ideas would face in the tourism industry in Kerala.

Despite their ill-luck with this niche market offering, they by and large resisted the temptation to move on to a more standard tour operating company catering to tourists who seek those standard vanilla type tours, focusing exclusively on beaches, backwaters, and traditional medical treatment. Although they never actively solicited orders of that type, they still handled occasionally tours of that type which came to them automatically. Fortunately, this gave the firm essential fodder for its survival.

Necessity is the Mother of Inventions

Meanwhile they kept on the search for new product ideas mainly by searching the Internet and by studying closely the latest trends happening in the adventure side of the tourism sector. This is how they got the idea to sell adventure to any ordinary person, packaged in such a way that the person could participate in it without much exertion or risk: a shift from hard adventures to soft ones. To make things clearer, the adventures themselves did not change much, but more visible and assuring protective layers were brought in so that tourists could participate in those seemingly risky activities with confidence. It was a great awareness that tourists seek adventurous experience, by within the protection of an environmental bubble.

By packaging heavy adventure as light and risk-free, maintaining nonetheless its excitement, they thought it would appeal to a wider market, especially when along with the adventure experience tourists also have an opportunity to enjoy natural and cultural products. While a hardcore adventurer partaking in typical adventure tourism activities would love to climb an un-climbable mountain not bothered about coming across anyone else in the process, their idea was to offer tourists climbable mountains, terrains and routes easier to bike and trek, at the same time providing tourists a unique experience of Kerala's local culture and nature by having opportunity to meet local people, and rest and camp in scenic locations. In short, they decided to sell Kerala with adventure as a vehicle. 'What better way to see the beauty of Kerala at close quarters and interact with its people than from a cycle or a kayak', they reasoned. From this idea they worked out various tour packages offering exclusive cycling, trekking, birding, wildlife, and natural history tours. So from a pure adventure company, they moved on to become an eco-adventure and nature travel company.

Conceptualizing the product was one thing, but actually designing the product package, taking into account the details of the tour package in its minute level was quite another thing. With their passion for the product idea and the commitment to make it an outstanding tour package, they devoted their whole efforts to the operational aspects of setting up such tours. The toughest part in the process was identifying routes or trails. In their efforts to come up with an array of tour routes, they used the various available cartographic devices, in the process studying the geography of Kerala in its minute detail possible to identify and mark out the roads, canals, inland waterways, secluded tourist spots—not much heard of—which offered a lot of appeal in experiencing the nature in its pure and exotic state. Once a route is identified for its trekking or biking potential, they personally travel the route, and get more accurate data about the route. This route information is then fed in to GPS compatible devices and to maps suitable for conveying tourists the actual route profile when they demand it. As part of selecting a few routes from the many they have identified, routes are examined for the scenic view they offer, availability of amenities like hospitals and nearby evacuation points, and suitable accommodation points. In many cases, it has taken almost a year to convert a product idea to a final package ready for offering to tourists. And there are cases where, before launching the product, trials were taken with student volunteers to see if any modifications were to be made later. Appropriate camp site selection, arrangements of suitable home stay properties for the tourists stay en route, planning interactions for tourists with the flavor of local life which the villages and small towns in Kerala can offer were all parts of their package design and development efforts.

Niche Marketing: The Solution

The solution adopted by Kalypso, in technical terms, is called niche marketing. The market niche defines the specific product features aimed at satisfying specific market needs, as well as the price range, production quality, and the demographics that it is intending to impact (Novelli, 2005). Small businesses, being close to their customers, are in a strong position to know their needs and therefore are in a better position to exploit niche marketing opportunities (Anderson and McAuley, 1999). However, as the Kalypso case shows us, niche markets are not easy to identify in their infancy

(McKenna, 1988). Studies have shown that developing niche markets in tourism is a difficult process, requiring a level of marketing expertise often not possessed by small business firms (McKercher and Robbins, 1998).

By specialization along market, customer, product or marketing mix lines, a company can match the unique needs of a small part of a larger market whose needs are not fulfilled. Kotler (1991) suggests that the key idea in niche marketing is specialization and he provides the following ways by which to specialize:

- end-user specialization;
- vertical-level specialization;
- customer-size specialization;
- geographic specialization;
- product or product-line specialization;
- product-feature specialization;
- quality/price specialization;
- channel specialization.

Specialization is the key factor in niche marketing. In designing the niche product Kalypso specialized on end-user, product- line, and service dimension. This approach especially mirrors Kotler's (1991) idea of specialization needed for successful niche marketers.

Niche markets shares certain characteristics: They are small markets not served by competing products (Keegan, Moriarty, and Duncan, 1992). It can serve a small market consisting of an individual customer or a small group of customers with similar characteristics or needs (Dalgic and Leeuw, 1994) and posses the following attributes:

- of sufficient size to be potentially profitable
- having no real competitors
- having growth potential
- demonstrating sufficient purchasing ability
- having a need for special treatment
- possessing customer goodwill
- presenting opportunities for an entrance
- company to exercise its superior competence

With the growth potential, many niche markets can technically grow into larger markets (McKenna, 1988). But, many a time, due to the fear that they might lose the unique competitive advantages, niche marketers prefer not to do that.

Because of its small size, a niche is some times referred as 'super-segment'. Shani and Chalasani (1992) however point out that rather than being an extension of segmentation, niche marketing is an inversion of the practice. The distinction can be drawn by focusing not on the characteristics of each but on the philosophies that underpin them. Whereas segmentation is a top-down approach to marketing that breaks mass markets into allegedly manageable portions, niching involves a bottom-up approach whereby the marketer starts by identifying the needs of a few individuals and builds on this to satisfy the needs of a group with similar demands. The niche, therefore, rather than the segment, would appear to have a place in many postmodern marketing contexts by allowing a focus on the experience needs of the individual. With post modern contemporary forms of tourism consumption resulting in fragmentation of markets, niche marketing as an alternative to segmentation has gained prominence, notes Shani and Chalasani (1992). Kalypso's Marketing efforts were focused on meeting the unique needs of each tour groups they handled. This is an important characteristic that distinguishes a niche approach from segmentation.

In principle, both small and large firms can adopt niche marketing (Sorenson, et al., 2006). For many large firms, however, niche marketing is a conscious strategic response and develops niche as a finer level of segmentation. On the other hand, for many small firms possessing creative entrepreneurship, the need for niche marketing grows out organically as a natural response suited to their strengths and weakness. And, the small firm approach is closer to the bottom-up approach that underpins the true spirit of niche marketing. The bottom-up perspective on niching suggests that niche marketing and relationship marketing are promising strategies to deal with fragmented markets as alternatives to segmentation. They argue that the two strategies might complement each other in the creation of a marketing tool to deal with a turbulent business environment. A niche strategy avoids competition/confrontation with larger competitors and enables a firm to devote its energy to serving a unique market.

Over the last few years, the practice of niche marketing has been increasing in tourism. Changing behavior patterns and lifestyles, demographic shifts and increasing consumer choice are some of the factors causing a fragmentation that has rendered consumption patterns unpredictable (Jacobsen, 2003). Alongside increasing diversity in the nature of tourism consumption, tourism providers have increasingly sought to identify niche markets and to develop products specifically for them. Many tourism product-markets such as rural, nature and adventure tourism are getting evolved into smaller niche markets. This trend is further evidenced by the emergence of a large number of new destinations; an increasing tendency among tourists to move away from traditional tourism destinations; and a surge in what is termed as 'new age tourism' with a more socially responsible approach to vacationing (Poon, 1993). Many tourism markets have already been fragmented into smaller niche markets. In rural tourism, for example, research suggests that there may be identifiable market niches more likely to be associated with rural values and activities (McKercher and Robbins, 1998).

Developing reputation early on is very crucial for a niche marketer (McKenna, 1988). Some of the early efforts of Kalypso were particularly aimed at developing a strong goodwill with the first group they started. Also this reputation has to be maintained with relationship marketing for developing long term strong relationship with the customers (Novelli, 2005).

Kalypso Niche Products: A Brief Description

Products and package add-ons proceeded. Starting with bicycling and trekking tours, they soon added birding tours, kayaking etc. The following are Kalypso's current products:

- *Mountain Biking:* With over 6 packages in cycling tours ranging from easy to very difficult packages, through various routes in Kerala, the packages include cycling on the plains, through the hills or a combination of both. It is one of the most sought after activity of the company. A 14 day itinerary would start from the plains, climbing to altitudes of up to 7000 ft, and then descending through the undulating terrains of the Kerala country side, till they are back on to the plains. As mentioned before, it is not just cycling, tourists see and experience the life of the Kerala people from very close quarters as they stop over en-route, interacting and mixing with the local populace.

- *River & Backwater Kayaking:* Here again kayaking as an adventure sport is developed to discover Kerala backwaters and lagoons and rivers in a new light as the tourists watch and interact closely with the local community. There are frequent stop over at a tea shop, or coir spinning yard or a school while kayaking on the backwaters. This package again is positioned in their brochures as the best way to explore the country side, tasting of the local cuisine or taking visits to ancient temples and churches en route. There are three Kayaking itineraries: Backwater kayaking – a 4 day trip; River kayaking a 3 day trip; and Kayaking along the lagoons for 2 days.
- *Trekking & Camping:* This package is offered along some of the interesting yet not popular wilderness trails around Munnar and Periyyar, promising picturesque views of the country side, interesting people, and forests teeming with exotic birds, animals and plants.. This is again an innovative tourism product in the Kerala tourism map using some of beautiful trekking and walking tracks which is rarely exploited by the tour packagers in Kerala. Within this package they offer 4 trails each covering different route. Most itineraries have a mix of home stays and camps by way of accommodation.
- *Bird Watching:* Some of the birding spots in Kerala and the southern states are combined into a package tour offering tourists a possibility of spotting at least

250 species of birds including all the rare species endemic to the region. This is a two week tour catering to birding enthusiasts, taken along with a expert birding guide and offers tourist an opportunity to observe and photograph most of these birds found in Kerala. This tour is an exclusive birding tour aimed at keen bird watchers. In addition to there also 3 day and 5 day tours covering limited spots.

- *Wildlife & Nature Safaris:* This include packages like a three day trekking and camping in the periyar tiger trial conducted by mainly by earlier poachers who have turned protectors of the forests, Wild Kerala safari, one of the package, offers opportunity to view the rich bio diversity of flora and fauna in this region.
- *Small Family Adventures:* Specially targeting to families, this package offers an all round package entertainment with a mix of soft adventure, rest and relax in secluded beaches, fun and interesting sites at an elephant camp, and a glimpse of wildlife, cultural and historic attractions very popular in Kerala. This package is conceived sensing the growing global trend of families wanting to travel together and have an experience that is enjoyable both for the adults and for the children.
- *Eco and Culture Tours:* With the adventure part removed, and offering a more intimate experience of the country side living, this package options are for those travelers seeking more meaningful cultural interactions with local communities, seeing and taking part in their village life, local festivities and traditions. The routes are typically away from the normal tourist circuits with a range of staying options like home stays, plantation bungalows, traditional homes near backwaters, eco lodges maintained by tribal communities and tree houses.
- *Charity Challenges:* The company in its quest for coming up with innovative tour packages has pioneered in Kerala a new concept of travel business called Charity challenges, a unique concept of fund raising for charities through challenges. Originated in the UK,

The concept of Charity challenges is a novel way of fund raising, in which the task of collecting money is distributed amongst many people who in turn were rewarded with a challenging trip to some exotic part of the globe. Kalypso Adventures started operating Charity Challenges in 2005 when they arranged the tripfor 30 Britons on behalf of the International Childcare Trust. The challenge entailed the participants to cycle from Cochin to Kodaikanal, a distance of over 400 kms in 5 days. Subsequently, they have started doing more challenges both cycling and trekking and so far over 1000 people have done the charity challenges through Kalypso.

- *Gap Year Adventures:* Another unique form of tour package devised by Kalypso is the Gap year adventures, catering to a slowly rising trend of gapers, mainly in western countries. A gapper is a person who may be a professional or a student seeking planning to take a gap of say c᾿ one year, and to work, and live in developing country often offering the voluntary work through various NGOs. Are coming up with unique packages for gapers offering multicultural experience voluntarily working and living with indigenous people and other distinct ethnic communities, they
- *Kalypso Outbound Training:* The two partners utilizing their vast experience in the navy and the outdoor adventure infrastructure has also started an outbound Experiential training firm offering outdoor and adventure based activities as a group learning exercise for corporate teams. One of their colleagues, Cdr Madhusoodanan, a deep sea diver by profession and a product of Jamnalal Bajaj Institute for Management Studies, left his career in shipping and joined the team to look after this operation.

Niche Tourism Marketing: What Did Kalypso Learn?

Being committed to a niche product in the tourism market like adventure tourism, the company faced specific challenges.

Right from accessing the market to communicating the product offerings and gaining the trust of international tour operators required innovation not just in the product but also in the marketing tactics. Early on, they jumped into the Internet as a leading channel to communicate and promote their product. With limited funding and consequent low marketing budget, attending international travel fairs in the initial 2 to 3 years was very difficult. Given the unique aspects of the product, they knew that, direct visits to international markets and meeting personally tour operators and travel agents, would have helped get inquires and groups faster. However with limited marketing budget Internet was relied largely and as a result package sales took more time than otherwise.

The First major break for them came with a requirement for a cycle tour from an international tour operator. But, in the process of handling that inquiry they realized how important it is to have the "right" equipment for the activities liking bicycling, and kayaking. The best of locally available cycles they bought were evaluated by the tour operators as inferior for kind of cycling tours they promoted and therefore found it inadequate. To market cycling tours internationally, they realized, it is a must to have imported world class cycles to satisfy the international tourist market needs. Fortunately the first major tourist group they got agreed to bring with them the bikes on a condition that Kalypso should buy it after their use. Still, with all the risks inherent in it, they accepted it and that decision was rewarded soon when this same tour operator brought a bigger group next time. That was a start of a long lasting relationship with that international tour operator who has remained their top client even now. Their customer centric approach also generated lot of positive word of mouth. For instance, when the first major tour group they handled went highly satisfied, many of the same members in that group came with different groups again. This trend continued, and later many bookings came mainly on the basis of strong positive word of mouth generated by highly satisfied tourists who took their tour.

With the growth in the business established, they stated attending regularly international travel fairs at the rate of 3 to 4 every year. At the same time, they frequently upgraded their websites adding many dynamic features, incorporating the complete details of the tour with specific photos and videos. Today besides the main website, they have also specific websites for almost all individual activities of the company.

Being a niche product they also found that standardization is very difficult. Even though the company has developed standard packages of different durations under each product package type, a typical client, mostly an international tour operator seek many clarifications and changes regarding amenities, trip dates and duration. Most bookings are preceded by extensive consultation through emails regarding price, accommodation, food and other facilities. These aspects of the typical booking patterns make offering standardized packages difficult, and for this reason most of the enquiries required negotiating skillfully with clients which are handled exclusively by the two partners.

Even though there is preference for a large groups for bicycling, kayaking and trekking, With their customer specific approach, they never turn down an enquiry just because size of the group is unviable, For instance they have even taken pains of conducting a cycling tour for just one member, a professor from Cambridge, mainly because of his background the peer influence he can exert to generate more tourists of similar profile in the future.

Human Resource Development for A Niche Business

Given the unique nature of product with its high level of interaction and activities, the role of the accompanying guiding person is very crucial. There are separate guides for bicycling, trekking, and kayaking. For birding they rely on outside experts for guiding. The feedback company often receives from tourists' carries lot of appreciation for the guides for their skill in tour handling and the high level of personal service they deliver. This is the result of intensive personal and technical training the company gives to their guides'. It is a rigorous training process which develops them to excellent guides, and this also includes trying guides initially with a smaller tourist groups before letting them take charge of a bigger group.

The unconventional method of selecting a guide and the kind of people they select are also responsible for getting such excellent rating for their guides. Almost all of the guides have no professional qualification, but are handpicked from the local communities, often coming from a poor family. The subsequent training and the job as a guide offers to them a respectable career which they value very highly, and this in turn engenders high commitment and the loyalty among the guides. Some of the guides before joining Kalyopso were coolies and road construction workers, and they view they job as a highly rewarding career, far above their previously low paid jobs. Many Guides often have opportunity to move out of Kerala to handle tours coordinated by Kalypso in other locations in India. As an added payoff, Kalypso further uses these guides to recommend more like-minded people they know, as part of taking new members as guides.

A similar unconventional approach is used for selecting the mangers that are responsible for coordinating tours. All of them selected have no tourism, travel or hospitality experience, instead, as the owners' state, all of them have that fire in the belly to take on with an overriding passion, the kind of challenge Kalypso offers. This avant-garde style is witnessed even in the style of functioning of two partners. Both of them mostly work in one room with a common table and have no formal titles displayed anywhere, reflecting a sort of informal working environment inside the office.

A significant human resource management issue facing the promoters is this: niche tourism customers do not want employees to interact with them in a way mass market tourism employees interact (Kotey and Slade, 2005). In sum, they want differences in everything! To achieve this, promoters have to give special training to all the recruits. When it comes to train employees who have already got work experience with a mass tourism operator, the resistance to unlearn what had been learned in the past is so huge. Employees who might want to leave a niche business like Kalypso to join a mass market operator or even yet another niche tourism operator too encounter problems because of the difficulty to port their knowledge, skills, and attitudes to the new environment (Hill and Stewart, 2000).

Responsible Tourism: The Niche Way

As far as possible the firm tries to practice responsible tourism, a growing movement in the tourism sector. One of the practical outcomes of responsible tourism is to leave no trace (Frey and George, 2009; Medina, 2005). While designing the activities as part of the tour package, they claim, they take into account this principle of responsible tourism by adopting practices that are respectful of natural and cultural environment and which contribute in an ethical manner to the local economic development. Sourcing the food provisions locally, encouraging tourists to use home stays instead of hotels, and recruiting guides from the local community are ways through which they tries to contributes in a positive and equitable way to the development and fulfillment of individuals living, working and staying in the areas they operate in. In many cases involving home stays, they estimate that, by way of offering tourists various service and entertainment, at least 10 to 15 families adjacent to particular home stay benefit directly or indirectly.

The Future

From a very humble beginning with very limited capital and no business experience, the company has by now achieved impressive growth. Currently, the average annual rate of growth is 300%. From making a comprehensive website to identifying new routes, both partners were doing everything on their own, and they enjoyed the process, unhindered by the fear of a looming failure. As they look at it, they have survived the initial leg of race to take their fledgling operation to a respectable position in the tourism industry map of Kerala. They took the company to the growth mode when Kerala had never been sold as an adventure destination: of course, this made their work very difficult to get across to travel agents who were sending people to Kerala. Hard work, determination, commitment, and belief in the product paid off well and in the year 2006-07 alone the company has sold 10,000 room nights.

Starting 2009, they would be offering similar activities in Goa, and varied activities like Scuba diving and Sea kayaking in The Andaman islands. Kalysos adventures has also joined hands with Concord Exotic Voyages, a reputed tour operator in Kerala to start Kalypso Eco- Lodges & Camps, a new company aimed at providing exclusive non-hotel accommodation across the country. These would include Luxury Tented Camps, Bungalows, and ecolodges and would cover most of Kerala, Karnataka, Tamil nadu, Goa, and The Andamans.

Now, as they aim for the next level of growth, they know things will not be that easy as in the past. They have various marketing options before them: to go beyond UK, their main market currently, and tap many other European and US markets; provide more novel and innovative products; adding new itineraries and new destinations in their offerings; expanding the operations and offices in other countries; and, venturing into hospitality business. More importantly, for them to focus more on the expansion and marketing part of the business, they want some one senior with good managerial experience, decision making capability and commitment to manage effectively the operation side of the business, which they were doing so far. Another side of the business they failed to give proper attention was the financial and accounting part of the business. Here too they need a senior person with good finance management acumen who can advice the partners on all aspects related to finance and accounting. They admit that in the past they have taken many important decisions related to marketing, sales, and operations without proper financial information due to which they have committed many mistakes. With new people planning to be selected, they hope, all these short comings could be avoided.

REFERENCES

- Direct interviews with the promoters of Kalypso and other stakeholders directly or indirectly involved with Kalypso.
- Official website of Kalypso Adventures. http://www.kalypsoadventures.com
- Dalgic, T. and Leuw, M. (1994). Niche marketing revisited: Theoretical and Practical Issues. *European Journal of Marketing,* 28(4), 30-46.

- Frey, N. and George, R. (2009). Responsible tourism management: The missing link between business owners' attitudes and behavior in the Cape Town tourism industry. *Tourism Management*, 31(1), 20-35.
- Hill, R. and Stewart, J. (2000). Human resource development in small organizations. *Journal of European Industrial Training*, 24(2/3/4), 105–117.
- Jacobsen, J.K.S. (2003). The tourist bubble and the Europeanization of holiday travel. *Tourism and Cultural Change*, 1(1), 71-87.
- Keegan, W., Moriarty, S. and Duncan, T. (1992). *Marketing*. NY: Prentice-Hall.
- Kotler, P.H. (1991). *Marketing Management*. NJ: Prentice Hall.
- Kotey, B. and Slade, P. (2005). Formal human resource management practices in small growing firms. *Journal of Small Business Management* 43(1), 16-40.
- McAuley, A. and Anderson, A. (1999). Marketing landscapes: The social context. *Qualitative Marketing Research: An International Journal*, 2 (3), 176-188.
- McKenna, R. (1988). Marketing in an age of diversity. *Harvard Business Review*, 66(5), 88–95.
- McKercher, B. and Robbins, W. (1998). Business development issues affecting nature-based tourism operators in Australia. *Journal of Sustainable Tourism*, 6(2), 173-188.
- Medina, L.K. (2005). Ecotourism and certification: Confronting the principles and pragmatics of socially responsible tourism. *Journal of Sustainable Tourism*, 13(3), 281-295.
- Novelli, M. (2005). *Niche Tourism: Contemporary Issues, Trends, and Case Studies*. UK: Butterworth-Heinemann
- Poon, A. (1993). Tourism, *Technology, and Competitive Strategies*, UK: CABI.
- Shani, D. and Chalasani, S. (1992). Exploiting niches using relationship marketing. *Journal of Services Marketing*, 9 (3), 33-42.
- Sorenson, O., Mcevily, S., Ren, C.R., and Roy, R. (2006). Niche width revisited: Organizational scope, behavior and performance. *Strategic Management Journal*, 27(10), 915-936.